LINGUIST ON THE LOOSE

LINGUIST ON THE LOOSE

Adventures and Misadventures in Fieldwork

Lyle Campbell

EDINBURGH
University Press

Edinburgh University Press is one of the leading university presses in the UK. We publish academic books and journals in our selected subject areas across the humanities and social sciences, combining cutting-edge scholarship with high editorial and production values to produce academic works of lasting importance. For more information visit our website: edinburghuniversitypress.com

© Lyle Campbell, 2022

Edinburgh University Press Ltd, The Tun—Holyrood Road,
12(2f) Jackson's Entry, Edinburgh EH8 8PJ

Typeset in 11/15 Adobe Garamond by
Servis Filmsetting Ltd, Stockport, Cheshire,
Printed and bound in Great Britain.

A CIP record for this book is available from the British Library

ISBN 978 1 4744 9414 4 (hardback)
ISBN 978 1 4744 9415 1 (paperback)
ISBN 978 1 4744 9416 8 (webready PDF)
ISBN 978 1 4744 9417 5 (epub)

The right of Lyle Campbell to be identified as the author of this work has been asserted in accordance with the Copyright, Designs and Patents Act 1988, and the Copyright and Related Rights Regulations 2003 (SI No. 2498).

Contents

List of figures	vi
Foreword by Wade Davis	x
Preface	xvi
Acknowledgements	xviii
1 Introduction: What's a linguist do, anyway?, What's linguistic fieldwork?	1
2 Fieldwork adventure	26
3 Discoveries	39
4 Finding language consultants and working with them	75
5 Perils, parasites, politics, and violence	117
6 Eating, drinking, and matters of health	164
7 Surviving fieldwork: Travel and living in the field	179
8 What next?: What is needed in endangered language research?	235
References	262
Subject index	273
Languages, language families, and ethnic groups index	285

Figures

1.1 Lyle Campbell, fieldwork in Misión La Paz (Salta Province, Argentina, 2010) — 10
1.2 Alphabet posters for the school: team production (led by Nancy García, graduate research assistant) (Misión La Paz, Salta Province, Argentina, 2008) — 18
1.3 Fishing with diving nets, Chorote, Nivaclé, and Wichí speakers (Pilcomayo River, Misión La Paz, Salta Province, Argentina, 2005) — 19
2.1 Lyle Campbell with armadillo (Misión La Paz, 2007) — 27
2.2 Don Francisco Calvo Pérez (Trinitaria, Chiapas, Mexico, 1986) — 35
3.1 Don Altín getting honey (Misión La Paz, Salta Province, Argentina, 2006) — 63
3.2 *Lhte'ech* bloodletting bone tool (April, 2021; gift from don Altín, Misión La Paz, Salta Province, Argentina, 2010) — 67
3.3 Piranha bite (Misión La Paz, Salta Province, Argentina, 2007) — 69

3.4 Trough for making chicha (with Luis Díaz, Misión La Paz, Salta Province, Argentina, 2007) 71
3.5 Don Altín making tinderhorns (for when there are no matches) (Misión La Paz, Salta Province, Argentina, 2007) 72
4.1 Language revitalization materials: booklets in Chorote, Nivaclé, and Wichí produced in the Chaco language documentation project. (Misión La Paz, Salta Province, Argentina, 2008) 76
4.2 Felipa and Beatriz firing pots (Pipil) (Santo Domingo de Guzmán, El Salvador, 1976) 86
4.3 Don Rafael Hernández, guide (on the left), with Tojoloabal speakers (Chiapas, Mexico, 1986) 88
4.4 Luis Díaz with fish (Misión La Paz, Salta Province, Argentina, 2007) 94
4.5 Don Altín with caiman hide (Misión La Paz, Salta Province, Argentina, 2005) 96
4.6 Don Altín singing with drum and rattle (Misión La Paz, Salta Province, Argentina, 2007) 97
4.7 Don Laureano Segovia (Wichí) (Misión La Paz, Salta Province, Argentina, 2006) 99
4.8 Hugo Gonzáles singing Chorote songs (Misión La Paz, 2007) 100
4.9 Fieldwork with Teresa Ramos and Josefa Ampú (doña Teresa does not know Spanish, but speaks Nivaclé and understands Chorote) (Misión La Paz, Salta Province, Argentina, 2004) 112
5.1 Scorpion (Misión La Paz, Salta Province, Argentina, 2008) 123
5.2 Vinchuca bug (Misión La Paz, Salta Province, Argentina, 2005) 125
5.3 Anaconda skin (with don Altín and Franco, Misión La Paz, Salta Province, Argentina, 2006) 126

5.4 Snake that tried to visit me in the night (Misión La Paz, Salta Province, Argentina, 2013) 127
5.5 Snake track (Misión La Paz, Salta Province, Argentina, 2007) 128
5.6 Snake skin (with Fernando Ángel, Misión La Paz, Salta Province, Argentina, 2013) 129
5.7 Coral snake (Misión La Paz, Salta Province, Argentina, 2004) 130
5.8 Fernando Ángel recording (Misión La Paz, Salta Province, Argentina, 2008) 131
5.9 Asencio (Misión La Paz, Salta Province, Argentina, 2007) 132
5.10 Clay slingshot balls (Misión La Paz, Salta Province, Argentina, 2007) 140
5.11 Owl (with Franco, Misión La Paz, Salta Province, Argentina, 2007) 141
5.12 Dog with vampire bat bite (Misión La Paz, Salta Province, Argentina, 2007) 143
5.13 Lyle Campbell with Chorote-speaking parrot (Misión La Paz, Salta Province, Argentina, 2006) 144
5.14 Coca sign: "There is coca and lime (bicarbonate of soda)" (Tartagal, Salta Province, Argentina, 2013) 156
5.15 Coca leaves for sale (Tartagal, Salta Province, Argentina, 2007) 157
6.1 Cooking our dinner in Misión La Paz (Salta Province, Argentina, 2008) 166
7.1 *Piqueteros* roadblock (main highway north of Tartagal, Salta Province, Argentina, 2007) 191
7.2 Fieldwork with Mam while seeking Chicomuceltec (Lyle Campbell with Mam-speaking immigrants, Paso Hondo, Chiapas, Mexico, 1986) 193
7.3 Combing hair with bundled hair of an anteater's tail

(don Altín, Misión La Paz, Salta Province, Argentina, 2007) 208
7.4 Puppy investigating the recorder (Misión La Paz, Salta Province, Argentina, 2007) 211
7.5 Cooking fish (Misión La Paz, Salta Province, Argentina, 2007) 220

Foreword

An invitation to write a foreword for an important book is always a singular honor, but in this case it's also something quite personal, for Lyle Campbell is and has always been one of my heroes, a rare scholar who throughout his career resisted the pressures of academic orthodoxy to do the work that he knew to be vitally important.

As a chronicler of the imagination, Lyle has devoted his life to the celebration and revitalization of what is arguably humanity's greatest legacy, our astonishing linguistic diversity, the seven thousand languages that encode the totality of our collective experience. As this book marvelously recounts, Lyle embraced his mission with both humor and joy, not to mention considerable wisdom and humility. Modest to a fault, he would be the last to agree with my assertion that his unflagging support for language documentation and fieldwork over the last half century has been of truly historic significance. But he would be wrong. His presence has been that important.

In 1992 Michael Krauss, then head of the Alaska Native Language Center in Fairbanks, published one of the most important and disturbing academic papers ever written. Based in part on his address the year before to the Linguistic Society of America, his paper "The World's Languages in Crisis" began with a litany of loss. Among the Eyak of the Copper River delta of Alaska, where Krauss had worked, there remained but two speakers of the language, both elderly. The Mandan of the Dakotas had but six fluent speakers, the Osage five, the Abenaki-Penobscot twenty, the Iowa five, the Tuscarora fewer than thirty, the Yokuts fewer than ten. Altogether some six hundred extant languages survive with fewer than a hundred speakers. Over 3,500 of the world's languages, Krauss reported, are kept alive by a fifth of 1 percent of the global population.

My background in anthropology notwithstanding, I was astonished to learn that fully half the languages of the world are not being taught to children. Within the linguistic community I could find no source to challenge Krauss's bleak assessment. This academic consensus was itself haunting. When I spoke to Ken Hale, an eminent linguist at MIT, he agreed without hesitation that 50 percent of the world's languages were endangered. A language, he stressed, is not just a body of vocabulary and a set of grammatical rules; it's a flash of the human spirit, the means by which the soul of a culture comes into the material world. Every language is an old-growth forest of the mind, a watershed of thought, an ecosystem of social and spiritual possibilities. To lose a language, Hale said very simply, is like dropping a bomb on the Louvre.

From my perspective as an anthropologist, language loss was the canary in the coal mine, a sure indicator of what was happening to cultural diversity throughout the world. It was something that everyone could understand. Audiences invariably gasped when they heard the dire statistics. How would it feel, I would ask during public lectures, to be the last speaker of your native language, enveloped in silence, with no means or ability to pass on the wisdom of your ancestors, or to anticipate the promise of your descendants? To those who suggested that the world would be a better place if we all spoke one language, that communication would be facilitated, that it would be easier for us to get along, I responded: fine—but let's make that universal language Haida or Yoruba, Lakota, Inuktitut or San. Suddenly people got a sense of what it would mean to be unable to speak their mother tongue.

When I finally reached Michael Krauss in Alaska, he compared the loss of languages with the erosion of biodiversity. No biologist, he noted, would dare suggest that 50 percent of all plant and animal species are on the brink of extinction, certainly across the entire world. Yet this, the most apocalyptic assessment of the future of biological diversity, scarcely approaches what is known to be the best conceivable scenario for the fate of the world's languages and cultures. Newspapers, Krauss added, devote columns of print to the fate of the spotted owl, yet barely a word to the plight of the world's endangered languages. The American government spends one million dollars a year to save a single wildlife species, the Florida panther. The total budget for the study, documentation and revitalization of the 175 extant native languages in the United States was at the time, as Krauss noted, a mere two million. Why does a species of bird or a flower, he asked, matter more than the poetry, songs, and stories encoded in the memories of the surviving custodians of an ancient language?

My question for Krauss was rather different. If he was correct, it surely implied that half of humanity's intellectual, spiritual, and social legacy would disappear within a generation. Yet no one outside a small circle of academics was even talking about it. If virtually all linguists agreed with this dire prognosis, why on earth were they not screaming about it? Krauss responded with one word: Chomsky.

Noam Chomsky, a colleague of Ken Hale's at MIT, had been a hero during the heady days of student protests at Harvard, a prominent academic who consistently joined the ranks in the streets and spoke with great insight and passion at many of the most heated anti-war rallies. He was a darling of the New Left and this burnished his already formidable reputation as the most influential linguist of his generation. To critics he was virtually unassailable. His ideas and theories transformed and in time utterly dominated the entire field of linguistics.

Until Chomsky, linguists assumed that infants acquired language as they responded behaviorally to rewards and affirmation. Chomsky didn't buy it. He noted that language acquisition is an extraordinarily complex process that children throughout the world all manage to do at roughly the same age, as if designed to accomplish the task. He believed that the ability to learn language was in fact encoded in the human brain at birth as an immutable set of rules he called a universal grammar. This language organ did not exist in a physical sense, but it might be studied through the detailed analysis of the abstract structures underlying language. By doing so, he suggested, it might even be possible to learn something fundamental about intelligence and human nature.

Chomsky's theory was insightful and novel, and it became hugely influential in part because it suggested that linguists might be able to act as real scientists. Of enormous consequence was its premise that culture had no role to play in the study of language. To go off to the field to compile dictionaries and grammars of dying languages spoken by a handful of survivors was to Chomsky and his acolytes a completely pointless exercise. What mattered was linguistic theory and whatever might help reveal the nature of the universal grammar.

As Michael Krauss explained, Chomsky was interested not in what distinguished languages but rather in what they had in common. Krauss used an analogy from biology. A microbiologist interested in the fundamentals of life studies DNA and doesn't really care where the DNA comes from because it is so similar across the animal kingdom. Why go to the effort to get panda DNA, for example, when you can conduct the same experiments with the DNA of laboratory rats, which is so much easier to obtain? What matters to the microbiologist is the universal structure of DNA, not the fact that its phenotypic expression produces creatures as varied as pandas, rats, and fruit flies. Biodiversity was important but it could be left to the conservation biologists and ecologists.

Such was Chomsky's influence that the entire field of linguistics for some thirty years focused exclusively, if you will, on the micro. Linguists pursued the Holy Grail of a universal grammar, blithely unconcerned that the actual expressions of that imagined deep structure—the languages of humanity—were disappearing by the day. Those who challenged this orthodoxy, who argued that language documentation, the creation of dictionaries and actual grammars, was indeed the real work of linguistics, found themselves for the most part ostracized by the academic world. Michael Krauss was an exception, as were Ken Hale and, of course, Lyle Campbell. In time, these three scholars would inspire a new generation of linguists for whom language loss would be seen as one of the most pressing challenges of our times. But this change came slowly, and for the longest time Krauss, Hale, and Campbell remained as lone voices in the wild.

Only today, an entire generation on, can we fully grasp the significance of those who stood their ground, insisting that every language was by definition of inherent importance. Studies of the human genome have revealed beyond doubt that the genetic endowment of humanity is a single continuum. We are all brothers and sisters. Race is an utter fiction. Virtually every human alive is a descendant of a relatively small number of individuals who walked out of Africa some 60,000 years ago and then, on a journey that lasted 40,000 years, some 2,500 generations, carried the human spirit to every corner of the habitable world.

But here is the key revelation. If we are all cut from the same genetic cloth, then by definition all cultures share essentially the same mental acuity, the same raw genius. Whether this intellectual capacity and potential is exercised in stunning works of technological innovation, as has been the great achievement of the West, or through the untangling of the complex threads of memory inherent in a myth—a primary concern, for example, of the Aborigines of Australia—is simply a matter of choice and orientation, adaptive insights and cultural priorities.

There is no hierarchy of progress in the history of culture, no social Darwinian ladder to success. That Victorian notion of the savage and the civilized—with European industrial society sitting proudly at the apex of a pyramid of advancement that widens at the base to the so-called primitives of the world—has been thoroughly discredited, indeed scientifically ridiculed for the racial and colonial conceit that it was. It is no more relevant to our lives today than the notion, fiercely held by clergymen in the nineteenth century, that Earth was but six thousand years old.

The other peoples of the world are not failed attempts at modernity, let alone failed attempts to be us. Every culture is a unique answer to a fundamental question: What does it mean to be human and alive? When asked this question, the peoples of the world respond in seven thousand different voices, and these collectively comprise our human repertoire for dealing with the complex challenges that will confront us as a species in the coming centuries. Every culture has something to say, each deserves to be heard, just as none has a monopoly on the route to the divine. As Lyle Campbell has always known, to lose any one of these voices is to lose something of ourselves.

Wade Davis, 2021

Preface

Fieldwork with little-known languages has been one of my life's greatest passions. It has taken me far and wide and involved me with numerous fascinating peoples and their intriguing languages and cultures. From unusual encounters both delightful and dreadful I learned a great deal. With some considerable reluctance I finally decided to write about things I had learned from doing fieldwork, the sorts of things that are never talked about in other writings about linguistic fieldwork. My motivation was the hope that these things will be useful for others who do or want to do or just want to know about fieldwork. By recounting true-life linguistic fieldwork adventures, discoveries, adversities, and perils, I hoped to bring readers face to face with heartbreaks involved in working up close and personal with endangered languages, with the great satisfaction and excitement that language documentation and revitalization can afford, and with its importance.

About that reluctance, a writer friend once told me that I make high adventure sound like a postcard. I think that and my reluctance here has to do with growing up with the Code of the West as the prime directive, with its proscription against showing off or talking big about yourself, right up there with the mightiest of the "thou-shalt-nots." Because of that, nothing reported in this book is embellished or exaggerated. That postcard style of reporting—I'd prefer to think of it as objective scientific expository prose tempered by the Code of the West—is far more natural and comfortable to me than the fish-story approach so often deployed by some who like to try to make their fieldwork experiences sound more colorful, glamorous, and self-laudatory than warranted by reality.

And having mentioned the Code of the West, perhaps I should clarify that it has nothing to do with the bad history of the Old West with hideous treatment of American Indians, just the opposite; it requires respect and fair treatment for all. The Code of the West is just an informal set of notions about expected conduct shared by many Westerners. My father was a cowboy; he worked on cattle ranches and horse ranches when I was a child, and he and my other relatives inculcated these attitudes about proper behavior in me. Though informal, the Code of the West is well-known—a Google search for "Code of the West" returns many hits. (References to Zane Grey's book with that title can be ignored.) Some of its tenets include: your word is your bond (if you make a promise, keep it); don't talk too much, don't talk much about yourself, and never brag; treat all with fairness, justice, and respect. It's always been a part of me. I mention the Code of the West in a few instances in the book where it plays a role, useful guiding principles that stood me in good stead in various fieldwork situations and interactions.

I hope you enjoy this book and find something worthwhile in it for you.

Acknowledgements

First and foremost, I thank all those speakers of languages and members of their communities who worked with me in the fieldwork talked about in this book. I owe them more than I can ever express. I thank also Susan Wurtzburg and Daniel Campbell for helpful advice, and I owe special thanks to Laura Williamson of Edinburgh University Press for encouragement and abundant insightful feedback on earlier drafts. I also thank three anonymous reviewers for helpful comments and two later anonymous readers for their kind and valuable suggestions and comments. Finally, while not directly involved in this particular work, I thank the National Science Foundation, the Endangered Languages Documentation Programme, National Endowment for the Humanities, and other funding agencies for a number of grants over the years that supported fieldwork talked about here.

1

Introduction: What's a linguist do, anyway?, What's linguistic fieldwork?

Introduction: identity

In my mind I have always been a country boy; I grew up mostly in the woods in Oregon. However, my business card—rarely used though provided by my university—says I'm a Professor of Linguistics. I'm the kind of linguist who has done a lot of fieldwork, on a fair number of languages. In connection with this fieldwork I've been called a "witch" (shaman) and a "swashbuckler"; it was said both that I "bring 'em back alive" and conversely that I "step over dead bodies to save endangered languages." This book is about linguistic fieldwork experiences. These things said about my fieldwork get explained along the way, but they are not central to the book. Though the experiences lying behind those things convey some of the excitement of linguistic fieldwork, the real goal of this book is to relate some of what I have learned from the fieldwork that I have done. I believe that some of the insights gained from that fieldwork may be useful for others who do or are contemplating doing linguistic fieldwork. A second goal is to make clear the need for language documentation and the fieldwork that goes with it and to increase understanding for the plight of endangered languages. I hope, too, that what I relate here will be interesting and motivating to readers interested in linguistics, languages, Indigenous peoples and their cultures, travel and geography, and especially fieldwork, and, also, that it might prove entertaining in a general way.

Some context

Something to make clear here at the beginning is that there is nothing in this book for anyone who would wish to appeal to imagined higher, purer spirituality or mystic wisdom presumed to be possessed by Native Americans and other Indigenous peoples with whom I have worked and lived. I loathe the behavior of those few anthropologists and linguists who feign some special mystical or spiritual connection or knowledge or ability acquired in their fieldwork with some Indigenous group.

I once lost a girlfriend over this. She assumed that the speakers of Mayan languages with whom I worked must have some deep spiritual comprehension beyond the grasp of us spiritually bankrupt modern mainstream Americans. When I insisted that they were just my friends, just ordinary people, with troubles and illnesses and fears and hopes and needs and joys and values and successes and failings parallel for the most part with our own, she was certain that I was either holding out on her and unwilling to share or that I just wasn't able to understand the levels of spiritual enlightenment beyond ours that they must surely have attained. Every group of Indigenous people I have worked with has fascinating beliefs and stories, important values, and cultures that are captivating in so many ways, distinct from my own. However, none, in my view, has control over or special understanding of anything supernatural or beyond the reach or ken of other human beings, even of spiritually decrepit average Americans. Mostly they deal with the vicissitudes of life in a normal, natural world. Where they differ in religion and belief systems—and many differ mightily; some examples are mentioned in later chapters—those differences are not beyond the ability of others to comprehend, though they can and often do involve spiritual matters of extreme importance to the groups involved.

Let me bring up one final clarification in this context. There is often sensitivity concerning the names used to talk about cultural groups. For example, some avoid the word "Indian" and instead refer to "Native Americans" or "first peoples" or "first nations," or just "Indigenous people." However, at the same time there are members of these groups who prefer to be called "Indians" or "American Indians"; some are offended by the alternatives that are in use. In this book I most often say "Indigenous" when talking about people or languages, attempting to avoid any terms that might be thought objectionable, disrespectful, or offensive. However, I do occasionally use "Indian" in contexts where the people involved prefer "Indian" or where "Indian" is in general use. "Indian" is found in the official names of many Native American tribes and federal reservations, and is used by the US Bureau of Indian Affairs and other government agencies. It would be difficult to avoid "Indian" entirely, and, as mentioned, there are American Indians who prefer to be referred to as Indians. Given that no term is entirely satisfactory to everyone in all contexts, it is important to make it clear here that in no way is any term used in this book meant to be disrespectful of anyone, especially not of the people referred to.

This applies also to the names of languages. Most of the languages mentioned in this book are known by names long used in the linguistic and anthropological literature; however, in a number of cases, members of the groups whose languages are involved have advocated for change, that those names given by people outside the group should no longer be used and that the groups' own names for their languages and for themselves be used instead. For example, though long called Papago, the language and people are now called Tohono O'odham; the people and language formerly called

Nootka are now known as Nuu-chah-nulth. Many other such examples could be mentioned and several are pointed out in this book. I use the people's own names where I am aware of them though I also mention the traditional names by which languages have been known so that readers can find them if they are not familiar with the newer names. I apologize for any case where an ethnic group may have a preference for a name that I may not yet be aware of. No disrespect is intended. Let me add here that as a non-indigenous guy from the US, I cannot and would never dream of attempting to speak for Indigenous peoples on their preferences with regards to names, terminology, or in fact anything.

What's a linguist?

So, first, what is a linguist? To linguists it often feels like the general public thinks that a linguist is a person that you ask, "How many languages do you know?" Linguists hate that question . . . anyway, I always have. If you answer it truthfully, it probably sounds like you're either bragging or being evasive. You end up having to explain the different ways one can "know" a language, and that starts sounding pedantic. Some have said it would be better just to answer a different question, like "How many languages can you read novels in?" For me that's around half a dozen, though "can" is a less operative word here than "do" or "would" or "have (read novels in)." That is, I have read novels in some half dozen languages, but, then, foreign language novel reading isn't at all what identifies linguists—linguistics isn't about novels—and anyway, the languages I have done fieldwork on have no novels written in them, at least not yet.[1]

To that dreaded question of "How many languages do you speak?" I usually give an evasive answer like, "Oh, I've had to study several." The Code of the West disdains pretentiousness, self-importance: bragging or acting big can lose you your friends and probably some kin, too, where I grew up. So, I have always found being asked about the number of languages I might "know" exceedingly uncomfortable, making me almost tongue-tied.

I guess a sort of answer to that question is on my CV, which lists around sixty languages, a number perhaps larger than that of many linguists but smaller than that of others. However, that CV lacks detail about to what degree the word "know" might apply to the languages listed, so it's not a real answer to the question "How many languages do you know?" You can "know" a language in various ways; you can know a language well or only poorly. It recalls the guy who bragged that he knew three hundred languages . . . because he could say "coffee" (or in a different version of the story he could say "Coca-Cola") in a sizeable number of languages. The words for "coffee" in many languages are similar, since the word for "coffee" tends to be a widespread loanword that sounds similar in languages around the world. Same story for "Coca-Cola."

A linguist, as academics use the term, is definitely not just someone who knows a bunch of languages, as is sometimes thought and seems to be implied by that dreaded question. That's a polyglot; some linguists are also polyglots but most are not. However, if they do speak several languages, they would not call themselves "polyglots"; they might speak of themselves just as being multilingual.

And a linguist, in our sense, is definitely not the military's "linguist," someone who can help military operations that depend on foreign language support. US Army recruitment websites tell us that "the job title 'military linguist' sounds pretty impressive, right?" (Lange 2018). They ask, "Wouldn't you love to get paid to go to school to learn a language and then travel the world with your newfound knowledge?" (Fisher n.d.). They offer the headline enticement, "Military linguists: rapid training track with no experience required" (US Dept. of Defense 2018). The military's notion of what a linguist is makes academic linguists cringe.

The answer to the question "So what's a linguist?" really has nothing to do with knowing a language or about the question "How many languages do you speak?" Rather, linguists investigate and analyze languages for particular purposes, and different linguists have many different reasons for choosing and studying the languages that we do and for doing the kind of research we do.

Linguists don't need to "know" or study any more than one language; they can investigate a single language in several ways—for example, to find out how children acquire their native language, how the language has changed over time, how its grammar works, how foreigners learn it (called second language acquisition), how it varies in society, how to analyze it acoustically, how to apply computational techniques to it for various purposes (machine translation being only one of them), and so on and on. These are some of the many purposes for which linguists investigate and analyze languages. In my case, for many of the languages I got involved with my purpose was to describe (to document) endangered languages, those languages at risk of being lost, to discover as much as I could about what is possible in human languages, how their pieces fit together, what makes them tick, how and why languages change and what their histories tell us about the history of the people who speak them, and to provide source materials for communities and individuals interested in conserving or revitalizing their languages and using the documentation for educational purposes.

Let me hasten to add one further clarification here in the context of endangered languages. Most linguists working with endangered languages and languages that no longer have any native speakers today try to avoid using the word "extinct" in talking about languages, especially ones that have lost their last fully competent speaker recently. We say "dormant" or "sleeping" instead. The word "extinct" is offensive to many and can have negative impacts we hope to avoid. Unfortunately, people often misinterpret "extinct language" to mean the people whose heritage language it is are also "extinct," though in most cases the people survive, having shifted to another language. Today many of these groups are trying to revive their languages based on materials available, often documentary materials collected by earlier linguists when there still were native speakers. Unfortunately, calling such a language "extinct" has a dampening impact on people trying to learn their heritage language. Calling it "dormant" or "sleeping" has a more positive feel, suggesting that the work to learn it can help bring it back, hence the various "awakening language" projects now to recover these languages, no longer called "extinct."

What is linguistic fieldwork?

There are lots of definitions of linguistic fieldwork and they vary widely one from another. Some feel like characterizations of what might happen in fieldwork more than like definitions. At the less elaborate but probably actually the more accurate end of the spectrum we have definitions of linguistic fieldwork that go something like:

> The investigation of a little-known language based on interviewing a native speaker.

At the more elaborate end we have more idealized definitions of linguistic fieldwork that might include all the following:

> The collection of accurate data through direct interaction with a community of speakers of the language under investigation. It is conducted by interviewing and observing speakers in a place where the language is spoken, in their real, natural environment, with the goal of documenting, describing, and analyzing the language based on the data collected. It is done in an ethical manner, producing results approved of by both the community and linguists, often with community-oriented applications relevant to language revitalization, educational programs, etc.

So, all well and good; this latter one is a fine, ideal, aspirational definition—except that some linguists, especially in the past, have been accused of and criticized for doing fieldwork in ethically and culturally inappropriate ways; it was fieldwork just the same, just not the ideal sort that the profession would be proud of today. The data collected by some fieldworkers has not been accurate; in some cases, the results have not been acceptable to the language community or to other linguists. And there are many cases, some very famous ones, of fieldwork that was not done where the language was spoken and did not involve the fieldworker interacting with a community of speakers, but was done in hotels or universities, conducted with refugees, émigrés, students, and others, often with single individuals.

One famous example is Edward Sapir's fieldwork with Tony Tillohash on Southern Paiute at the Carlisle Indian School in central Pennsylvania. It resulted in Sapir's *Southern Paiute, a Shoshonean Language* (1930), which has been called "the most beautiful grammatical description ever written of an Amerindian language" (Darnell and Irvine 1997: 284). Another is Leonard Bloomfield's Tagalog fieldwork, done in his office at the University of Illinois with a single speaker, Alfredo Viola Santiago, an engineering student at the university. It resulted in Bloomfield's *Tagalog Texts with Grammatical Analysis* (1917), a three-volume description of the language. This has been described as "the best treatment of any Austronesian language . . . a description of Tagalog which has never been surpassed for completeness, accuracy, and wealth of exemplification" (Wolff 1987: 173).

I think the definition of linguistic fieldwork has to be less restrictive and more open so that it fits better the kinds of linguistic fieldwork that have been done and the cases about which there is agreement that it constitutes fieldwork. It would be along the lines of:

> Investigation undertaken with a speaker or speakers of a language in order to gain knowledge of that language for linguistic purposes.

We can take the long, elaborate view given above as appropriate to aim for in fieldwork, typical of the aspirations many today have for what fieldwork should be, but not allow it to exclude other kinds of things that are also generally acknowledged to be fieldwork.

Why do linguistic fieldwork?

A few reasons among the many for why linguists do fieldwork are because it's fun, pleasurable, intellectually stimulating, satisfying, and rewarding. Linguists' reasons include:

- They want to document languages to contribute to understanding of linguistic diversity, to determine what is possible in the world's languages, a major goal of linguistics. Language is a window to the mind, and understanding what is possible in human languages helps us understand better the potentials and limitations of human cognition—to better comprehend our very nature as humans.
- They want to document an endangered language so that important information is not lost if that language might cease to be spoken, if it should lose all of its speakers.
- They do fieldwork for altruistic motives, to collaborate with and support communities whose languages are at risk by providing descriptive materials on the languages that can be used for language teaching and learning; they want to use their materials to collaborate with these communities in their language reclamation and language revitalization efforts.
- They do it for the intellectual satisfaction of language analysis and problem solving. They do it for the rewarding sense it gives them personally, both from discoveries about the language investigated and from collaborations that can benefit communities that speak the language.
- They want to be able travel to unusual locations, interact with interesting people, learn an interesting and unusual language, and experience cultures different from their own.

Figure 1.1 Lyle Campbell, fieldwork in Misión La Paz (Salta Province, Argentina, 2010)

- They do fieldwork from a sense of commitment to and hopes of defending social justice, to slow down or reverse the trend towards language loss ongoing in so many communities and to counteract the socio-political causes behind language loss.
- They collect linguistic data to contribute to documenting endangered knowledge systems; to understand interconnections between language and culture and the role of language in ethnobotany, ethnozoology, traditional medicines, etc.; to investigate how the structure of the language and society co-vary with one another; to learn about language ecology, language contact, contact-induced language change; and for a host of interests in language that connect linguistics with other disciplines.
- They do linguistic fieldwork in pursuance of missionary interests—for example, for Bible translation, religious instruction, or proselytizing.

Each of these reasons, except the last, at different times and in different situations, has been a motivating factor behind fieldwork that I have conducted. I have always found fieldwork intellectually stimulating, personally rewarding, and professionally fulfilling. The many challenges and difficulties that I have encountered in various fieldwork projects, several recounted in subsequent chapters, have never overshadowed the sense of satisfaction.

The need for language documentation

With languages becoming dormant at an ever faster and alarming rate and with so many in threat of imminent loss, it is easy to comprehend the sense of urgency linguists feel for language documentation to be done on the undescribed or poorly described endangered languages of the world and why we do fieldwork to achieve that end. That is generally recognized as the most compelling and urgent task for linguists right now and into the future. Language documentation is also urgent for communities who want materials on their languages so they can attempt to learn the languages, teach them, revitalize them, and reverse the trend towards language loss. Collaborating with communities whose languages are under threat to provide adequate documentation is one of the greatest services linguists can render.

It is difficult to overstate the seriousness and severity of the language endangerment crisis.[2] The full status of language endangerment in the world is made particularly clear in the *Catalogue of Endangered Languages*.[3] It reports endangered languages on all continents except Antarctica and in nearly all countries of the world with very few exceptions. The *Catalogue of Endangered Languages* lists 3,113 currently endangered languages.[4] This is 45 percent of the 6,851 living languages in the world as listed by *Ethnologue* in 2018.[5] That is a shocking proportion of the overall linguistic diversity of the planet that is at risk. Of these, 815 languages are severely or critically endangered; that's 26 percent of all the endangered languages—437 languages are critically endangered; 12 percent of all living languages are severely or critically endangered.

The terrible consequences of language endangerment can be seen also from the perspective of whole language families. There are, or were, c.398 independent language families known in the world, including language isolates, language families which have only one member. Of these, 91 have lost all their mother-tongue speakers—no language belonging to any of these families has any remaining native speaker (Campbell 2018). This means that 23 percent—nearly a quarter—of the linguistic diversity of the world, calculated in terms of language families, has been lost. Moreover, of all the millennia in which languages could have ceased to be spoken, two-thirds of these 91 language families have lost their last mother-tongue speaker in only the last 60 years. This confirms the reports of the dramatically accelerated rate of language loss in recent times. Many other languages and language families are on the brink of total dormancy and so these numbers representing the world's linguistic diversity will change soon, dramatically for the worse (Campbell 2020: 277; Barlow and Campbell 2018).

Though not really comparable, the loss of a specific language can be likened in gravity to the loss of a single species, say the Siberian tiger or the right whale. However, the loss of whole families of languages is a tragedy similar in magnitude to the loss of whole branches of the animal kingdom, say to the loss of all felids (feline animals) or all cetaceans. Just imagine what the distress of biologists would be, attempting to understand the animal kingdom with major branches missing. Yet what confronts us is the staggering loss already of essentially a quarter of the linguistic diversity of the world, gone forever.

Why does it matter?

Why do fieldwork to document endangered languages? Why should the issue of language endangerment matter to us? The following are some of the main answers to these questions that we can reflect upon.

Social justice and human rights

Language loss is often not voluntary; it frequently involves violations of human rights, pushed by political or social repression, oppression, suppression, aggression, prejudice, violence, and at times by ethnic cleansing and genocide. It is simply a matter of right and wrong—and that should matter to us all.

A closely related reason for grave concern for language endangerment is because their languages matter immeasurably to the people who use them and identify with them, full stop. Language loss is typically experienced as a crisis of social identity. For many communities, work towards language revitalization is not about language in isolation, but is part of a "larger effort to restore personal and societal wellness" (Pfeiffer and Holm 1994: 35).[6] Some scholars and community activists insist that ongoing language loss leads to damaged communities and dysfunctional behaviors. They argue that one's psychological, social, and physical well-being is connected with one's native language; it shapes one's values, self-image, identity, relationships, and ultimately success in life. Indigenous voices testify to the crucial role language plays in their cultural and personal identity and to the personal heartbreak of language loss.[7]

Human concerns

Languages are treasure houses of information for history, literature, philosophy, art, and the wisdom and knowledge of humankind. Their stories, ideas, and words help us make sense of our own lives and of the world around us—of human experience, of the human condition in general. When a language becomes dormant without documentation, we lose incalculable amounts of human knowledge.

I illustrate this from two important areas of the humanities, literature and history, although examples from other areas of the humanities could also easily have been chosen.

The life-enriching value of literature is well understood—"by studying literature, we learn what it means to be human" (CliffsNotes n.d.). This is equally true of the oral literatures of the Indigenous peoples of the world. They, too, have struggled with the complexities of their world and the problems of life, and the insights, discoveries, and artistic creations represented in their literatures—whether written or oral—are of no less value to us all. When a language loses all of its speakers without documentation, taking into oblivion all its oral literature, oral tradition, and oral history with it, all of humanity is diminished.

We study history "to gain access to the laboratory of human experience" (Stearns n.d.). Great reservoirs of historical information are contained in languages. The classification of related languages teaches us about the history of human groups and how they are related to one another, and we gain understanding of contacts and migrations, the original homelands where languages were spoken, and past cultures from the comparison of related languages and the study of language change—all irretrievably lost when a language is lost without adequate documentation.

Loss of knowledge

The world's linguistic diversity is often considered one of humanity's most valuable treasures. This means that the loss of the hundreds of languages that have already been lost is a cataclysmic intellectual disaster, on many different levels. To cite a single example, encoded in each language is knowledge about the natural and cultural world it is used in. That knowledge is often not known outside the small speech communities where the majority of endangered languages are spoken. When a language is lost without adequate documentation, it takes with it this irreplaceable knowledge. It is argued that loss of such knowledge could have devastating consequences even for human survival.

A telling example comes from Seri, a language isolate of Sonora, Mexico, with about seven hundred speakers. The Seri have knowledge of "eelgrass" (*Zostera marina L.*) and "eelgrass seed," which they call *xnois*. It is "the only known grain from the sea used as a human food source . . . eelgrass has considerable potential as a general food source . . . Its cultivation would not require fresh water, pesticides, or artificial fertilizer" (Felger and Moser 1973: 355–6). Seri has a whole set of vocabulary dealing with eelgrass and its use. According to the argument, it is all too plausible to imagine a future in which some natural or human-caused disaster might compromise land-based crops, leaving human survival in jeopardy because of the loss of knowledge of alternative food sources such as the knowledge of eelgrass reflected in the Seri language.

This Seri case is an example of the specific knowledge that is often held by the smaller speech communities of the world—knowledge of medicinal plants and cures, of plants and animals yet unknown to Western science, of new crops, etc. Documentation of the languages of small-scale societies and of the knowledge they hold has significantly benefitted humanity.

For example, it is reported that 75 percent of plant-derived pharmaceuticals were "discovered" (meaning came to the awareness of Western medicine) through the examination of traditional medicines, where the language of curers often played a key role (Bierer et al. 1996). If these languages had become dormant and knowledge of the medicinal plants and their uses had been lost with them, all of humanity would be impoverished and human survival would be less secure.

I hasten to add in this context that today there is grave concern for Indigenous peoples' intellectual property rights and with biopiracy, the theft from and exploitation of Indigenous groups for their ethnobotanical knowledge and their medicines. At the same time many pharmaceutical companies now concentrate their research and development efforts on producing drugs synthetically in the laboratory. The good side of this is that it means less unscrupulous exploitation of Indigenous groups' intellectual property rights. It would seem also to increase risk that knowledge of effective new medicines based on Indigenous ethnobotanical knowledge stands a greater risk of being lost, even if the ethnobotany and traditional medicines of Indigenous peoples could be treated in legal and ethical ways.

When a language is not learned by the next generation, typically the knowledge encoded in the language fails to be transmitted. Most obvious in many cases is loss of the cultural knowledge about traditional medicines, the environment and ecology, about uses of plants and animals, modes of subsistence, fishing and hunting, horticulture, and also the many aspects of culture involved in ritualistic, poetic, esthetic, artistic, and other cultural functions of the language being lost. Loss of linguistic diversity and with it these kinds of knowledge means loss in the range of potential ways of understanding the world.

Another example comes from Paul Alan Cox (then director of the National Tropical Botanical Garden, in Hawai'i), working with Epenesa Mauigoa, a *taulasea* (healer) on Upolu, Western Samoa. They described 121 herbal remedies. In particular, their ethnobotanical research revealed knowledge of the mamala plant (*Homalanthus nutans*), used to treat yellow fever, and to discovery of the antiviral drug prostratin. The National Cancer Institute found healer preparations of *Homalanthus* to be active also against human immunodeficiency virus-type 1; in trials at that institute, it proved effective against HIV Type 1. Another healer led to the bark of *Erythrina variegata* and its use in healing. The Schering-Plough company found it effective against inflammation and isolated flavanone from it (Cox 1993, 2001; Cox and Balick 1994). Disappearance of this kind of knowledge would have been a loss for all of humanity.

So, it is argued that reduction of language diversity diminishes the adaptive strength of humans as a species because it lowers the pool of knowledge from which we can draw for survival.

Consequences for scientific understanding of human language

A major goal of linguistics is to understand human language capacity and human cognition through the study of what is possible and impossible in human languages. The discovery of previously unknown linguistic features as we document little-known languages contributes to this understanding and advances knowledge of how the human mind works. Conversely, language loss is a horrendous impediment to achieving this goal. The following example illustrates this well.

The discovery of the existence of languages with Object-Verb-Subject (OVS) and Object-Subject-Verb (OSV) basic word orders forced abandonment of a previously postulated language universal. Joseph Greenberg had proposed that "whenever the object precedes the verb the subject does likewise" (1978: 2). However, it was discovered that Hixkaryana, a Cariban language of Brazil with only 350 speakers, has OVS basic word order, as seen in the following sentence:

toto yonoye kamura
man ate jaguar
"The jaguar ate the man." (Derbyshire 1977)

We now know that several languages have OVS or OSV basic word order; most of them are spoken in small communities in the Amazon. Discovery of languages with these basic word orders not only forced abandonment of the postulated universal, but also required revision of a number of other theoretical claims about language. However, it is easy to imagine, given what has happened to Amazonian Indians at the hands of unscrupulous loggers, miner, and ranchers, that the

Figure 1.2 Alphabet posters for the school: team production (led by Nancy García, graduate research assistant) (Misión La Paz, Salta Province, Argentina, 2008)

few languages with these word orders could easily have become dormant before they were documented, leaving us forever with erroneous assumptions about what is possible and impossible in human languages and how that reflects on our understanding of human cognition.

Documentation of endangered languages has frequently and repeatedly demonstrated the importance of getting adequate documentation of these languages. The discovery of previously unknown linguistic traits is helping linguists to comprehend the full range of what is possible in human languages, a central goal of linguistic theory.[8]

Of crucial importance is making the fieldwork sensitive to and responsive to the needs and interests of the people whose languages are involved, collaborating for language revitalization and language conservation.

This look at the status of the world's languages and at why linguists feel so strongly about language documentation and about collaborating with communities to help strengthen or revive their languages provides the context and background for the fieldwork experiences reflected in the chapters of this book.

Where is fieldwork done?

As mentioned, most countries of the world and all continents except Antarctica have minority languages and languages that are endangered.[9] Languages in all these regions can be and widely are the targets of linguistic fieldwork; many are in need of much more fieldwork.

Figure 1.3 Fishing with diving nets, Chorote, Nivaclé, and Wichí speakers (Pilcomayo River, Misión La Paz, Salta Province, Argentina, 2005)

Most of the fieldwork I have done has been with Indigenous languages in Latin America, though I have also worked with some languages spoken in the US and Canada, Africa, Asia, the Pacific, and Europe.[10] Experiences involving fieldwork with languages of these regions is referred to in the chapters of this book.

How fieldwork is done is not a focus here, although a few things relevant to methods do show up in later chapters. There are a number of useful guides and manuals on linguistic fieldwork and related topics, each typically covering a different range of topics with varying orientations, but most offer guidelines and advice for how to do fieldwork.[11]

I also do not focus much direct attention here on ethics and ethical behavior in fieldwork; however, that should not be taken to mean that ethics is not important—it is extremely important. Several of the guides and manuals on fieldwork and also other sources provide valuable discussions and recommendations concerning ethics in fieldwork (see Rice 2006).

What is ethically appropriate for language fieldwork depends not just on Western notions of right and wrong, but also upon what is proper and what is not in the communities where the fieldwork is done—and little if anything in institutional review board (IRB) training addresses these culturally determined local aspects of ethics. The bottom line is that outsiders doing fieldwork need to figure it out and then do only what is ethical, nothing that is unethical, because that's the right way to do things, and, secondarily, because if they don't, it will very likely have negative consequences for them and their project, and potentially for other scholars and projects and for how linguists are viewed, positively or negatively, in the community, region, and country in general. It can have lasting negative consequences for the profession and for anyone ever being able to document certain languages critically in need of attention or for helping communities to deal with their language needs.

Preparation for fieldwork

When I was a student, lack of preparation for fieldwork was notorious and linguistics students were pretty much expected to learn how to do it on the spot . . . the spot being the deep end into which we were thrown. In a number of university programs a field methods course was available, but these courses tended to concentrate exclusively on elicitation and on analysis of what was elicited with little if any attention to anything else—valuable training to be sure, but far from adequate preparation for the many obstacles and difficulties typically encountered in doing actual fieldwork in the field. Most field methods courses today are still like that for the most part, concentrating on elicitation and analysis, sometimes also with attention to recording equipment, software programs that aid data management and analysis, and archiving. A few programs also offer courses involving language revitalization, grammar writing, dictionary making, and maybe with some practical guidelines for writing grants. More is available now in some linguistic programs with particular interest in language documentation, but still hardly ever are the sorts of issues addressed in this book brought to students' attention.

In my graduate training I was fortunate enough to have multiple linguistics field methods courses. The first had Tibetan as the language of the class. No guidance or instruction was given; rather, one-on-one time with the consultant was provided with the expectation that the student would write up the results of his or her analysis and submit it at the end of the course. The consultant for that class had been the Dalai Lama's bodyguard when he left Tibet, and I found him, his culture, and the stories he told so fascinating that it was hard to use the time allotted effectively for linguistic elicitation and analysis. So, my first field methods course was dive in, alone, and have at it, swimming in the deep end.

My next linguistics field methods course had Nuu-chah-nulth (then called Nootka) as its language, spoken on Vancouver Island,

British Columbia. It was a required year-long course for the MA in linguistics then at the University of Washington. In this case the instructor refused to reveal the name of the language to us students, for fear that we would go read whatever had been written about it. Of course, we eventually did figure out what language it was and we did eventually read what had been published on it. This is just wrong-headed as advice for making the most of fieldwork. Some do hold the opinion that you should not read anything by anybody else on the language in order not to be influenced by their potential mistakes, at least not in the beginning. Most, however, think that you should read everything you can get your hands on to be as prepared as possible for what to expect and to be able to progress faster, and to advance beyond whatever documentation there may already be on the language. Of course, you're not to believe or accept as accurate anything you read but rather you are to test and confirm or reject whatever data and analyses those who came before you may have provided.

The instructor of our course also insisted that nothing be tape-recorded. His idea was that doing it the hard way would make us better at hearing and transcribing the language. Of course, audio and video recording can and does greatly facilitate how much and how fast you can progress in your fieldwork. Today this admonition to avoid recording would seem close to criminal to some ardent proponents of language documentation who advocate recording everything and archiving the recordings for preservation and for potential use by members of the language community and others.

Later, I had a quarter-long field methods course with Tohono O'odham as its language (then called Papago), a Uto-Aztecan language spoken in Arizona and northern Sonora, Mexico. It was a fine course, but the same as the others, just jumping into elicitation and analysis with no discussion of anything else—and a quarter goes by frustratingly fast, especially if the language has complex phonology or morphology.

These field methods courses never addressed the unexpected things that are talked about in this book, with nothing about how to find language consultants, interactions with people, transportation, maintaining health, and a whole array of socio-political-geographical-medical matters fieldworkers typically have to contend with, things that figure centrally in the chapters of this book.

I believe that today most seasoned fieldworkers would advise anyone embarking on new fieldwork to learn as much as possible from as many sources and people as possible in advance to help get prepared for what to expect and for what might be encountered in the fieldwork.

More about preparation for fieldwork comes up in subsequent chapters. We turn first to fieldwork adventures and discoveries, and then continue on to the many other kinds of fieldwork challenges and complications not considered in other publications about linguistic fieldwork.

Notes

1. I've also heard it said that a better question would be, "How many languages have you made love in?" Sharing my father's Code of the West, I could not answer a question like that. The Code of the West demands respect for women; that includes avoiding anything that could harm a woman's reputation and not telling off-colored jokes nor using foul language around women and children. So, that question simply doesn't compute, for me, and in any case, again, if there is any connection between language and love-making, it has nothing at all to do with linguistics. Also, I have taught five languages (Finnish, K'iche', Nahuatl, Quechua, and Spanish) in courses at universities, but no one ever asks a question about how many languages you have taught, and, anyway, teaching languages also is not what defines a linguist either.
2. Campbell and Belew (2018) and Rehg and Campbell (2018) can be consulted for details concerning the crisis affecting the endangered languages of the world.

3. <http://www.endangeredlanguages.com/>. (Accessed June 28, 2021.)
4. More precisely, it listed 3,428 total languages but this includes 251 dormant or awakening languages, that is, languages with no known native speakers, and 135 for which the number of speakers is unknown.
5. As of 2018, *Ethnologue* listed a total of 7,097 languages in the world (https://www.ethnologue.com/statistics/status, accessed August 8, 2018), but when this is adjusted to remove the 245 with no remaining speakers and the one constructed language, its number of living languages is actually 6,879. The figure of 45 percent of the world's languages being currently endangered is calculated based on *Ethnologue*'s total number of living languages compared with the *Catalogue of Endangered Languages*' total number of endangered languages.
6. See also, for example, Galla and Goodwill (2018).
7. Some of the Indigenous voices that make this abundantly clear include Jenny L. Davis (2019), Darrell Kipp (2008), Barbra Meek (2012), Anton Treuer (2020), Lucille Watahomigie (1998), and Ofelia Zepeda (1990), among others.
8. Several examples can be seen in Palosaari and Campbell (2011); there are others also in Chapter 3 of this book.
9. Details on these can be found in the *Catalogue of Endangered Languages*, at <http://www.endangeredlanguages.com/>. (Accessed June 28, 2021.)
10. Not so long ago, some students asked me how many countries I had traveled to or worked in, so I counted—ninety-two (of the UN's 193 official sovereign states). I went to most of these for professional reasons, to do research, to teach, or to participate in academic conferences, though some involved just curiosity and enjoyment (tourism). In my case, there has been something to the notion of "join linguistics, see the world," parodying the US Navy's old recruitment slogan, "join the Navy, see the world," seen on hundreds of recruitment posters in its time, and related to the Army's "get paid to go to school to learn a language and then travel the world," mentioned earlier. I feel very fortunate for the travel opportunities my profession as a linguist has afforded me.
11. Some examples are: Abbi (2001), Bouquiaux and Thomas (1992),

Bowern (2015), Burling (1984), Crowley (2007), Dixon (2007), Gippert et al. (2006), Grenoble and Furbee (2010), Healey (1975), Meakins et al. (2018), Payne (1997), Sakel and Everett (2012), Samarin (1967), Thieberger (2012), Vaux and Cooper (1999), and Vaux et al. (2007), among a few others. They each provide useful information for doing fieldwork. Crowley (2007), Dixon (1983, 2011), Macaulay (2005), and Newman and Ratliff (2001) give personal accounts, tales by linguists about doing fieldwork, mostly quite different from the sorts of experiences talked about in this book.

2

Fieldwork adventure

Introduction

The accusation of "swashbuckler" mentioned in Chapter 1—always embarrassing to me—has to do with accounts of some of my fieldwork experiences that got out. In some cases they got told by colleagues or students who participated in research projects with me in the field; in others, in unguarded moments I mentioned some happening that got retold and probably embellished as it was passed along, usually to my embarrassment. I'll recount a few instances here. I hope they show that linguistic fieldwork can indeed involve high adventure and great fun. However, it needs to be clear that not all fieldwork all the time is glamorous or glorious—and most of the instances related here involve also considerable discomfort and often danger.

What may seem like adventures in fieldwork as we tell about them should not be allowed to overshadow the bug bites, dangers, illnesses, lousy food, crumby shelter, thefts, threats, travel problems, and a litany of hardships and icky stuff also often encountered, though not often included in zealous talk about fieldwork experiences and the wonders of doing fieldwork—though they are talked

Figure 2.1 Lyle Campbell with armadillo (Misión La Paz, 2007)

about in subsequent chapters here. Much of the work involves just plodding on, sheer drudgery, in bad living conditions, where lots of things often go wrong. Even in such instances, however, there is some good news, I think. Even when things become really difficult and trying, or go wrong, we still learn from those experiences. Several examples of the kinds of hardships I encountered doing fieldwork and what I learned from them are related in later chapters.

The bush-plane flight to Apolo, Bolivia, and a mystery variety of Quechua

Much of my research has been on Indigenous languages of Latin America. Very often it involved searching for possible remaining speakers of endangered languages, where travel to research sites was often not only challenging but sometimes difficult in the extreme. On some occasions it involved flights in bush planes.[1]

Early in my academic life, when I was a graduate student just about to go off to do my dissertation research, I was invited to participate in a survey of Quechua dialects in Peru and Bolivia. I had experience with Quechua from being a graduate research assistant on a project to write a pedagogical grammar of Cuzco Quechua for the Peace Corps. As we did our survey, we kept being told of a strange and different dialect in Apolo, Bolivia. We resisted going there because the only ways in were either a trek of many days on foot over the Andes or a bush plane. However, we were told so often of this unusual dialect that ultimately we decided it was necessary to go there to check it out.

Apolo is on the jungle side of the Andes, at about 7,000 feet (2,000 meters) elevation. At that time, guerrilla activity had been announced in the area, and this required us to obtain a *salvoconducto*, an official document from the government in La Paz, a permission to enter the dangerous area. The bubonic plague—no joking—was also announced in the area. The flight was, unsurprisingly, delayed. When we showed up at the scheduled departure time, pieces of wing and the plane's tail were scattered around on the ground with the pilot and his assistant filing down bits here and there so, for example, flaps would move without sticking. Eventually the plane was reassembled with all its pieces. Before take-off, the plane was sprayed with DDT—for the bubonic plague. We, naturally enough, knew nothing about bubonic plague nor about what DDT might be able to do to keep a plane from catching it—only later did I figure out that the DDT was for killing fleas, for keeping the plague-bearing critters from coming back over the mountains with the plane to infect other areas.

The smallish cargo hold of the plane was filled with beef carcasses to be flown out to Apolo—and, yes, due to the combination of DDT and beef carcasses, the plane stank, fiercely; fortunately once airborne, the smell was no longer so noticeable. The plane itself had only four seats for passengers—we were five passengers.

The section behind the seats had been loaded with iron elbows for construction, tied down with ropes. Being a gentleman, I ended up seated on the iron elbows, grasping onto the ropes that tied the iron elbows down.

And off we went, flying through mountain passes, seemingly with the plane's wings nearly scraping mountains on either side. The international airport in La Paz, our starting point, is the highest in the world, at an altitude of 13,325 feet (4,062 meters). The flight to Apolo had to cross the Andes, over 21,000 feet (6,000 meters) high, flying through mountain passes of around 17,000 feet (5,500 meters) altitude, unpressurized and with no oxygen, of course.

Upon arrival over Apolo, the plane's landing gear would not come down, though I did not understand this until after we had flown around and around for a long time. Finally, as darkness was coming on, the pilot flew the plane up quite high and just let it fall nose-first for what seemed a great distance, and then sharply pulled the plane up out of its nosedive as we got close to the ground. This was done some three times, with me clutching frantically onto the ropes tied around the iron elbows. Finally the wheels came down and we landed. Seatbelts on commercial flights have never seemed to have the same character since then.

Upon arrival in Apolo, we were met at the airstrip by the *comandante* (military commander) in charge of the outpost there, drunk. He alternated between aggressively demanding our *salvoconducto* document in Spanish and demanding "the contraband" in Portuguese—contraband activity in the area being something we were unaware of until it was demanded of us in this way—all the time with the *comandante* intermittently shaking his rifle at us, three gringo linguists just hoping to investigate the local dialect of Quechua briefly. After a seemingly long time, though probably actually only about half an hour, of aggressive harangue, we finally convinced him that we definitely wanted to do everything properly and so we would appear in person in the morning and bring our *salvoconducto* to the *comandancia*—the official headquarters, actually a small wooden building—where it could be recorded officially in the registry as it should be. At the *comandancia* the next morning a junior officer officially registered us and our documents; the *comandante* was apparently sleeping it off.

It turns out that the guerrillas were nowhere near this area; reportedly they were much further east and south of there. No one knew of nor was there any sign of bubonic plague, either.

The dialect of Quechua in Apolo, though interesting, was not as unusual as we'd so often been told. It appeared to be the result of immigrants from further north, in Peru, whose dialect sounded unusual to those speaking Bolivian varieties of Quechua.

Apolo was a very pleasant place—sunny, warm, not hot, not so high as to cause altitude sickness, with lots of orange trees and beautiful waterfalls. However, it turned out we were stuck there for several days. We had planned on being there just a couple of days until the same plane we arrived in would make its return trip. We had to wait until they could get another plane out there, one without the landing gear problem.

This one was an even smaller plane, but again with only four seats for passengers, this time with a Quechua woman in one of them with a stereotypic large round basket on her lap with chickens' heads sticking up through the netting covering it, gawking around nervously. This time, however, the mountains were completely socked in with clouds and the pilot flew by his wristwatch—he consulted it, making slight turns every few minutes to adjust the direction of flight. I still had shocking images in my mind of nearly scraping mountains on either side of the plane on the flight out to Apolo when the visibility had been good. This return flight through the clouds with the pilot flying by his wristwatch evoked varied emotional reactions of the most negative and unpleasant sorts.

I have flown on other bush planes elsewhere, including another, in Chiapas, Mexico, that had pieces of it strewn about, with filing and hammering on plane parts going on before take-off. However, these were few, and I always avoided them unless there was no other choice.

"Witch" and people-eater

The "witch" (shaman) attribute mentioned in Chapter 1 came from fieldwork with Guazacapán Xinka of southeastern Guatemala. I was there attempting to document Xinkan languages. There were once four languages in the Xinkan language family; today there is no longer any native speaker of any of them. At that time three of the languages, though extremely endangered, were still spoken by a few elders of their communities. The fourth language, Yupiltepeque, no longer had any speakers though a few elders could still remember a handful of words and phrases that they had learned as children from old people in the community, long ago.

Though extremely little had been written on Guazacapán Xinka at that time, a scholar had published a story about *naguales* from there. A *nagual* (also spelled *nahual*) is an animal alter-ego, animal companion spirit or guardian spirit, an animal with which one is associated from birth. "Witches" are believed to have the ability to shape-shift into their animal companion and change back again to human form at will. "Witch" here is a translation of Spanish *brujo*, but *brujo* is very different in meaning from English "witch," and thus is sometimes translated instead as "shaman," "sorcerer," or "curer," as "witch-doctor" in former times.

Unlike most other places in Mesoamerica where *naguales* are usually wild animals, in Guazacapán the belief was that people's *naguales* were domestic animals, and that one could tell when witches had shifted to their *naguales* because their ears would remain human ears in form. For example, don Lucio, one of the principal Guazacapán consultants, was believed to be a "witch" whose *nagual* was a domestic pig and people of the town, reportedly, knew when don Lucio had shifted to his pig alter-ego because they would see a pig walking around town with human ears.

I asked the main consultants there if they could tell me this story about *naguales* in Xinka. However, they just clammed up, said nothing. I assumed it was a delicate topic and so just let it drop. Not long after that, while I was working with don Cipriano, one of the principal consultants, he asked me why I had asked about that story when I had all those gifts/powers (*dones* in Spanish). I had no idea what he meant. Eventually it came out that people there believed that I had the power to leave my body asleep at night and go off in my spirit to do my deeds, "be they good or evil," and they could tell when I returned, because, according to what they reported, they could hear my spirit land on the roof.

I foolishly made the mistake of mentioning this to some linguist friends also working in Guatemala. For a long time after that I was mercilessly and relentlessly teased about being a witch (*brujo*/shaman), that is, for being believed to be a witch by the Guazacapán consultants.

People-eaters

When I was working with Guazacapán Xinka, I encountered very trying difficulties in attempting to analyze the glottalized consonants.[2] In frustration one day I gathered a group of eight of the most knowledgeable remaining speakers together to ask them questions to try to solve the problem. In this meeting of several elders and me, don Alonso, the oldest and most respected of the group, just announced to everyone present that apparently the gringos, meaning North Americans in this context, were not the people-eaters, it must be the *ingleses*, the English. I wasn't sure what this was all about, but I was happy to discover that they no longer thought I was a people-eater (*comegente*), though I hadn't previously been aware of this suspicion about me.

I believe that the pronouncement that I was not a people-eater had something to do with don Alonso having had a broken wrist that had not healed properly and had not been attended to for the several weeks since he broke it and which pained him severely. When I discovered this, I felt very sad that he was suffering and I arranged to take him to the nearest town with a clinic, where they set the broken bones and put his arm in a cast and got rid of the constant severe pain, treatment which I happily paid for . . . and he survived that experience, uneaten.

The idea of foreigners as people-eaters, I learned later, seems to have come from hospitals and from the practice of using cadavers of some Guatemalan Indians in medical training. Often the Indigenous people there would resist going to the hospital, often located far from where they lived, delaying until their conditions were very severe, and consequently many died after reaching the hospital. The bodies of some of them that went unclaimed were used for training of medical students. Some of the doctors involved in this training were apparently foreigners, "gringos," and dissecting cadavers was somehow equated with eating people, ipso facto, that some gringo doctors were involved in this kind of medical instruction meant that gringos were people-eaters.

When don Alonso made the announcement that apparently it was not the North American gringos who were the people-eaters but rather probably it was the English, I was so taken back that I had no ready response. I could only get out something to the effect that I personally knew of no evidence that the English ate people either. It turns out these Indigenous men in Guazacapán had no clear conception of who the *ingleses* might be; they had heard the name but to them it just referred to some vague, distant group somewhere, and they were uncertain to which precise people the name might apply.

Notions due to cultural mismatches

The cases where I was thought to be a witch or maybe a people-eater illustrate some of the sorts of things fieldworkers not from the community where the language is spoken can encounter as they, representing other parts of the world, and local beliefs come into contact with one another. I'll recount here a few additional instances of this sort of mismatch of ideas in cultural contact, though they involve no "swashbuckling."

In another instance don Cipriano, the important Guazacapán Xinka consultant mentioned above, told me the story of *El Gran Rey Catarral del Mar* (The Great Catarrhal King of the Sea). Guazacapán is near the coast, and the upshot of the story is the belief that there is a giant king standing out in the ocean with a tortilla griddle in each hand to heat up and evaporate seawater so that it will not flood the land ever again. Don Cipriano's story ends with the line, "and that's why we don't want you gringos screwing around with him [the great king] with your jet planes, so that it won't flood anymore," a seemingly incongruent juxtaposition of modern technology with local beliefs.

In another case, when I was interviewing some elderly men in La Floresta, in Chiapas, Mexico, one of the southernmost towns where Tzotzil (a Mayan language) is spoken, one of the men asked me if I had a dollar with me. I did happen to have one and so I pulled it out of my wallet and showed it to him. At first he was dubious about whether this could be a real dollar. I was surprised as he told me that he had heard so much about the famous *dólar* in news reports on the radio that he believed dollars were *globos de oro* (balls of gold).

A different sort of contact interface was an encounter I had with traditional medicine. I had been working with don Francisco Calvo Pérez of Trinitaria, in Chiapas, Mexico, one of the last speakers there of Southeastern Tzeltal. Don Francisco was the *encargado* (leader) of pilgrimages (*romerías*) in which Tojolabal and Tzeltal participated,

Figure 2.2 Don Francisco Calvo Pérez (Trinitaria, Chiapas, Mexico, 1986)

trekking to sacred sites (caves, mountain tops, etc.) to make ritual offerings, and he was a famous curer (*curandero*), much sought after by Tojolabal, Tzeltal, and even *ladinos* (people of European ancestry). While there, I got a bad cold, and don Francisco volunteered to *pulsar* ("pulse") me. Pulsing is a kind of curing practice in which the *curandero* feels the patient's "pulse," feeling not just the wrist but various points on the arms and legs and elsewhere on the body. The feeling of the "blood" in the "pulse" reveals to him not just what is wrong and how to treat it, but the overall condition of the patient's "spirit."

It felt sort of odd but very interesting, being pulsed. In my case don Francisco prescribed as the remedy a drink made of several ingredients, fennel being an important one and *aguardiente* as the largest ingredient. *Aguardiente* is booze, almost literally "firewater" (from Spanish *agua* "water" + *ardiente* "burning"), a powerful alcoholic beverage usually made from sugar cane. I concluded that whether it could cure a cold or not might come to seem irrelevant; if the patient drank a sufficiently large quantity of this remedy, he or she might no longer care about the illness nor much about anything else, either. I did drink it, and found it not particularly unpleasant. However, I am among that small portion of the world's population who cannot drink alcoholic beverages without nasty effects, in my case severe headaches. So I didn't drink it in sufficient quantity to reach a state of blissful oblivion where the illness would seem irrelevant to anything at all.

Cases such as those recounted here show surprising and unexpected differences when the local culture and a non-local fieldworker's culture interact. From such cases I learned that I should always be on watch for unexpected culturally mediated differences in outlooks and views. Remaining on good terms with the people I worked with or even being permitted to continue the investigation sometimes depended on being alert to such differences and on how I behaved in such situations.

Realism

Stories such as those shared here show that linguistic fieldwork can be fun and involve adventure and exciting interactions with other cultures and peoples, though later chapters reveal that it can also be arduous and unpleasant in many ways. Some fieldworkers like to recount their fieldwork experiences as high adventure, though that isn't an accurate image of what most linguistic fieldwork is like. Claire Bowern in her book on field methods chastises the Indiana Jones image of the fieldworker as "some rugged individual who . . . lives a life of deprivation and austerity, comforted and nourished by weird insects and by the satisfaction that they are preserving a knowledge system for humanity" (2008: 2). She declares this to be "rubbish," reminding us that in any case Indiana Jones was "a terrible linguist" (2008: 2, 225). She is correct that the excesses of the linguistic swashbuckler image need to be tempered with realism about the difficulties and dangers brought more centrally into focus. The following chapters of this book definitely highlight many of the more challenging and icky aspects of fieldwork, too. Balance is needed.

It is good to recognize that linguistic fieldwork can involve adventure, romance, discovery of new knowledge, contribution to linguistics generally and to communities of speakers whose languages we work with, and can give a sense of personal reward and fulfillment from practicing our craft for the benefit both of science and of other human beings. It is these and other positive aspects that make fieldwork so exciting. However, it is awareness of the often trying, distressing, challenging, and downright horrible aspects of fieldwork, recognition of what one is getting into, that can help the fieldwork to succeed.

Other "adventures" in fieldwork are recounted in different contexts in other chapters of this book, along with the "realism" foreshadowed here.

Notes

1. Other difficulties involving travel are taken up in detail in Chapter 7.
2. Glottalized consonants, also called "ejectives," are not found in English or most better-known languages of the world. They are produced by closing the vocal cords and producing a consonant not with air from

the lungs as in the case of most speech sounds, but with only the air trapped above the closed vocal cords. Because some of the people with whom I was working were imperfect learners of the language, called semispeakers, they glottalized some consonants in words where other speakers lacked them or they lacked glottalized consonants in words where others had them. The difficulty for analysis stemmed from the fact that some of the consultants had just never learned which words should have glottalized consonants and which ones not. Since Spanish, their dominant language, has no glottalized consonants, some, due to imperfect learning, simply glottalized almost any consonant in Xinka words randomly. I asked the speakers of the language in that group in turn to pronounce words where glottalization appeared to vary and was unclear. This is, incidentally, a terrible fieldwork tactic; it can go badly wrong for a number of reasons. For example, a speaker may just mimic whatever an earlier speaker said or some speaker may not want to say anything that might conflict with what another had said before them, and so on. By this technique, the uncertainty can be compounded rather than resolved.

3

Discoveries

Introduction

One of the reasons linguists do fieldwork is to discover new things. To discover new knowledge is a big reason why most academics do the research that we do. The general public, however, might associate the word "discovery" with big, monumental new findings, thought of more as "breakthroughs." At the same time it seems that anything of more than passing significance is often said by journalists and reporters to have "astounded" scientists and experts—sensationalizing the news seems sometimes to be their main mission in life. While to linguists some of our findings do seem sensational for linguistic reasons, rarely would any of us think of them as so sensational as to astound all fellow linguists. Some discoveries in my own fieldwork have excited me—intellectually stimulating and rewarding, though not hugely sensational, not even to sensationalizing journalists. Some things that I consider to be discoveries involve just small points of analysis in languages whose names hardly anyone has ever heard of, though some other discoveries do feel somewhat grander. This chapter is about some of them. The purpose of presenting them here is to help demonstrate the value and excitement of linguistic fieldwork, of language documentation.

Several things found in the structure of the languages that I have investigated in fieldwork have significant implications that require some theoretical claims made about language in general to be abandoned or significantly modified. These are in my estimation among the most substantial discoveries that I have made. However, some of them are hard to explain without relying on linguistic terminology that may not be familiar to all readers. I try to touch more lightly on such cases. To those readers for whom the discussion of some topic presented here may seem too opaque, feel free just to skip on to the cases that are easier to follow. The main points won't be missed.

A new language

Perhaps situated at the higher end of some hypothetical significance scale when it comes to the public's sense of sensation might be the discovery of a new language. I discovered a new language, Jumaytepeque Xinka, one of four Xinkan languages in southeastern Guatemala—and that is exciting. It does happen from time to time that a new language is discovered, though ever more rarely in modern times, and extremely rarely now in Mesoamerica. "Discovery" of a language, of course, does not mean unknown to its speakers and their communities, but rather only that the wider world, especially the world of scholarship, was previously unaware of it.

I had come across indications in colonial records from the 1700s that an unidentified language may have been spoken earlier in the department of Santa Rosa, and elders that I worked with in Guazacapán, where one of the Xinkan languages was spoken, told me that they remembered from their childhood men who spoke a language that sounded similar to their own coming from Santa Rosa with goods on mules to trade in the Guazacapán market. In surveying the zone carefully, I discovered Jumaytepeque Xinka, spoken in a small village very near the top of the volcano of Jumaytepeque. It is a relatively small volcano, 5,955 feet (1,815 meters) high, with corn planted on much of it and with coffee grown higher up. It had only one road, which washed out each year in the rainy season and wasn't repaired again until the next coffee harvest. So entry usually was by foot, hoofing it the 4.5 miles (7 kilometers) up from nearby Nueva Santa Rosa.

As an aside, once when I was able to enter with a jeep loaned to me from the Proyecto Lingüístico Francisco Marroquín (PLFM) in Antigua, Guatemala, the unexpected struck, as it often does in fieldwork. When I attempted to leave, at the end of a day, it turned out that the lights on the jeep just wouldn't work and I couldn't fix them. Fortunately, an elderly woman who lived there gave me permission to spend the night in her storage shed, where I slept on sacks of corn—very cold, but this time without the fleas so common elsewhere.

Language loss in Jumaytepeque was quite advanced but there were a few very old people who were fully competent native speakers. Terrence (Terry) Kaufman and I were able to work with them on their language and succeeded in completing major documentation of it. This discovery was gratifying, and I'm truly glad that I found this language in time to work with competent speakers and to get good documentation of it. Today, the language is no longer spoken; there are no surviving native speakers.

Several years later, Terry and I returned to Jumaytepeque, hoping to check some of the words and other things we had recorded earlier and to collect additional information, and to say hello to our old friends. We were told somewhat aggressively by a pair of elderly women that the two speakers of Jumaytepeque who had gone with us to work in Antigua were now dead—we were very sad to hear of the death of our friends. It was also disturbing that there was no longer anyone who knew the language.

The implied accusation was that these men had died because they had gone with us to Antigua, that their deaths were our fault. To those making the allegation it was apparently irrelevant that both men were already in their late eighties when they had worked with us and, had they still been alive at the time of our later visit when we were told this, they would have been in their nineties. As people seem often to do, the accusers took a correlation as causal, further fanned, I am guessing, by some suspicion of us wielding some sort of witchcraft, what I assume that they assumed was the real cause of the deaths.

A new speech sound

Perhaps somewhat lower on that hypothetical public-perception significance scale would be the discovery of a new speech sound. To linguists, however, such a finding is exciting. To us, the discovery of a previously unknown speech sound is like finding a new species of mammal or bird is to biologists. I encountered a unique speech sound, unknown in any other language, in Nivaclé (a Matacoan language of Argentina and Paraguay): $\widehat{kl}$, a simultaneously articulated and released "k"-sound and "l"-sound produced together as a single sound.[1]

Nivaclé, with /kl/ ($[\widehat{kl}]$) and voiceless "l" ($[ɬ]$) but with no plain voiced "l" ($[l]$), constitutes an exception to a number of proposed crosslinguistic generalizations about laterals ("l" sounds) and liquids ("l" and "r" sounds), providing valuable information relevant to the question of possible sound systems generally. For example, Maddieson (1984: 88) proposed the following:[2]

1. A language with two or more liquids is expected to have a contrast of a lateral and a non-lateral. However, in Nivaclé both liquids are laterals and there are no non-lateral liquids—no "r" sounds.

2. A language with one or more laterals typically has one voiced lateral approximant: for example, a marked lateral in a language implies the presence also of plain "l," and that voiceless "l" also implies the presence of plain "l." As Maddieson and Emmorey put it, "voiceless lateral approximants always occur together with a voiced lateral approximant in the inventory" (1984: 182; see also Ladefoged and Maddieson 1996: 198). This, however, is not true of Nivaclé; although it has two laterals, its /ɬ/ ([l̥]) is a voiceless approximant, not a fricative (see, e.g., Ladefoged and Maddieson 1996: 198), and the other, its /k͡l/, is not an approximant. Nivaclé has no plain (voiced) /l/.
3. A language with two or more laterals contrasts them either in point of articulation or in manner of articulation, but not in both. The Nivaclé laterals, however, differ both in point of articulation and in manner of articulation.

Thus Nivaclé laterals illustrate how the discovery of a new speech sound in the documentation of little-known languages can have an impact on general claims about language. Given the counterexamples just mentioned, all of these proposed generalizations about laterals need to be re-evaluated.

Nivaclé has a number of other unique or highly unusual traits, all of value for helping linguists towards the goal of understanding the full range of what is possible and impossible in human languages.[3] As already mentioned, knowing what is possible in human languages contributes to understanding potentials and limitations of human cognition and through this more about us as humans. This is one of the principal reasons why many linguists do fieldwork to document languages.

A new dialect and its implications

The discovery of a previously unknown dialect may be quite low in the general public's assessment on a hypothetical significance scale for discoveries. Finding new dialects of poorly known languages is not too uncommon, but discovery of new dialects of well-known languages is rare. I discovered a new dialect of Tzeltal, Southeastern Tzeltal. This was surprising because Tzeltal and Tzeltal dialectology has had a lot of attention from linguists and anthropologists and missionaries for decades, and so discovery of a new variety was unexpected.

Southeastern Tzeltal was spoken in a wide zone of southeastern Chiapas, Mexico, from Trinitaria to the lakes of Monte Bello to the east and to the Guatemalan border and even a bit beyond in the south and southeast from Trinitaria, in a zone where the Indigenous languages had been thought to have ceased to be spoken long ago, in the colonial era. Southeastern Tzeltal was very endangered when I worked there; nevertheless, I found elderly speakers in locations across the zone, and I was able to get considerable information about it from speakers in a good number of places. This dialect has several features of its own that make it quite different from the other Tzeltal dialects (Campbell 1987, 1988).

I discovered, contrary to all beliefs and expectations, that the Tzeltal-speaking territory had extended even into current-day Guatemala.[4] Although the language was all but lost there by the time I visited, I was able to interview don Demetrio Martínez, speaker of Southeastern Tzeltal in Gracias a Dios, an *aldea* (village) that belonged to the *municipio* (like a county) of Nentón in Huehuetenango Department, Guatemala. As part of the linguistic survey I was making in the region where Southeastern Tzeltal is spoken, speakers I interviewed in Carmen Xan, later spelled Carmen Xhan, a remote place in Chiapas near the Guatemalan border, told me about Tzeltal speakers in Guatemala, in Gracias a Dios.

There was no border-crossing station there, so I left the jeep on the Mexican side of the border, just crashed the border on foot, and set off to look for the Tzeltal speakers reported to be there. There was a military outpost in Gracias a Dios, just a mile and a half (a couple of kilometers) from the border, with a few soldiers stationed there with little to do. I bumped into the Guatemalan soldiers and explained what I was doing. Though I expected to be ushered harshly back across the border for entering unofficially with no visa, if not just arrested, instead they were delighted, as apparently any distraction from the ordinary was welcome, and four of them helped me locate don Demetrio and they hung out with him and me while we talked.

The ruins of Chaculá are quite near Gracias a Dios, only a few miles' walk from there, and I was invited by a couple of the Guatemalan officers to go with them to visit the ruins, but word spread and I ended up being accompanied by pretty much the entire group of the some fifteen Guatemalan soldiers stationed there, apparently a fun outing and temporary escape from boredom for them all. Chaculá is a quite large, unrestored Maya ruin, but with a lot to see.

Later when I told colleagues in Chiapas about crashing the border, they were horrified, imagining jail, prison, or possible death, though subsequently when I returned there for additional fieldwork with Tzeltal in Gracias a Dios some of those who originally were aghast accompanied me, for additional border crashing—big treat. That obviously would not happen today; subsequent violent conflicts and refugee problems led to crackdowns along this border.

Coxoh

Meanwhile, the discovery of Southeastern Tzeltal led to other discoveries, exciting, at least to me. Coxoh had always been identified as the name of a Mayan group and their Mayan language, once spoken in several towns in southern Chiapas, that had disappeared in the colonial period. Almost nothing is known of this language other than frequent mentions of its name in colonial documents. Through painstaking scouring of colonial sources that mentioned Coxoh (in various spellings, Coxogh, Coxog, Coxoc, Coxot, Coxhog, Cochox), I was able to pull together enough evidence to identify Coxoh as Southeastern Tzeltal, not a separate, independent, and now dormant Mayan language. From evidence from the geography, several place names associated with Coxoh, and the extremely few words mentioned—Coxoh names for two trees—I could show that Coxoh was actually the divergent dialect of Tzeltal, no longer spoken in those towns, but still spoken by a few elderly people in locations not far away.

For example, the earliest colonial documents indicate that Coxoh was spoken in Comitán and Zapaluta (modern Trinitaria), and in four other towns that no longer exist, Aquespala, Coapa, Coneta, and Escuintenango. Comitán and Trinitaria are today and always have been Tzeltal-speaking towns, though they have shifted mostly to Spanish now. The Comitán *Libro de Bautismos* (Book of Baptisms) from 1569, the earliest source from there, speaks of Comitán being administered in Coxoh, but all the non-Spanish things written in this book are indisputably in Tzeltal. The two tree names mentioned in early documents from Coxoh towns appear to be Tzeltal, as are the place names mentioned in these sources, and the local Spanish of this region has a number of loanwords for local plants that are Tzeltal in origin, names not known in the Spanish of other regions. The conclusion that Coxoh was actually Southeastern Tzeltal seems safe (Campbell and Gardner 1988).

One lesson I took from the discovery of this new dialect was to not assume that received views are necessarily complete or accurate and to be alert to the possibility of new, as yet unrecognized things when we do the fieldwork that we do.

Language structure discoveries

I will mention here just a few additional discoveries made in the course of doing fieldwork to investigate little-known languages. They involve the structural aspects of languages and have significant implications for theoretical claims about language in general. These, too, are of the sorts of things that excite linguists but might not seem sensational to others, since it can require a linguistic background to understand their significance.

In one example, the Mayan languages of highland Guatemala have an imploded voiceless uvular stop; in the International Phonetic Alphabet this is [ɠ], produced by closing the vocal cords, placing the tongue in position for the uvular *q*, like *k* pronounced further back in the mouth towards the back of the throat, and lowering the vocal cords slightly to create a reduction in pressure in the air trapped between the uvular *q* and the vocal cords so that when the "q" and the vocal cords are released simultaneously, air comes rushing into the mouth, "imploding," creating ingressive "q." Before this imploded "q" sound was understood in these Mayan languages (Campbell 1973), it was claimed that imploded sounds had to be voiced (like "b," "d," "g") and could not be voiceless (like "p," "t," "k") (Maddieson 1984: 121; Ladefoged and Maddieson 1996: 87–9). This discovery had implications for claims about what is possible in human languages and for proposed language universals.

These languages with implode "q" further show that the claim is erroneous that says that if a language has an imploded stop articulated further back in the mouth (as [ɠ] is) then all the stops articulated further towards the front of the mouth in the glottalic series must also be imploded (Greenberg 1970). That is, by this claim, the presence of imploded "q" ([ɠ]) in several highland Mayan languages would mean that these languages must also have imploded [ɓ, ɗ, ɠ]; however, several of these languages have only imploded "b" ([ɓ]) and imploded "q" ([ɠ]) but no imploded "d" or "g"—that is, their glottalic series of consonants has [ɓ, t', k', q]—against the expectations of the proposed universal (Campbell 1973).

Another example is the unique system of vowel harmony in Xinkan languages in Guatemala. In languages that have vowel harmony, there are restrictions on which vowels can co-occur with other vowels within a word. These languages distinguish classes of vowels defined by certain phonetic traits that the harmonic sets of vowels share. Within a word, vowels from one harmonic class cannot occur in combination with vowels belonging to a different harmony class; only combinations of vowels that are members of the same class can co-occur with one another in a word. For example, in some languages, the vowels of a word must all be front vowels, or all back vowels, but words with combinations of both front vowels and back vowels together are not permitted.

The vowel harmony of Xinkan is like that of no other language. Xinkan languages have three vowel harmony sets: //i, u, a//, //e, o, a//, and //ɨ, a//. That is, /a/ is neutral and can co-occur with any of the other vowels, while *i* can co-occur with no other vowel other than itself and neutral *a*. Otherwise, words have only combinations of these high vowels (*i* or *u*) or of mid vowels (*e* or *o*), with or without neutral *a*, but words containing combinations with both high vowels and mid vowels together do not occur. In most languages with vowel harmony, vowels within a word agree in frontness vs. backness or in roundness vs. non-roundness, or in having advanced tongue root (ATR) or lacking ATR. Xinkan's vowel harmony, that depends on high vs. mid vowels, with the low vowel /a/ as neutral, is unknown in any other language.

This has implications for theoretical claims about vowel harmony in languages generally. The fact that Xinkan harmonic sets of vowels are split based on vowel height but with /a/ as neutral, occurring with both high vowels and mid vowels, runs counter to the claim that vowel harmony is due to specific articulatory motivations—it is not possible to talk of a high vowel vs. mid vowel articulatory motivation when the low vowel /a/ can occur with vowels of either set. The fact that the high central vowel /i/ patterns differently from the other high vowels, and indeed from all other vowels, compromises any claim about articulatory motivation involving high vowels. This patterning is unique, not known from any other language that has vowel harmony.[5]

The examples just mentioned involve sounds, the phonology, but cases involving grammar could also be presented, though they require much more space to describe. For that reason I'll mention only one. In Nivaclé there is no marking for tense on verbs; in fact, the language has no grammatical tense at all. Rather, tense is inferred from the demonstratives. There are several contrasting demonstratives, including among them *naʔ* "this, that, the" [visible to the speaker], *xaʔ* "this, that, the" [seen previously but not currently visible to the speaker], as in the following two sentences (DEM = demonstrative):

(1) yoy **naʔ** siwɑnɑk
 escape DEM.VISIBLE dorado.fish
 "the dorado-fish is escaping" [VISIBLE TO THE SPEAKER]

(2) yoy **xaʔ** siwɑnɑk
 escape DEM.NOT.VISIBLE dorado.fish
 "the dorado-fish escaped" [NOT VISIBLE but seen previously]

Here, (1) and (2) are identical except for the demonstrative. There is no tense marking on the verb; tense is inferred from the demonstratives. In (1), *naʔ* [VISIBLE TO THE SPEAKER] implies "present"—if it can be seen currently, it is present. In (2), *xaʔ* [NOT VISIBLE but seen previously] implies "past," seen previously but no longer present. The tense is inferred from the demonstratives. Languages with nominal tense are rare, where tense is seen in the noun phrase, here seen in the demonstrative that modifies the noun. Languages like Nivaclé that have nominal tense but have no other grammatical markers that signal tense directly are very rare, and cases where tense is inferred exclusively from properties of the demonstratives are exceedingly rare, almost unique.

As mentioned, Nivaclé has several other unique or typologically highly unusual traits (Campbell et al. 2020). The discovery of each one of these was a thrill.

Who speaks what to whom

One discovery was not about language structure or new languages or dialects, but about language use and choice in multilingual settings. I consider the finding and analysis of the combination of dual-lingualism and linguistic exogamy practiced in Misión La Paz, Salta Province, Argentina very significant.

The language situation in Misión La Paz (henceforth MLP) is surprising. Chorote, Nivaclé, and Wichí, all Matacoan languages but not closely related to one another, as well as Spanish, are spoken there. Most conversations in MLP are multilingual. Each participant in a conversation typically speaks his or her own language, regardless of the language spoken by the person(s) addressed, and the other participants in the conversation each speak their own particular language in return. People communicate regularly with speakers of different languages, but commonly not in the same language as the one addressed to them. This kind of communication has been called "dual-lingualism," non-reciprocal language use where each person speaks his or her own language but understands the other's language in return. Also, linguistic exogamy characterizes marriages in MLP—a person marries someone whose language is different. In MLP each spouse speaks his or her own language and is addressed in and understands the other spouse's language in return—a spouse does not accommodate by speaking the other spouse's language (Campbell et al. 2020; Campbell and Grondona 2010).

In general, people "identify" with a single language and speak it with all others. They claim to understand but not speak one and in many cases both of the other two Indigenous languages spoken in MLP. This is remarkable, since the other two Indigenous languages are spoken around them constantly and they usually have perfect comprehension in the languages which they claim not to speak. Most households in MLP have constant multilingual conversations involving spouses who speak different languages and family members who identify with different languages.

There are other cases of dual-lingual interactions known from around the world and some instances of linguistic exogamy from elsewhere, and there are also cases where spouses speak different languages to each another. Nevertheless, the MLP case is fundamentally unique. Nowhere else is the combination of dual-lingualism and linguistic exogamy institutionalized and stable as it is here. Most other cases of dual-lingualism involve interactions among speakers of closely related languages and typically do not involve people in long-term relationships. Most cases where spouses speak different languages to one another are temporary, where typically the spouse who goes to live with the other spouse's kinspeople eventually learns and uses the other spouse's language.

It is important to document unusual and unique situations of language choice and patterns of language use such as this one in MLP. Given the increasing threat from Spanish and ongoing population change, this pattern of multilingual language use is beginning to fade and it is probable that it will be lost not long from now. If it had been lost without being documented, we would have known nothing about the existence of this unique pattern of multilingualism and language choice. That would have been unfortunate, since MLP's pattern of language choice and use has important implications for various claims concerning language contact and multilingualism (Campbell et al. 2020; Campbell and Grondona 2010).

For example, an interesting discovery is that the intensive long-term language contact and multilingualism in MLP do not conform to some assumptions about languages in contact. Linguists generally agree that "when two speech communities are in continuous communication, linguistic convergence is expected, and any degree of divergence requires an explanation" (Bloomfield 1933: 476). It is expected that in intensive language contact, languages become more similar to one another and should not undergo changes that make them less similar. However, contrary to these expectations, the three Indigenous languages of MLP, though in intensive daily contact with one another, have undergone several changes in both their phonology and grammar that make the languages more different from one another, diverging rather than converging. I'll mention just a couple of examples.[6]

The other two Indigenous languages have a voiceless "l" ([ɬ]). Voiceless "l" is like a regular "l" that is whispered or like blowing through an "l," a counterpart to a regular plain voiced "l" but without vibration of the vocal cords. However, Chorote in MLP has changed its former voiceless "l" to a consonant cluster, *xl* (/x/ + plain "l"), which word initially and word finally optionally becomes just a plain "l" alone. This changed in spite of Chorote speakers being in constant intensive contact with speakers of the other two languages spoken there that have the voiceless "l." This Chorote change goes against expectations of languages in such close, intensive contact. We would expect the presence of voiceless "l" in these other languages of close contact to exert pressure on Chorote not to change its voiceless "l" in this way.

In another example, both Nivaclé and Wichí distinguish first person plural inclusive ("we" including "you") and first person plural exclusive ("we" but not including "you") pronominal forms throughout the grammar, marking subjects of verbs, possession of nouns, and independent pronouns. However, Chorote in MLP has lost this contrast and now has only a single first person plural category, like the "we" of English. Again, we would not expect one of the languages to lose a grammatical contrast so prevalent in the other two languages, a contrast that speakers of Chorote hear and understand constantly in the other two languages of MLP.[7]

It would be expected that the intensive multilingual interactions of MLP would influence these languages not to change in ways that would make them different from one another but instead would influence them to maintain traits that the other languages spoken there have.

In short, it is not the case that languages in intensive contact must necessarily change only in the direction of more convergence (Campbell and Grondona 2010; Campbell 2017a; Campbell et al. 2020). Clearly, then, the MLP case of language use and choice in its multilingual setting merits additional sociolinguistic investigation to attempt to determine what is behind its seeming avoidance of convergence though convergence is expected.

I learned from cases like this that we should not take claims about what to expect for granted in doing fieldwork and allow them to deter us from seeing what is really there, to distract us so we miss important facts about the languages we investigate. Linguists need to be alert also to sociocultural aspects of language use and language choice. Linguists need to be alert to the possibility that what they encounter in their fieldwork may have implications that require the modification or even abandonment of certain general claims about language, about proposed language universals.

Old language document discoveries

Some discoveries I made involve uncovering previously unknown old written documents in and about languages that I was investigating. I often searched local church archives as well as larger archives, national and international ones, in attempts to learn as much as possible about particular languages—for example, about where speakers might be found or were previously located—and to find descriptive materials or texts written long ago in or about otherwise little-known languages. I'll mention just a couple of cases here.

While surveying all the locations where Xinkan languages had ever been reported to have once been spoken in hopes of finding more speakers, I visited Santa María Ixhuatán, in southeastern Guatemala. There were no speakers of any Indigenous language there and had not been in living memory, though the town has a Xinkan name, *šan piya* "place of clay pots" in Guazacapán Xinka. However, there was an important ancient manuscript there, guarded in a wooden chest by the town's *síndico* (town treasurer and secretary). This was a document of 221 folio pages, written in Nahuatl over several years starting from around 1620. Its contents are varied, but include an account of Pedro de Alvarado's conquest of Guatemala and a long history of this area. Nahuatl, the language of the Aztecs of Mexico, was never a spoken language of this region but it was a language of administration across Guatemala in early colonial times, and many locations had scribes who knew Nahuatl. This is an important historical document and the Nahuatl employed in the document appears to be sufficiently unusual to merit investigation.

Many communities in Guatemala have or have had revered ancient documents guarded in chests and kept secret. I was allowed to travel with this one in the company of the *síndico* to Guatemala City where I was allowed to make a photocopy of it in the National Archives building there. I learned that others who had visited Santa María Ixhuatán later were denied permission to see the document. It deserves careful and extensive attention from scholars, with a full translation, for its historical contents and for what it can tell us about the Nahuatl in which it is written.

In the Museum Library of the University of Pennsylvania, in Philadelphia, I discovered an important colonial grammar of Pipil, also called Nawat, a Uto-Aztecan language of El Salvador, related to Nahuatl of Mexico, the only colonial document in existence written about that language. It may sound strange to speak of "discovery" in relation to a document held in a library, but in this case the document was mislabeled. Because it was wrongly catalogued, it remained unknown until I rediscovered it among the rare books in the Museum Library there. It was mislabeled as being about Pochuteco and written by Franz Boas. Anything additional about Pochuteco, once spoken in Oaxaca, Mexico, would have been extremely valuable, since nothing is known of that language beyond what Boas published on it in 1917, after which it became dormant—it is the most divergent language of the Nahua branch of the Uto-Aztecan family. However, upon seeing the document in the library there I understood immediately that it was a short colonial grammar of Pipil of Central America and had nothing to do with the Pochuteco of Mexico. Since it is the only old document on the Pipil language, its rediscovery was important.

Its real title is *Arte de la Lengua Vulgar Mexicana de Guatemala qual se habla en Escuintla y otros Pueblos deste Reyno* (Grammar of the Vulgar Mexican Language of Guatemala which is spoken in Escuintla and other villages of this kingdom). *Vulgar* here means "of the people," related to *folk*; in colonial times and even later, Nahuatl was frequently called *Mexicano*. Unfortunately, the name of the author of the manuscript and the date when it was written are unknown, though from the writing style it appears to be from the early 1700s. The manuscript was in turn the property of Abbé Charles-Étienne Brasseur de Bourbourg (1814–74), Alphonse L. Pinart (1852–1911), and Daniel G. Brinton (1837–99)—all famous for their studies on the languages and cultures of the Americas.[8]

Philological discoveries

Linguists examine old documents with the goal of obtaining information about the history of the language in which the documents are written. This is called "philology." Philological investigations of older written attestations in and about several Mayan languages led to discovering or further confirming several things about their history, exciting findings for linguists, especially Mayanists, though probably low on any hypothetical scale of sensational discoveries in general.

For example, investigation of colonial documents from the 1600s and 1700s confirmed that although modern Kaqchikel has tense markers, Old Kaqchikel had no grammatical tense (time of an event or state), but only aspect (manner, how the action of the verb is performed). So Old Kaqchikel did not have "present" vs. "past," for example, but had "completive" vs. "non-completive"—something can be non-completive in the present (as in "he is eating [now]"), past ("she was eating"), or future ("he will be eating"), or can be completive in the present ("he eats it up each day"), past ("she ate it up"), or future ("she will eat it up"). Here tense (time) is not relevant, only aspect. Sequences of *tan* "now" + *t-* "incompletive prefix for transitive verbs" over time went through a series of changes until it was eroded down to *nd* and then *n*, while *tan* "now" + *k-* "incompletive prefix of intransitive verbs" changed to *ng, ny, y*, leaving these as present-tense markers, in contrast with *x-* ("*sh*"), the former completive marker, reinterpreted as "past" (Campbell 1978, 1990).

In one further example, today Q'eqchi', Poqomchi', and Poqomam have *s* where their relatives have both *ts* and *s*. However, sources on these languages from the 1600s and 1700s reveal that in earlier times these languages did have *ts*, only just beginning to merge *ts* with *s* back then. They show that this sound change took place later and independently in these three languages, and consequently that this sound change is not evidence of these three languages being more closely related to one another than to their other relatives (Campbell 1977, 1978).

Last speakers

I would not consider finding speakers of known languages a "discovery," at least not the kind of discovery in focus in this chapter. Nevertheless, it would be difficult to describe the thrill that it has been to find and be able to work with speakers of languages thought to be dormant or not known to have remaining speakers. I have done fieldwork with several languages whose last speaker, as far as anyone can determine, has subsequently passed away and the languages are now dormant.

The elated feelings from finding speakers of languages that are in such a precarious state and working with them to provide language documentation while it is still possible are ones that I would never be able to communicate adequately. I also am unable to describe well the range and depth of emotions that come with the death of the last speaker of a language—all the sorrow for the people affected by that loss, the personal grief felt for the death of someone I knew, worked with, esteemed, and in several instances considered a friend, sadness for the loss of unretrieved knowledge lost with that death, and doubts about whether I did enough, could have done more, should have tried harder to document more about the language. Each time it weighed very heavily on my mind and on my heart—a great privilege and great sadness and sorrow in each case.

The languages whose last speakers have now passed away that I have worked with include the following that are now just gone, unless or until attempts to revive them, "awaken" them using the data collected, are successful: Chiquimulilla Xinka, Guazacapán Xinka, Jumaytepeque Xinka, and Chilanga (Salvadoran Lenca). I also worked with remembers of now dormant Honduran Lenca, Cacaopera (Misumalpan language of El Salvador), Chicomuceltec (Mayan language of Mexico), Chiapanec (Otomanguean language of Mexico), and Subtiaba (Otomanguean language of Nicaragua). Rememberers are people who were never fully competent speakers of the language in question, but learned some words and fixed phrases from grandparents and elders. Several other languages that I worked with now survive only with extremely few elderly speakers or semispeakers.

Other cool stuff

Here I'll just relate a few odd but interesting things, mostly involving unusual words that I've come across in the languages I've worked with. These words are not really personal discoveries, just word that surprised me when I encountered them, ones that sometimes shocked me or amused me. I'll relate some of them here as further indication that fieldwork is fun and interesting because of the sorts of things we happen upon while doing it.

Skletsex

I find the Nivaclé word *skletsex* interesting and revealing in ways that perhaps resonate more strongly with scholars concerned with loss of knowledge systems encoded in endangered languages. *Skletsex* is the name of a plant, *Jacaratia hassleriana*, a plant with a bulky tuber that contains much liquid. It's called *cipoy* in Spanish, also *músculo*, which means "muscle." It is not because this word contains an example of Nivaclé's unique speech sound $\widehat{kl}$ nor because it has the unusual *-ex* lexical suffix for certain kinds of plants that I find it interesting, though these things about the word are interesting. Rather, it's because of what it represents for loss of knowledge of environment, ecology, plants, and medicines. Elders used the *skletsex* to get liquid to drink, to avoid suffering from thirst while out hunting and gathering in the bush or traveling from one place to another in this very arid landscape.

Young people no longer know this plant's name nor how to identify it or what its uses are, though they still live in the same precarious environment—as one of the elders told me, "los jóvenes no conocen los secretos de la selva como sus padres" (young people don't know the secrets of the bush like their parents). Loss of this knowledge could be a threat to their personal survival. To me, then, what makes *sklctsex* a particularly interesting word is that it serves as a symbol of our duty to document endangered knowledge systems before it's too late and it is a symbol of the sorts of information we lose if we don't do that and the possible consequences of such loss.

Part of the disappearing knowledge involving water in this arid region, also potentially relevant for survival, is what elders but not younger members of the community know about getting drinkable water in the bush. Elders know how to dig a small depression near a pool or puddle of dirty, stagnant water with a small channel (*ôyinach*) to allow a very small amount of water to flow from the puddle to the small depression. The process of the water's leaving the dirty puddle or pond and flowing through the small channel into the small depression dug to retain this water, then left to settle, results in relatively clean, drinkable water.

Pleiades in Nivaclé

One of my favorite examples from anywhere is Nivaclé *k'utsjaklaya lhawank'ekleshjanja'wat* [k'utsxaklaya ɬawank'eklešxanxaʔwat] "Pleiades" (the star cluster, Seven Sisters constellation), a compound. It is not unusual that Pleiades would have mythological connections; it does in many cultures around the world. However, the Nivaclé name is interesting, at least I find it so, for what it reveals not just of part of the Nivaclé belief system, but for how those beliefs connect with more mundane aspects of life. I suppose the name appeals to me, in some twisted sense, because of how utterly unexpected it is from an outsider's perspective and because what it depicts of a revered mythical figure seems irreverent, and that strikes me as humorous. *K'utsjaklaya lhawank'ekleshjanja'wat* "Pleiades" means literally "old woman's place for cleaning herself after defecating." This refers to the track left in the dirt where after defecating, one sits in the dust and wiggles around to clean their bottom. It is composed of *k'uts-ja-klay-a* [old-LIGATURE-AUGMENTATIVE-FEMININE] + *lha-wank'e-klesh-janja-'wat* [his/her-INTRANSITIVE-clean-FEMALE.AGENT-PLACE.OF]. The "old woman" referred to in this case is *kati'is lhamimi* [katiʔis ɬamimi] "Venus," literally "mother's star," a mythological figure.

This example involves local astronomical knowledge with cultural connections that can easily be lost as the language and the knowledge system it entails become more and more threatened.

"Earthquake" and "hurricane" in K'iche'

The word for "earthquake" in K'iche' is *kab'raqan*, composed of *kab'* "two" and *r-aqan* "his-foot/leg." There is a lot behind this word which makes it interesting and offers some explanation for why "earthquake" in K'iche' bears that name. It takes us to the *Popol Vuh*, the most famous example of Indigenous literature in all of the Americas, whose title is sometimes translated as the *K'iche' Book of Counsel* and called "the sacred book of the Maya." It tells of K'iche' mythology and history starting from before the arrival of the Spanish. In the *Popol Vuh*, *Kab'raqan* (Cabrakan) is one of the evil gods of the underworld, the god of earthquakes and mountains. As the story goes, *Juraqan* (Hurakan) (from *xun* "one" + *r-aqan* "one foot/leg"), wind and sky god, one of the creator gods, asks the hero twins Hunahpu and Xbalanque to dispatch the arrogant underworld god Vucub Caquix (*wuqub' kaqiš*), described as a powerful bird, often called "Seven Macaw"; *wuqub'* is "seven." The hero twins do defeat him. Then later *Juraqan* comes to the hero twins again, this time to ask them to take care of *Kab'raqan*, destroyer of mountains and god of earthquakes, the arrogant younger son of Vucub Caquix. They also defeat him.

Though not parallel in rank in the *Popol Vuh*, there is an interesting parallel in the names *Kab'raqan* "two legs/feet" and *Juraqan*, from *Jun-raqan* "one leg/foot," meaning "earthquake" and "hurricane" respectively.

We might suspect that K'iche' *juraqan* as the source of *hurricane*, borrowed first into Spanish as *huracán* "hurricane" and then from Spanish into English. However, it is usually thought that the word for hurricane comes originally from Taino, the language Christopher Columbus encountered on arrival in the Caribbean. Some have assumed the source must be this K'iche' word, and it has even been claimed that Taino must have gotten it first from the Maya before the Spaniards got it from them. That is unclear and probably unlikely. In any event, the pairing of "one-foot" and "two-foot" as the gods of hurricane and earthquake, respectively, give us the K'iche' names for these forces of nature with their mythological connections, and that is interesting.

Tsuntekumat "head" in Pipil

The word for "head, skull" in Pipil is *tsuntekumat*. It is composed of *tsun-* "head, hair" + *tekumat* "bottlegourd." This word has always struck me as humorous, conjuring up the image of a head like a bottlegourd, hollow inside, shaped sort of like an hourglass with a bottom part fatter than the top part. Bottlegourds are used like canteens by those working in the fields, filled with water, tied with a cord fastened around the center and long enough for the gourd to be carried over the shoulder, stopped up with a piece of corncob to prevent the water from leaking out. There is a somewhat related word that also strikes me as funny, *tsunehekat* "crazy, insane," composed of the same *tsun-* "head, hair" and *ehekat* "wind," wind-head seeming a fitting, descriptive way to refer to a crazy person. The Pipil *tsuntekumat* word is maybe not that unusual, associating gourds with heads, given, for example, that German *Kopf* "head" originally meant "mug," and French *tête* and Italian *testa*, both now meaning "head," originally meant "pot."

However, Pipil *tsuntekumat* "head" takes on added interest when it is discovered that this is also the name of a supernatural spook, the Rolling Skull (*La Calavera* "the skull" in Spanish), in the form of a disembodied head. "The Skull" rolls along at night and anyone who hears it dies. When I was doing fieldwork there, many people were genuinely frightened of going out at night for fear of hearing it. In Santo Domingo de Guzmán its name is *Tsuntekumat* "head, skull"; in Cuisnahuat it is known also as *tsunkechehchel*—as it rolls along it makes the sound *chi:kche:l, chi:kche:l* ([či:kče:l, či:kče:l]). So, I found the word interesting both for the funny image of bottlegourd-like "heads" that it calls up and because of how it intersects with the folklore, mythology, and beliefs of the speakers.

Bee and honey terms in Nivaclé

Nivaclé has a large number of terms for kinds of bees and honey, and a large associated vocabulary for bees, honey, and procurement of honey. There are at least fourteen species of bees that have names in Nivaclé, nearly all of which make honey, and elders in MLP harvest it. That's not such a startling discovery, but I found this terminology, the special knowledge associated with it, the complexity of the system, and the sheer number of terms associated with it really surprising and interesting. In addition to the names of the various kinds of bees and beehives, it has words such as:

> *waju* [waxu] "to search for honey"
> *wichiti* [wičiti] "agave fiber to sponge up honey from a hive"
> *fhtech* [ɸteč] "leather bag for honey, liquids"
> *wotsomech* [wotsomeč] "someone who knows how to handle the *lechiguana* bees"; *-mech* is a suffix for someone, often a ritual specialist, who has special knowledge of whatever it is attached to
> names for several kinds of chicha[9] made from different kinds

Figure 3.1 Don Altín getting honey (Misión La Paz, Salta Province, Argentina, 2006)

of honey—for example: *shinwonôk* [šinwonɑk] "chicha from dark honey," *shnakuwjatanôk* [šnakuwxatanɑk] "chicha from *extranjera* [killer] bee honey," and *wotsonôk* [wotsonɑk] "chicha from *chiguana* bee honey."

Today, the young men don't go out to get honey unless it's quite close to the village and found quite low in the trees, near the ground. The older men, however, will go considerable distances and will climb up tall trees to collect the honey.

One thing I found particularly amazing was the elders' ability to follow bees and find the honey. They sit near the ponds or puddles of water that have not yet dried up during parts of the year and watch for bees that come to get water. Though most of us unaccustomed to this could not even see the bees at all or would lose sight of them almost immediately after they took flight from the waterholes, the elders knew where to position themselves with respect to the sun and the bees' flight so they could watch the bees fly. From the direction, arc, and height of a bee's flight, they could predict exactly where the bee would go and land, where the hive with the honey would be, and unerringly they could go straight to it and harvest the honey. This is to me a truly impressive ability developed by these traditional hunters and gatherers.

Multilingual obscenity avoidance

Words can be avoided and even totally replaced because they sound like other words that are obscene. For example, English *ass* "donkey, jackass" has largely been replaced by *donkey* to avoid sounding like *ass* "buttocks, backside, the part of the body one sits on," because *ass* "backside" is obscene, originally from *arse*. Sometimes speakers of one language will avoid a word of their language because it sounds like an obscene word in another language in multilingual situations. I don't find the obscene words themselves of any particular interest, but the process of bilingual taboo avoidance does seem interesting. For example, *puta* in Spanish means "whore" and is very obscene. Nivaclé has the native word *puta* "hare, jackrabbit," but because this sounds like obscene *puta* in Spanish, many Nivaclé speakers have replaced this native Nivaclé word with *nônxatetax*, derived from *nônxate* "rabbit" + *-tax* "similar to"—literally "the thing like a rabbit."

Very occasionally, in language contact a word in one language takes on a new, obscene sense under influence from a word in another language whose meaning includes both the original sense of the influenced language's word and also the obscene sense that the influenced language did not originally have but comes to add. In some cases, after the word in the influenced language takes on the obscene meaning of the influencing language, the word goes on to be replaced in order to avoid the obscenity. For example, in Latin American Spanish the meaning of *pájaro* "bird" got extended to include also an obscene sense of "penis," and for that reason *pájaro* is now often avoided in the sense of "bird" in Spanish, frequently replaced by *pajarito*, originally the diminutive form of "bird," like *birdy* in English. The taboo "penis" sense of Spanish *pájaro* "bird" was taken on by the K'iche' word *ts'ikin*, originally meaning only "bird," under influence from Spanish. In K'iche', *ts'ikin* was then largely replaced by *čikop*, originally just "small animal," but now meaning "bird," to avoid the obscenity of *ts'ikin* that is due to influence from the obscene sense of the Spanish word corresponding to "bird."

There is a sort of unexpected irony in these changes, and that makes these words seem amusing to me.

"Horse" and "deer" in K'iche'

In K'iche', *kye:x* originally meant "deer"; however, with the introduction of horses with European contact, the meaning of *kye:x* was extended to mean "deer" and "horse." However, apparently it was not comfortable or convenient having the same name for the two different animals and so to distinguish "deer" from "horse," the term for "deer" became *k'i:che' kye:x*, literally "forest horse" ("wild horse"), and *kye:x* alone, which originally meant "deer" and only "deer," came to mean only "horse." Somehow the irony of "deer" ending up being called the equivalent of "wild horses" even though the name for "horse" comes from the original "deer" word strikes me as ironic and amusing.

K'iche' "shotgun" and "blowgun"

Somewhat like the horse/deer example, the K'iche' word *pub'* "blowgun" shifted its primary meaning from "blowgun" to "gun (shotgun)" in response to the introduction of this new item in acculturation. The onomatopoeia of this word also appeals to me.

Nivaclé "bicycle," etc.

To accommodate the new concept of "bicycle," Nivaclé extended the meaning of its word *siwôklôk* [siwak͡lak] "spider" to mean also "bicycle." Some speakers suggest that this is because the bicycle wheels with their spokes look like spiderwebs; some have imagined that the bicycle with a person mounted on it with elbows and knees poking out at funny angles looks spider-like. That image strikes me as comical.

The word for a species of ant, *tukus*, has been similarly extended to mean "soldier," said to be because soldiers walk in single file. Chorote *tokis* "ant" extended its meaning in the same way to include also "soldier." That image of soldiers as a string of ants going along in single file also appeals to my sense of humor.

The Nivaclé word to accommodate the new concept of "motorcycle" is *k'ututut*. "Motorcycle" in Chorote it is *pohpoh*, in Maká *qofqof*. All three of these are Matacoan languages. I like the sound of these onomatopoeic words. I also like two Nuu-chah-nulth (formerly Nootka) onomatopoeic words for animals acquired in acculturation, *mu:smu:s* "cow" and *oʕoʕo* "rooster."

Nivaclé -fhôjôy "to stab ritually (with sharpened bone)"

Nivaclé's verb *-fhôjôy* [ɸaxay] means "to stab in order to let blood in order to give one strength or increase luck in hunting." For example, when a boy killed a deer, he was stabbed with a sharpened bone so that he would never lack game, so that he would always have luck hunting. Also, you held the two front feet of an animal that you had shot together and then you jabbed them into your own forehead several times until it bled to guarantee luck in hunting. A man could be stabbed in this way to increase his strength. This is done with a *lhte'ech* ([łteʔeč]) "a sharpened bone (attached with a wooden handle) to stab with in order to let blood." The instrument is also

DISCOVERIES | 67

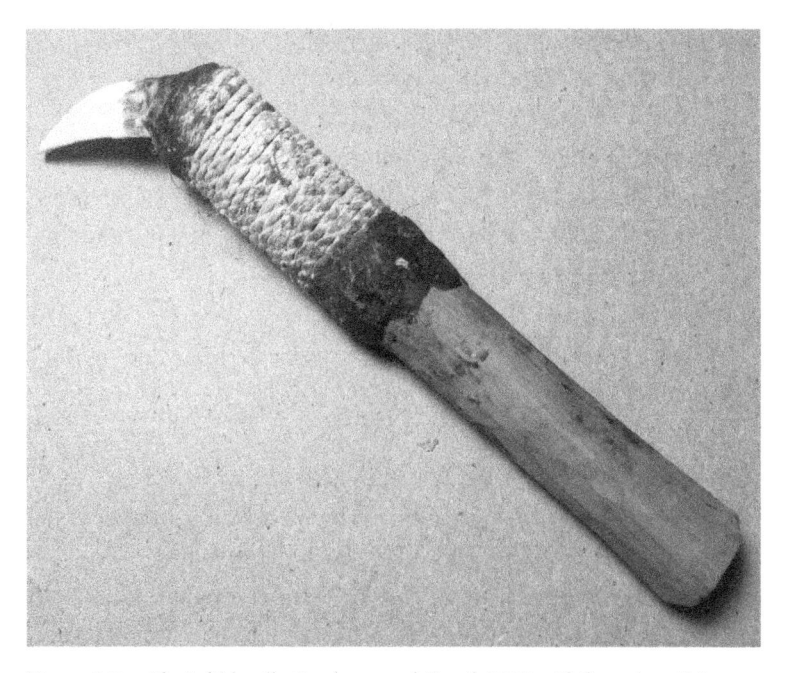

Figure 3.2 *Lhte'ech* bloodletting bone tool (April, 2021; gift from don Altín, Misión La Paz, Salta Province, Argentina, 2010)

called *fhôjôyjawo* [ɸaxɑyxawo] "pointed bone for ritual stabbing for bloodletting" (composed of *fhôjôy-ja-wo* [stab.with.bone-LIGATURE-INSTRUMENT]). There is an unrelated word for non-ritual, ordinary stabbing, for example, *jatsefheshesh* [xatsɸešeš] "I stab him/her/it" (*ja-tsefhesh-esh* [1ST.PERSON.ACTIVE-stab-VALENCY.INCREASING.SUFFIX]).

Words for medicinal plants

Nivaclé has several hundred words for medicinal plants, and elders in the community know their uses and how medicines are prepared from them. A few examples are:

> *yiklax* "quebracho blanco" (*Aspidosperma quebracho*), used to cure fever, flu, dysentery, and as a contraceptive

asaktsuk "bola verde" (*Capparis salicifolia*), a cure for flu, toothache, and intestinal worms

ninuk "sachasandía" (*Capparis speciosa*), whose soaked root is used as a cure for pain and for cough

tsanu'uk [tsanuʔuk] "duraznillo" (*Ruprechtia triflora Grisebach*), whose root is used as a cure for diarrhea, dysentery, and the bite of the dorado fish.

A few words among the several for medicinal plants in Pipil (Nawat) include:

i:xkwat [i:škwat] "night jessamine" (*Cestrum nocturnum*), whose leaves are toasted, made into a dough, and used to alleviate headaches and itch from athlete's foot

iyakmiku "guaco" (root) (*Mikania cordifolia*), a cure for diarrhea and stomachache

kuki:xtilu:ni [kiki:štilu:ni] "two-leaf nightshade" (*Solanum diphyllum*), used to treat skin diseases

siwa:pah "ericoma" (*Eriocoma tomentosa*), used to induce menstruation.

Nivaclé lexical suffixes

Lexical suffixes are rare. They are found in several languages of the northwest coast of North America. Nivaclé has about thirty of them. They are suffixes that must be attached to a noun or verb and cannot stand alone as independent words. The meanings of these suffixes refer to such concrete things that we would expect them not to be suffixes in languages; rather, we would expect them to show up as fully independent words. Lexical suffixes are rare in languages generally, therefore it is important to study their properties in any language which may have them. This makes Nivaclé significant for the typological understanding of the lexical suffixes in general.

The website *Das grammatische Raritätenkabinett* listed the Greek suffix *-itis* denoting a disease, inflammation, or infection of a body part as highly unusual and unexpected, seen in such English words of Greek origin as appendic***itis***, bronch***itis***, tonsil***itis***, and so on.[10] From a Nivaclé perspective this Greek suffix seems not particularly unusual at all. A favorite of mine in Nivaclé is the very productive suffix *-wash* ([-*waš*]) "wound," as in:

klesa-wash [k͡lesawaš] "knife wound" (cf. *klesa* "knife")
klutsshe-wash [k͡lutsšewaš] "gunshot wound" (cf. *klutsesh* [k͡lutseš] "weapon, gun")
k'utjaniwash [k'utxaniwaš] "wound from a thorn" (cf. *k'utja'an* [k'utxaʔan] "thorn")
pônake-wash [pɑnakewaš] "claw wound" (cf. *pônake* "claw")
namcha-wash [namčawaš] "axe wound from an axe" (cf. *namach* [namač] "axe")
wanja-wash [wanxawaš] "piranha-bite wound" (cf. *wônaj* [wɑnax] "piranha")

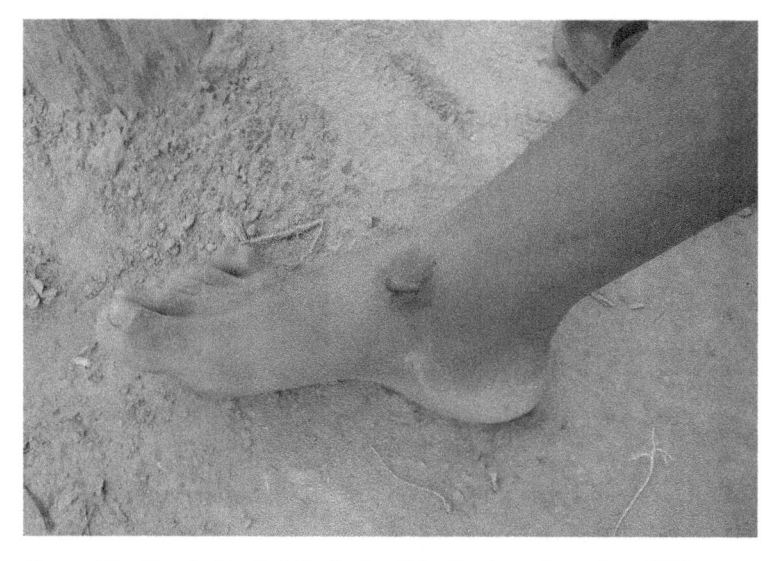

Figure 3.3   Piranha bite (Misión La Paz, Salta Province, Argentina, 2007)

jokita-wash [xokitawaš] "shovel wound" (cf. *jokitaj* [xokitax] "shovel")

yi'klô-wash [yiʔk͡lawaš] "wound from wood, stick" (cf. *yi'klô'* [yiʔk͡laʔ] "wood, tree").

Another favorite of mine is the "booze" suffix *-nôk, -inôk* for "fermented drinks" (called *chicha* or *aloja* in Spanish), which attaches to anything that can be used to produce such alcoholic drinks. A few examples are:

ajôye-nôk [axayenak] "mistol chicha" (cf. *axôyejx* [axayex] "mistol fruit" [*Ziziphus mistol*])

fha'ay-inôk [ɸaʔayinak] "algarrobo chicha" (cf. *fha'ay* [ɸaʔay] "algarrobo fruit" [*Prosopis alba*])

fhtsuk-inôk [ɸtsukinak] "palm chicha" (cf. *fhtsu'uk* [ɸtsuʔuk] "palm tree")

junshatanôk [xunšatanak] "tusca chicha" (cf. *xunšatax* "tusca fruit" [*Acacia farnesiana*])

shankujata-nôk [šankuxatanak] "killer-bee honey chicha" (cf. *shankujataj* [šankuxatax] "killer bee")

shinwo-nôk [šinwonak] "dark honey chicha" (cf. *shinwo'* [šinwoʔ] "dark honey")

wotso-nôk [wotsonak] "*chiguana* honey chicha" (cf. *wotso* "*chiguana* bee").

A few of the other Nivaclé lexical suffixes are:

-chat [-čat]/*-kat* "stand, grove of trees or plants"
-fha [-ɸa] "companion"
-mat "suffering from, defective in" (e.g. *fho'-mat* [ɸoʔmat] "injured foot"; cf. *fho'* [ɸoʔ] "foot")
-matsej [-matsex] "good in, efficient in, good because of" (e.g. *fho-matsej* [ɸomatsex] "good foot, well-formed foot, well-functioning foot"; cf. *fho'* [ɸoʔ] "foot")

DISCOVERIES | 71

Figure 3.4 Trough for making chicha (with Luis Díaz, Misión La Paz, Salta Province, Argentina, 2007)

-*mech* [-meč] "expert, person with power over or special knowledge of something, ritual specialist in something"; for example, *ita-mech* [itameč] is "person who knows fires, shaman who knows how to remove the ember that a patient is believed to have in his flesh" (cf. *itôj* [itɑx] "fire")
-*ta'a, -ita'a* [-taʔa, -itaʔa] "of no value, worthless"

Figure 3.5 Don Altín making tinderhorns (for when there are no matches) (Misión La Paz, Salta Province, Argentina, 2007)

> -*wałh* [-wał] "have large X" (e.g. *tsi-fho-wałh* [tsiɸował] "I have big feet," *tsi-* "I" + *fho'* "foot" + -*wałh* "have large X")
> -*yinjat* [MASCULINE], -*yinjate* [FEMININE] [-yinxat, -yinxate] "mourning kinship suffix for a deceased relative" (e.g. *chikla-yinjat* [čik͡layinxat] "late elder brother"; cf. *chikla'* [čik͡la] "elder brother").

Lexical suffixes cannot stand alone. They are clearly distinct from full words; most of them have no similarity to any free-standing words. For example, the lexical suffix -*wał* "to have large X," as in *tsi-ɸo-wał* "I have big feet" [1STATIVE-foot-HAVE.LARGE], bears no phonological similarity to any word in the language with meaning similar to "large, big." Compare -*wał* with *ux* "big, large," *tant'ax* "to be big, tall," and *xaʔt'ax* "to be of large physical stature." Or, to take another example, -*k͡laʔa* "little, small," as in *xa-ɸiʔič-k͡laʔa*

[1ACTIVE-hide-LITTLE] "I hid something small," bears no phonological similarity to words with meanings related to "small," "little": *tik'in* "little, small," *ɬawsuy* "small, simple," *tuk'a* "small, smallish, short, small of stature," *načax=waʔne* "to make smaller."

The cases presented here are only a small sample of "other cool stuff," of some of the words and related things that strike me as interesting that I have encountered while doing fieldwork on the various languages represented in these examples, though they show, I hope, how finding them in fieldwork can be surprising, thought-provoking, at times shocking, and often enjoyable and amusing. The other sorts of discoveries mentioned here feel far more significant.

Notes

1. This sound had been observed earlier (though usually mis-analyzed), but its unique character had not been recognized. For phonetic and phonological details, see Gutiérrez (2015), and Campbell et al. (2020: 29–31).
2. See also Ladefoged and Maddieson (1996), and Maddieson (2013).
3. These unusual traits are described in Campbell et al. (2020).
4. In colonial times, Chiapas was associated with Guatemala. It was not fully incorporated into Mexico until 1841.
5. Rogers (2018) describes this in detail. See also Palosaari and Campbell (2011).
6. Other examples can be seen in Campbell et al. (2020).
7. For details on this and for other examples where greater differences among these languages have developed without evidence of convergence, see Campbell et al. (2020).
8. It had even been mentioned by Daniel Brinton (1885: 63) in a footnote in his *The Annals of the Cakchiquels*, where he said, "I have in my possession the only grammar of this dialect probably ever written: *Arte de la Lengua Vulgar Mexicana de Guatemala* . . . in a handwriting of the eighteenth century, without name of author."

9. Chicha refers to fermented alcoholic drinks in much of Latin America made from several kinds of plants, as well as from honey.
10. The Grammatical Rarities Cabinet, <http://typo.uni-konstanz.de/rara>. (Accessed June 28, 2021.)

4

Finding language consultants and working with them

Introduction

Linguistic fieldwork depends on work with speakers of the language being investigated. They are typically called "consultants," sometimes "language teachers," or "language helpers" or "assistants," and now ever more increasingly "language experts." Traditionally in linguistics and anthropology they were called "informants"; however, that term is avoided now. It sounded too much like "informer" or "police informant," a snitch—something negative. So those who were formerly known as "informants" are called "language consultants" or just "consultants" in this book.[1] This chapter is about finding language consultants and working with them.

A traditional view of fieldwork involved an academic researcher asking questions of a native speaker of the language that was the target of investigation, for the purpose of collecting data on that language, usually with the aim of describing at least some aspects of it, often with the larger goal of producing a grammar, dictionary, and collection of narrative texts. Today the investigators may still be regular academics, but can themselves also be native speakers

Figure 4.1 Language revitalization materials: booklets in Chorote, Nivaclé, and Wichí produced in the Chaco language documentation project. (Misión La Paz, Salta Province, Argentina, 2008)

of the language, or can be members of a team involving academic linguists and trained community members, often language activists, working together to document the language and to help communities with their language revitalization efforts or language education aspirations.

Obviously, fieldwork can have many other objectives beyond traditional language description, and a range of methods may be needed to achieve these differing aims. The object of fieldwork can be language acquisition (to find out about how children "acquire" [learn] their language), dialectology (determining the dialects and varieties of the language), historical linguistics (collection of data relevant to the history of the language and its relationship to other languages), sociolinguistics (investigation of socially conditioned variation in the language), language conservation and language reclamation (production of learning and teaching materials for community language projects and needs), phonetic and phonological documentation (investigation and analysis of the sounds and sound system of the language), documentation of endangered knowledge systems, TEK (documentation of traditional ecological knowledge) and ethnobotany, linguistic anthropology (understanding of language use in its cultural setting), ethnogeography, and many others.

Most of the fieldwork I have done was aimed at documenting the languages, though some cases had other objectives, including investigating the history of the languages involved.

Finding consultants

Finding good language consultants can be challenging. They are like gold: you find them where you find them, if you're lucky. Obviously situations differ enormously and so what works well for finding consultants in one place or for one project may not be suitable for others. Most of my experiences reflect work with speakers of Indigenous languages in Mexico, and Central and South America, and some in North America and elsewhere.

Personally, I rarely had difficulty gaining people's confidence sufficiently for them to be willing to work with me as language consultants. I often wondered why they decided it would be OK to work with me, given that in several Mayan-language communities where I worked and where people seemed happy to work with me, an array of downright scary things were often believed of gringos at the time.

One belief was that gringos stole children. What is behind that seems to be some aggressive schemes to provide Guatemalan children for adoption by North American families. Illegal adoption has plagued Guatemala for decades. Another was some leftist propaganda that claimed foreign workers from aid organizations who were providing vaccinations against measles were actually sterilizing women to suppress Guatemalan Indians and poor people. Measles is serious but usually not fatal to healthy children in developed countries.

However, in Guatemala at that time malnutrition was so bad, and weakened conditions from intestinal worms, dysentery, and other endemic maladies were so prevalent, that for many rural children catching measles was fatal. These political efforts to oppose foreign organizations by suppressing vaccination efforts resulted in increased deaths of children from measles; it was heartbreaking.

Another belief was that gringos were people-eaters. As explained earlier, this one had to do with some Guatemalan Indians showing up at hospitals only after they were in such serious condition that recovery was often not possible. Many died there, and then, if not claimed by relatives, their bodies were sometimes donated as cadavers for training medical students, which involved some foreign medical doctors.

And, speaking of beliefs, there was often in many regions the general suspicion that gringos could be involved in witchcraft. In those days the amount of suspicion that someone might practice bad witchcraft increased according to the distance from that person's homeland to the Indigenous locale; hence, gringos, who definitely came from afar, were regarded with a high degree of fearful suspicion.

So, in light of all this, I was surprised over and over again that speakers of those languages generally seemed willing to work with me. For example, in the case of the Guazacapán Xinka elders mentioned in Chapter 2, why were they OK working with me when they thought I was a witch (*brujo*) who might do evil deeds or when they thought I might be a people-eater?

There may have been something about me that explains consultants' seeming to trust me when they distrusted others—after all, dogs and cats and farm animals and small children always seemed to like me. However, I have a different idea about that. In Central America the only gringos that many of the local people had seen were Catholic priests and Peace Corps volunteers. At the time, male Peace Corps volunteers tended to look scruffy, longhaired and bearded, but priests tended to be clean-cut, mostly beardless and without long hair, and so I, without beard or long hair, was often taken to be a priest. I hypothesize that people felt confidence in me because they thought I was a foreign priest, or at least the fact that to them I looked like one of those priests made me seem less dodgy or dangerous.

For example, in Guatemala there were many American Maryknoll priests, from Maryknoll Fathers and Brothers, Catholic Foreign Mission Society of America; in El Salvador Irish priests who are Franciscans, Poor Clares, and Jesuits; and in various places in Central America European priests, from Belgium, Italy, Spain, etc. It was difficult at times to convince people that I was not a Roman Catholic priest. On two occasions even while I was attempting to explain that I was not a priest, I got the response "sí padre, sí padre." It was very painful when sobbing women more than once asked me to perform the last rites for a close relative. I was also asked to perform baptisms in places priests got to only rarely if at all. Because of the depth of the petitioners' earnestness, I was sorely distressed that I could not provide what they so desperately wanted.

When I went to meet don Anselmo, the last speaker of Lenca in El Salvador, I was told by people of Chilanga, his village, that he had refused to talk to a number of outsiders who had come on various occasions wanting to talk to him, though he accepted me with no hesitation. Caution with regard to strangers was indeed understandable and from his perspective very much warranted. In El Salvador in 1932 there was a peasant uprising caused by economic collapse. The global economic situation caused coffee prices to drop, several coffee-growing plantations closed, and peasants lost their jobs, their livelihood; they were starving. They rebelled. The government took the position that the insurgents were communist-inspired Indians, and those identified as Indians because they looked Indigenous, wore Indigenous dress, or spoke an Indigenous language were rounded up by soldiers and executed, 25,000 people as reported in several representative estimates, in what is called the *matanza* (massacre).

In the years that followed the *matanza*, the repression aimed at Indigenous Salvadorans continued. Laws were enacted that made it illegal to speak an Indigenous language. They abandoned their native dress and languages for fear of further reprisals—a life-or-death matter of self-defense. Lenca, don Anselmo's language, was abandoned completely; he had not heard it nor spoken it since the 1930s. Cacaopera, a Misumalpan language, unrelated to Lenca, was also abandoned then and only a few rememberers remained. Pipil (Nawat) was severely curtailed. It is then no wonder that don Anselmo avoided strangers, and I still find it surprising that he unhesitatingly agreed to talk with me.

I also worked with Pipil (Nawat) speakers in El Salvador,[2] who still lived in fear, having the legacy of the *matanza* and subsequent brutality. There were extremely few remaining speakers when I worked there; vanishingly few remain today, most of them semi-speakers. I was very surprised that so many Pipil speakers were willing to work with me when clearly they were still extremely guarded with strangers and outsiders, and from their experiences they had serious reasons to be so.

For whatever reason or reasons, I usually had little difficulty getting speakers of Indigenous languages to talk with me and to work with me, even where others were often unsuccessful, even where speakers had very compelling reasons for being distrustful.

I sometimes worked together with other linguists, especially with Terrence (Terry) Kaufman, on particular languages at the Proyecto Lingüístico Francisco Marroquín (PLFM) in Antigua, Guatemala, a center dedicated to the Indigenous languages there. Often I went to find consultants of particular varieties of particular languages around the country to bring them to Antigua to work together with me and Terry and sometimes with other linguists at the PLFM. In a few cases the particular speakers I wanted to come needed some time to make arrangements before they were able to leave, and I gave them money for the trip so they could come later by bus. In no instance did any of them fail to show up. Nearly everyone thought this was quite amazing, since Guatemalan Indians typically did not trust outsiders or places they were not familiar with. In particular, it was surprising that those with whom I'd left money for the bus travel actually showed up—there is the Spanish saying, *Músico pagado toca mal son*—"a paid musician plays a bad song," that is, if you pay someone for goods or services in advance, you get bad goods or bad service, if you get them at all. Fortunately, no one decided not to come.

Other linguists there at the PLFM started calling me "bring 'em back alive," their response to my being able to gain the confidence of consultants and get them to come to work with us away from their homes, something that seemed so unlikely to be successful. "Bring 'em back alive" was a common catchphrase in English reflecting big game hunters. It is a refrain that goes back to Frank Buck, a hunter and animal collector who brought thousands of animals to zoos and circuses, and to his 1930 bestseller book, *Bring 'em Back Alive*. I did not like this. My interactions with those who came to work with us seemed ordinary and normal to me, and the "bring 'em back alive" epithet felt disrespectful of those who had sufficient trust and initiative to come to work with us.

Strategies for finding consultants

Probably the worst way to find consultants to work with is just to show up unannounced and unexpected. That approach might work in Papua New Guinea or Vanuatu, where it is often reported that some ethnic groups are eager for someone with linguistic training to come and work on their languages. It is rarely successful where people are suspicious or fearful of outsiders, and this includes much of the rest of the world, and especially much of Latin America.

Sometimes, a fieldworker may be fortunate enough to have some connection through personal networks. In some cases it may involve the researcher's heritage language and contacts may be possible via relatives or through local people who know members of the fieldworker's family. Some cases involve field methods courses, where the fieldworker makes local contacts through the language consultant of the field methods course whom he or she has gotten to know. Some contacts have been arranged through immigrants from Indigenous communities. In a few cases tribal councils or other Indigenous groups have sought out linguists to employ for work on their languages, with goals of providing results aimed at meeting community language needs. In most cases, however, circumstances do not provide such fortunate connections for finding consultants. More typically we have no ready-made connections and no one comes seeking linguists to work on their languages. Mostly serendipity reigns when it comes to finding consultants and being given permission to do fieldwork. I have found best success in a good number of cases with the tactics I describe next.

I found it useful, better said essential, to get and carry with me official letters, letters of several sorts. I discovered that it was valuable to get and take along letters from someone in authority at my university—for example, from the chair of the department or the dean of the college. It was good to have the letters in both English and in the dominant language where the research was conducted, in my case in Spanish for much of Latin America. These letters needed to look official, so they needed to be on letterheaded paper. Official letters in Latin America typically also bear various sorts of seals and stamps, and sometimes I was able to get official-looking stamps on some of these letters as well.

These letters worked best when they introduced me and explained my project and what I would be doing. It was valuable to have letters mention the educational value of the projects. One letter was addressed "To whom it may concern," to show, for example, to immigration and customs officials, police, and anyone with some authority that I might have to deal with. The contents were concise, stating that I was a faculty member and trusted employee of my university. For student participants in some of the research projects, their letters explained that they were students of the department and university in good standing. The letters explained that I would be traveling in the country to do research with a language or languages for educational or scientific purposes, and that I was traveling with a laptop computer, recorder, and other equipment necessary for this project, equipment that belonged to the university and which would be taken out of the country and returned to the university when I left the country on completion of the research. Importantly, this type of letter asked those to whom the letter would be shown to help to facilitate my project in any way that they could.

I also always attempted to obtain other official letters from relevant individuals or institutions with clout in the country where the fieldwork was undertaken. I would present the letter from my home institution that explained who I was and the purpose and legitimacy of my project to, for example, the minister of education, the director of a national Indigenous institute, prominent persons in relevant fields or positions of administration at universities in the country, leaders of Indigenous organizations, etc., and ask them if them could provide me with a letter of introduction in the official language of the country that I could then use to make contact with local leaders in communities where the language was spoken. Letters of this sort were immeasurably valuable for getting help to find consultants and for obtaining permission to work in the communities.

For making first contact with a community and attempting to locate speakers who would work with me, just showing up turned out often to have the opposite result from that hoped for—some people just scattered and hid, others refused to talk or just gave evasive answers, or just said "no." What usually worked best was to seek out someone with some authority or respected status in the community and present them the letter obtained in country from someone with some authority; or, when I didn't have such a letter, to show the letter of introduction from my home institution. The first choice of whom to approach was usually the local mayor, village chief, or whoever the head man or woman might be. In any case in most places it is necessary to obtain official permission from town or village officials to work there. If such a person of some authority didn't exist or couldn't be found or turned out to be unhelpful, the next choices, in no particular order of priority, were local priests, pastors/ministers, missionaries, health care providers, or as a last recourse local police or military personnel. These kinds of individuals tended to know the local people who were or were likely to be speakers of the language, or they knew people in town who could put me in touch with speakers, and they could provide the introductions to those people, often removing or at least reducing the fear of outsiders and helping to pave the way towards confidence.

While this approach usually proved best, it can also backfire. In some cases local Indigenous people may be afraid of or at least not trust local authorities, especially those from the police or military, leading to even greater distrust of the newly arrived linguist and his or her project. Also, local authorities can try to manipulate the linguist for their personal gain or advantage, sometimes outright asking for money, more typically taking the fieldworker to their kin or allies whom they hope the linguist will pay, instead of to good speakers, so that whatever pay might be involved goes to benefit them and their relatives. I found that the best solution to this kind of difficulty was just to be lucky and to be alert and flexible, and to keep trying, keep asking.

Availability and maybe boredom can be a factor in finding good speakers to work with. Being aware of factors affecting speakers' availability is important. For example, in places in Central America and Mexico, it is much easier to get people to work with during the dry season than during the rainy season, that is, especially not during planting and other times of heavier agricultural labor. In Guatemala and El Salvador, for example, it is extremely difficult to find people who will work on language matters during the planting season. On one occasion, when I arrived, consultants had agreed to work with me on Pipil (Nawat) in Cuisnahuat but only until the planting started, which happens just after the first rains. The rainy season in western El Salvador generally begins sometime between May 5 and 15. I hoped to complete a particular part of the project with them before that, though I calculated that I still needed more time beyond that date, probably at least until the end of May, to be able to finish. Well, that particular year I was in luck because the rainy season started late, at the end of May. Some of the townspeople suspected that I had used secret powers to delay the onset of the rains in order to get what I wanted, delayed until I could complete my project. Surprisingly, though, no one seemed to be bothered much by the idea that I might have caused the delayed beginning of the rain to serve my own wishes, so perhaps they didn't really think I had the powers to do that or that I personally had been the cause of the delay.

Availability, or more precisely unavailability, can be a serious obstacle. On several occasions when I was doing linguistic survey work, when in some town or village no one was available because of other obligations—for example, planting, weeding, harvesting, going to market, attending a funeral, etc.—I ended up working with people in jail. They were typically there for something relatively minor, for example public drunkenness, not for the serious sorts of crimes Americans and Europeans typically associate with jailed people. They were available, literally captive audiences. Sometimes, upon obtaining permission, I worked with them right through the bars in the jail, which often were just wood shacks with wooden posts for bars. In some cases I paid their fines, usually small amounts, and sprung them from jail under the condition that they would work with me in order to pay back the amount of their fine. Usually they were very happy about this and often turned out to be good language consultants, though not always.

Sometimes, when most people were unavailable, engaged in necessary agricultural pursuits, it was still possible to find some elders willing and able to work as consultants. That is, there seemed to be a sense that after a man had worked long years and his children were grown and his children and grandchildren could take care of the fields, especially if physically he was no longer in good shape for such hard labor, then he was free. In this freedom, however, life's daily routine can get tedious. I found that often such elders were happy to work with me, I assume just for the novelty of it, even happy to travel to other places to work with other linguists and Indigenous persons, something different and interesting, an adventure of sorts for them. I don't think elderly women of these communities ever felt the same sort of freedom, though I did often work with elderly female consultants, but in their own communities. However, even work with these elderly people had to conform with their availability. For example, in my work with Pipil (Nawat) women consultants in Santo Domingo

Figure 4.2 Felipa and Beatriz firing pots (Pipil) (Santo Domingo de Guzmán, El Salvador, 1976)

de Guzmán, El Salvador, time needed for making and firing ceramic pots always took precedence over fieldwork sessions, ceramics being a major occupation for many women in the town.

Another approach to making contact and gaining the confidence of speakers of a language is to hire a local guide to help. That used to be done with some frequency, particularly in older anthropological research. I didn't like the idea much; I did it only twice. Through archaeologist friends working near where I needed to do a linguistic survey in southeast Chiapas, Mexico, I hired a local man, don Rafael Hernández, from the region and known to many people there. Don Rafael understood completely the local expectations for how social interactions were to be conducted and the region's cultural expectations. This turned out to be very successful. I was seeking speakers of languages and dialects of languages throughout the region, where it was not known whether any speakers remained. This involved going to numerous towns and villages where Tzeltal, Tojolabal, Chicomucelyec, Chuj, and Mocho' had been spoken, and in some there were still a few elderly people who knew the local Indigenous languages. I would show up with don Rafael in an old jeep on loan from an archaeological foundation and don Rafael would talk with people who knew him or knew people that he knew, and eventually we would be taken to meet people who were thought to be speakers of one of these languages.

I found the interactions fascinating. Don Rafael and whoever he was talking with would seemingly go on and on with greetings and questions not meant to elicit any real information, just intended, it seemed, to let the connection seep in gradually and to set the stage for bringing up the purpose of our visit. They did eventually get around to that purpose after long series of repetitions of everything said, with long pauses between speaking turns. After what seemed a long time in each of these stretched-out greeting and connecting interactions, don Rafael would ease into the topic of people who might speak the heritage language there.

Figure 4.3 Don Rafael Hernández, guide (on the left), with Tojoloabal speakers (Chiapas, Mexico, 1986)

With don Rafael's help and knowledge, and the confidence that people of the region had in him or developed from the initial connection-making interaction, I was able to visit the places where these languages had been spoken and to find remaining speakers, and to undertake considerable language documentation with them.[3]

In another situation, in searching for possible speakers of Honduran Lenca, I went accompanied by the local telegrapher from Guajiquiro, who introduced me to people in some of the villages and small settlements in those mountains that we traversed on foot and later on mule. Showing up with him was very helpful to make communication with people in these places possible, given that this was a region of exceedingly high distrust of outsiders.

Blundering through vicissitudes of ignorance

A major thrust of the discussion so far has been finding consultants to work with and getting permission to work in particular towns or villages. Success at this is unpredictable, but becoming informed in advance to the extent possible about local circumstances can help. There are cases, however, where it is not possible to know in advance about some things that can affect your reception and so you just have to blunder through, learn from your mistakes, and hope that they are not so grave that no one will talk with you. Here are a few examples of that sort from my work.

In early fieldwork in Guatemala, surveying dialects of seven Mayan languages (Kaqchikel, Tz'utujil, K'iche', Poqomam, Poqomchi', Uspantek, and Q'eqchi'), I carried a small briefcase-like bag with the usual stuff used for collecting data: tape recorder, questionnaire, pens, pencils, notebooks, batteries, tapes. When I entered Indigenous communities and people saw me coming with that bag, they ran away and hid. I learned that portfolios/valises/briefcases were, in the view of the locals, what outsiders carried when they came to deceive people into giving up their lands, to extort payments of who knows what sort, or to attempt various other sorts of frauds, scams, and swindles—bags like my briefcase were associated with these carpet-baggers and cheats. After I discovered this, I carried instead a *morral*, a bag woven by local people with Indigenous designs and a woven shoulder strap, used by the Indigenous men there.

I learned a similar lesson about umbrellas. I had hiked into Las Pacayas, an Uspantek-speaking village (*aldea*), some hours' walk from the nearest road in those days, and because it was raining heavily, I had my umbrella out. To enter the village it was necessary to walk up a long low slope, coming over the horizon of the hill and gradually into view of those who lived there. As I emerged over the top of the hill, villagers saw my umbrella coming over the horizon and they all instantly dashed off into hiding; no one would talk with me. It turns out that umbrellas were to them also a symbol of the carpetbagger outsiders who would come to cheat them. So, after that, I abandoned the umbrella and ended up wearing what local men wore in the rain, a *nailon*, the name of which is a loanword borrowed from English *nylon*. It is really just a sheet of thin plastic, about 10 square feet (a square meter) in size, with two of its corners tied together under the chin, leaving my front mostly exposed so that I often got soaked, at least in the front. I also wore a broad-brimmed hat, like the local men, which was in fact the most effective part of the protection against the rain. As a rain cape, the *nailon* left much to be desired, but at least I no longer sent the people I hoped to talk with off in horror at my arrival.

Fortunately, later, I was able to return to Las Pacayas and was this time successful in getting some speakers there to work with me so that I could get the information that I had needed. It has a very interesting dialect of Uspantek (a Mayan language of the K'ichean branch), very useful for figuring out the tonal contrasts in the language.

A mistake from cultural ignorance that I never made, but that many others did, was knocking on doors of houses of Indigenous families. In rural areas of southern Mexico and Guatemala, one does not march up to someone's door and knock. Rather, you stand outside the fence or yard and shout the name of the owner of the house.

If anyone is home, they come out to see what you want or to let you know that the person you called for is not at home. Several times I saw foreign anthropologists march up and knock on doors, with the reaction of sending the occupants into panic, hiding from those doing the knocking who had wanted to talk with them.

Another example of a cultural ignorance that one couldn't know about in advance involves day names of the Maya calendar. Most towns in Guatemala where Mayan languages are spoken also have so-called calendar priests, daykeepers, who divine the days based on the twenty named days of the Maya calendar. This divination determines which particular days are propitious for planting and other things, and which are inauspicious (of *mal agüero*). This was esoteric knowledge, usually private, more important in some communities than in others. Also, there was some variation in the names of the days and the associations they had in different Mayan languages and different locations. Thus I never knew whether I would be arriving somewhere on a favorable day or on a day of bad luck. I have no idea how much this may have affected the kinds of receptions I got. I tend to believe it mostly did not prevent people from being willing to talk with me, when approached gently; however, I suspect that it must have played a factor in some people's reticence to deal with me on inauspicious days in some of the places I visited.

Kinds of consultants

It is good to understand that not all language consultants are born equal; each has his or her own unique personality and talents or lack thereof. Some, for instance, can be very good storytellers but not good at answering questions about how to say things; some seem intuitively to grasp right away what it is that the linguist is after, while others seem never to get it. For example, for good recordings of items on wordlists usually things need to be repeated, said at least twice and for some purposes it is better if they are repeated three times. However, some consultants seem unable to grasp this and so do not repeat even with much coaching and constant coaxing. Often it is necessary to explain that when you ask how to say, for instance, "I broke my leg" that you want to know how "I broke my leg" is said in their language, not "you broke your leg," which is a frequent response to the question, "How do you say 'I broke my leg'?" When the difference is explained to them, most consultants soon understand this and then respond appropriately from then on. Some, however, seem incapable of ever grasping this and so give a response that means "you broke your leg" when asked how to say "I broke my leg," and give the equivalent of "I broke my leg" when asked for "you broke your leg." Some consultants seem incapable of providing more or less accurate translations of what they say instead of just vague circumlocutions, and some seem unable to repeat things in the same words as first offered, even though you need the repetition in order to get it transcribed accurately.

Some consultants are just not good at all at thinking about language, whereas others are excellent. This should hardly be surprising, since everywhere in the world individuals who speak the same language differ considerably from one another in their ability to answer questions about their language. We have to realize, however, that it is never the consultant's fault that their ways of dealing with questions about language may not match what would be most advantageous for our fieldwork purposes.

Here is an example. I once was doing some fieldwork on Huastec (a Mayan language), in Veracruz state, Mexico, accompanied by a Mexican linguist who had not done much fieldwork. We began working with two speakers of the language who had been contracted for the task by town officials in the mayor's office. We were attempting to go through a very long wordlist to verify whether we had all the data and whether it was correctly recorded—frustratingly, it was taking hours to make only limited progress, though my Mexican colleague thought all was going swimmingly, that fieldwork must all be like this, very slow, difficult to get forms repeated, difficult to get translations that actually correspond reasonably well to what was said, and so on. Then we got the opportunity to work with a different consultant, a man who had interest in preserving his language. He was a remarkably good consultant, seemingly able to anticipate what we would ask next, and able to correct us if we made transcription or translation errors. We were able to complete the entire task in a matter of a few hours, where with the original consultants it appeared it would take several days to complete it. The Mexican colleague confessed astonishment that there could be such huge differences between consultants of the same language, though as I said, such differences ought not to surprise anyone.

Obviously we linguists all want to work with the most able and reliable consultants. It is reported that Edward Sapir began working on Hopi with a student at the Carlisle Indian Industrial School in Pennsylvania but gave it up in order to work with Tony Tillohash on Southern Paiute at Carlisle, "choosing the ideal linguistic informant over the language as such" (Darnell and Irvine 1997: 284).

Often with luck and some trial and error, it is possible to find able consultants. In circumstances where the consultant may be the last speaker of his or her language, there is no choice. Sometimes all the remaining speakers of a language have either no or only a few teeth, not ideal for discovering the proper analysis of languages that have several sibilant sounds—the hushing and hissing sorts of sounds, like "s," "sh," "z," "ch," "j." We have to be ready to make the most of what those we work with are able to provide.

It should also be said that consultants should never be underestimated. The experiences some consultants have had and the abilities we ultimately discover that they have can be quite astonishing.

A case that illustrates this well is that of Luis Díaz, one of the main consultants for Nivaclé. Luis was very quiet, sometimes seemingly inert. He often insisted that he didn't know Spanish well, though in working with him I came to learn gradually that he had a

Figure 4.4 Luis Díaz with fish (Misión La Paz, Salta Province, Argentina, 2007)

remarkably extensive command of Spanish vocabulary, able to identify and provide the Spanish names for a huge number of obscure plants, birds, and animals, with far broader knowledge than that of most native speakers of Spanish from that region of Argentina. One thing about Luis that truly amazed me, and amazes me still each time I think about it, was that he learned the International Phonetic Alphabet (IPA) solely by seeing me write IPA transcriptions in my notebooks of the things from his language that he said to me, seen upside-down from where he was sitting and written in my cumbersome handwriting! I discovered more or less by accident that Luis had learned this when I came to realize that he was repeating things, sometimes several times, when I wrote something he had said down inaccurately in a phonetic transcription, his way of letting me know that I should change it if I wanted to get it right. That he learned to read and understand this very complex and esoteric way of writing in this way astonishes me still to this day. Seeing how much many students in linguistics courses struggle even with extensive instruction to learn how to transcribe or read their own language in the IPA, Luis's learning it in this way seems truly amazing in contrast.

From then on, Luis became a project collaborator, a full team member, much more than just an ordinary language consultant. He learned to transcribe recordings and translate them, and to record himself and others. He had a number of insights that I considered brilliant, all from a guy from whose outward appearance and usual behavior you'd never ever suspect such things. Luis died in June, 2012, a dear friend, deeply missed.

To cite one other example, Nivaclé has a voiceless bilabial fricative (IPA [ɸ]), like "f" but pronounced with the two lips close together, not labiodental, with the upper teeth on the bottom lip as with "f." In the Nivaclé translation of the Bible this sound was written as "f," but that presented a problem. Some people insisted that because it was spelled with "f" it had to be pronounced as "f" in Spanish, as labiodental, not bilabial as it is in native Nivaclé. Luis had pondered this problem and came up with the recommendation that our orthography for Nivaclé should write this sound not as "f" but instead as "fh," parallel with "ch" and "sh." The "h" after some other letter indicated that the sound that the two letters together represent is not the same as the sound of the single letter without the following "h," though somewhat similar to it. Spelling this bilabial fricative as "fh" seemed to me a brilliant solution, a way to alert readers to the fact that this was not just an ordinary "f" as in Spanish but was a different sound though somewhat similar to "f" and that they therefore had no reason nor justification for insisting it should be pronounced as a labiodental "f" instead of as its native bilabial sound. I was extremely impressed with Luis's recommendation and the reasoning behind it, from a man who had never had any formal linguistic instruction and in fact had only had the first few years of primary school education.

Another amazing language consultant is don Altín, speaker of Chorote in northern Argentina. He had never seen a non-Indigenous person until he came out of the bush when he was around twenty years old. He is a remarkable repository of cultural knowledge. On the surface he seems rather unremarkable, blind in one eye from where a mule kicked him, although he has been known to repeat an

Figure 4.5 Don Altín with caiman hide (Misión La Paz, Salta Province, Argentina, 2005)

account of this in which it reportedly resulted from a fight with a jaguar. Although one would never suspect it from seeing him, don Altín has traveled to most major cities in Europe, from Moscow to Paris and beyond. He was one of only four elders who still played and sang traditional music, and an Argentinian ethnomusicologist arranged this extended European tour that his group participated in.

On another occasion, the group was taken to Guatemala for an ethnomusicology event involving various Indigenous groups from around the Americas, but something went dreadfully wrong. The organizers abandoned the four men in Guatemala. Don Altín speaks limited Spanish and was stranded on the streets of Guatemala City for several months until finally someone took the trouble to help him get in touch with the Argentinian embassy there, and they arranged for him to get back home. Don Altín is now the only survivor of

Figure 4.6 Don Altín singing with drum and rattle (Misión La Paz, Salta Province, Argentina, 2007)

that music group, the only remaining person able to play and sing the traditional music—we were fortunate to be able to make many recordings with him, many of them at his urging.

Don Laureano Segovia was another truly remarkable example. Don Laureano was a native speaker of Wichí. He had had only seven years of primary school education, but became a well-known homegrown scholar of Wichí. Over years, he interviewed elders and speakers with special knowledge of the language and cultural traditions and he published four books written in Wichí. He traveled throughout the Wichí area on his motorcycle, recording stories on hundreds of tapes. He rode his motorcycle the 20 miles (over 30 kilometers) each way over hideous roads to present his weekly radio show that featured tales, oral histories, and traditions in Wichí and sometimes also in other Indigenous languages of the Pilcomayo region of Northern Argentina—the only radio program in an Indigenous language there at the time.

Of his reason for writing his books don Laureano said, "For me it is important to write so that in this way our Wichí culture will not be lost. Young Wichí people follow the white culture a lot and thus our culture is being lost." Don Laureano was awarded the Ken Hale Prize from the Society for the Study of the Indigenous Languages of the Americas (SSILA) in 2007 for his work and for raising awareness about the threat to his language. A film was made about him in Argentina. Don Laureano collaborated with us on the Chaco Languages Project in Misión La Paz, and we in turn helped him with equipment and expenses for his "campaigns," as he called them, to travel the region to interview Wichí elders and to collect tales and data. He was often described as "amazing" by those who had met him. Don Laureano died February 4, 2020, at the age of eighty-three, a truly sad loss.

Another instance that amazed me involved Hugo Gonzáles, brother of the chief of Misión La Paz (henceforth MLP), in Argentina, where we were working to document three Indigenous

Figure 4.7 Don Laureano Segovia (Wichí) (Misión La Paz, Salta Province, Argentina, 2006)

languages. Hugo was an avid musician and a friend of our project, though because of work obligations at the school he did not work with us as a language consultant. He played guitar and sang, with a huge repertoire of songs in Spanish. Because we had good recording equipment, occasionally Hugo would ask us to record him, which we were happy to do, for him and the community, but also because he was a very good musician and for us it was entertainment in a place that otherwise had almost none.

I mentioned to Hugo once that he should do some songs in his native Chorote, and immediately, with no prior practice or even prior thought about doing that, he sang us a song in Chorote, one he knew in Spanish but converted to Chorote on the spot. To me this was an amazing feat. For Hugo, the very concept of music with rhythm and lyrics was a Spanish-language thing. Indigenous music was chanted with nonce syllables with only rattles or drums for accompaniment.

Figure 4.8 Hugo Gonzáles singing Chorote songs (Misión La Paz, 2007)

Later, we recorded Hugo singing a number of songs in Chorote, including some that he composed himself. One of his Chorote songs in fact was dedicated to Nancy, a graduate research assistant who worked on the project in MLP during two summers, and to me, thanking us for coming and for the work we were doing to help his community. I felt very moved when I first heard that song, totally unexpected; it is still gratifying when I think about it.

Hugo's ability to create Chorote songs spontaneously when the very idea of such a thing had never before occurred to him seemed to me then and still seems to me now truly remarkable.

A very different sort of example, though also involving a musician, has to do with the last fully competent speaker of Brulé Spanish in Ascension Parish, Louisiana, the language of the descendants of Canary Islanders who were settled there by the Spanish in the late 1700s before the territory was ceded to the French. We had wanted to document this unique dialect of Spanish before it was too late. We were very uncertain of what we might find there. We had been given the name of a person in Donaldsonville, Steve Medine, who agreed to meet us and help us try to locate some of the people whose names were mentioned as possible speakers. One of them was identified as a handyman who worked at the mayor's office, Jack Millen. Steve knew where Jack lived and took us to meet him.

Jack invited us in immediately when we explained what we were interested in. Though seemingly an ordinary and unassuming elderly guy, Jack was remarkable. He was a musician; in fact, he had appeared multiple times on MTV with The Dick Nixons band. We had come that day only in hopes of making contact, of locating someone who might be willing to make an appointment to work with us later, but Jack pulled out a boombox and some tapes and said let's get started right now—as a musician, he was ready to record, on the spot. He loved telling stories and performing. This was the start of much work that resulted in Charles ("Chip") Holloway's dissertation and articles that document this language (Holloway 1993). Today there are no longer any surviving speakers of Brulé Spanish in Louisiana.[4]

As mentioned, consultants have their own unique personalities and character. Some can be delightful to work with, some become lifelong friends, some become members of a project's research team, some even go on to become professional colleagues. Some prove to be amusing characters, and some are just unpleasant human beings. Of course, the consultants' culture has a big impact on their behavior in fieldwork situations.

For example, doing extensive work with various highland Mayan languages in Guatemala, I found people, especially women, to be rather formal, quite reserved, modest, even prudish in interactions with me, and so I felt it best not to attempt to elicit vocabulary for certain delicate body parts and activities that were on the wordlist questionnaires that I often used. In contrast, in fieldwork on Pipil (Nawat) in El Salvador with two elderly sisters, principal consultants, when they would see me skip over a delicate word on the questionnaire, they would stop me and ask what that word was, and they would without hesitation or any embarrassment give me the Pipil equivalent. In fact, frequently they would discuss the word with each other, sometimes with comments that much embarrassed me, along the lines of reminiscing about how they did certain things when their husbands were alive, things that I would never have asked about or talked about. The feeling of work with them was quite distinct from work with women who spoke Mayan languages. The point here is that because of cultural differences, consultants can differ greatly in terms of character and behavior as manifested in different fieldwork situations.

Fair compensation for language consultants

It should be self-evident that language consultants should receive fair compensation for their time, labor, and contributions. It is not always straightforward to figure out just what is fair and how to deliver that, and several kinds of complications can arise.

An initial serious consideration was always just how much funding a particular project had for paying consultants. Some projects supported by larger agencies tend to be relatively better endowed with funds for consultants, while other projects may have much less support, from small agencies or even from the researcher's own pocket.

This imbalance of amount of funding available for consultants can create problems. Research supported by institutions in developing nations usually cannot provide the same level of funding that grants from agencies outside the country can, and this has sometimes created difficulties. For example, if consultants on one project are paid significantly more than other projects can afford to pay, workers on other projects may demand payment matching that of the higher-paying projects. This sometimes has created considerable animosity in some places, though not with projects I worked on as far as I know. It has led some countries to institute controls or restrictions regarding such research, such as demanding surrender of a certain percentage of all external grants' budgets. The imbalance in consultant pay can create ill will in Indigenous communities and with local scholars, students, and government agencies. It may not be easy but those organizing fieldwork need to try, before making arrangements with consultants about payment, to find out if there are any local expectations about compensation, and then they need to try to work within those norms to avoid complications that can arise if they don't do that.

Determining fair compensation can be tricky also in several other ways. Situations vary hugely. In some cases payment in money is inappropriate. In a few places life doesn't operate on a cash economy, and fair compensation/payment cannot be handled with just cash; it is usually made in terms of gifts of things needed or wanted by individual consultants or by whole villages, often foodstuffs—a kind of a barter system. In such situations it can be difficult to determine what is appropriate to give, how much to give, when to give it, and how to get those goods/gifts to the people being compensated. For example, transporting sacks of flour or rice or sugar along with all the recording equipment and other gear can be a significant challenge, especially in places not accessible by road.

In some situations the tension over how much consultants are paid may come from inside the community. For example, even though grants or research support may provide substantial funds to pay consultants, some communities are strongly against that kind of payment for consultants working on the language. These communities take language documentation and language revitalization seriously and believe it is the obligation of community members who are speakers of the language to be willing to pitch in, to help the community work towards documentation of the language and language maintenance or reclamation, serving the community's language needs and interests. In such situations community leaders are opposed to elders being paid for this sort of language work, both because of the belief that the speakers of the language should be willing to do this for the greater good of the community and also because they don't want the same expectation of payment to continue after the fieldworker has gone, because normally the community doesn't have that kind of funding itself to be able to pay them for helping the community with its language aspirations. Usually in that type of situation, some appropriate way can be found to provide gifts to try to provide some sort of fair compensation without going against the community's opposition to direct payment and without creating envy or enmity among members of the community.

Even in situations where funds for consultants are available and the circumstances do allow if not require payment for language helpers' time, it can still be tricky figuring out how much compensation is appropriate. If we end up paying too much, that can cause jealousy in the community and create problems among community members that can be very disruptive. In most of my fieldwork in Central America and in Argentina, where we did have funding for consultants and where payment for their work didn't create problems of the sorts mentioned here, I attempted to find out what the salary of men working on local road crews was or what local school teachers were paid, and then I tried to pay something approximating those salaries. That is, I could easily have paid less, say what agricultural workers were paid, but I wanted to pay a bit more to try to help community members and the language consultants themselves to understand that their language was important, and the better salary helped to foster that view. It was necessary, nevertheless, sometimes to pay less than I would have wanted to in order to avoid the sorts of community disruptions that can arise when salaries are perceived as high. In some cases, because of the severe poverty in communities where I worked, I wanted to pay consultants the maximum amount that the grant budget would allow. This, however, would have caused disharmony in some of those communities and problems for the consultants themselves.

For example, witchcraft can be a serious problem in some places. Though community members themselves would not articulate it in these terms, in some places the concept of "limited good" is at play, the idea that there is only so much good to go around and that if one person gets more than another, that diminishes the amount of the good that the latter will be able to get that he or she feels entitled to. That is, it is seen as a zero-sum game, where one person's gain necessarily means another person's loss. This results in witchcraft against the one perceived as receiving more than his or her fair share and then countercharges from the person accused of getting too much against those others suspected of arranging the witchcraft against him or her. This may help exercise social control and be an effective way of ensuring egalitarianism in a community, but it is not something we linguists want our attempt at fair compensation for consultants' work to result in.

Language consultant compulsions

Some instances of remarkable and unexpected intellectual feats exhibited by consultants have been mentioned above. I also experienced what felt like almost the opposite of this with a few male consultants in Mexico and Central America from different language communities where many things asked about in fieldwork sessions routinely suggested to them something of a sexual nature.

For one elderly Jakaltek speaker from Paso Hondo in Chiapas, Mexico, almost anything I asked him seemed to bring forth an obscene reply. For example, elicitation of a list of animal names ended up with many obscenities and sex-laced comments. Since so many things apparently suggested sexual themes to this consultant, he once shouted loudly in the hearing of the several people, including children, who were listening in on our session that "a woman's monkey [obscene in Spanish] is called a 'rabbit' [indelicate in Jakaltek]" (*el mico de la mujer se llama 'conejo'*). That is, *mico*, a

Spanish word for 'monkey' on the questionnaire, is also used in the local Spanish as an obscenity referring to female genitals, and the Jakaltek word meaning 'rabbit' has similar connotations.

There were other occasions with different men and different languages but with the same sort of exuberant volunteering of forms involving sex and obscenities, best passed over without further comment here.

In another instance, I had gone to Guazacapán with two linguist colleagues several years after my earlier fieldwork there to see if any consultants could still be found who had learned Guazacapán Xinka well enough to be able to work with us on further language documentation. One of the linguists was Judith Maxwell, well-known Mayanist. One elder there knew considerably more of the language than the others, who were semispeakers of the language at best with limited competence in it. In trying to determine how well this man knew the language, I attempted to elicit verb forms that would illustrate the unusual grammatical property of Xinkan languages in which the first consonant of a verb root is glottalized in the imperfective form if that consonant can be glottalized. For example, in "she was cooking" it is glottalized, but it is not glottalized in the perfective, as in "she had cooked"; particularly unexpected is that in this glottalization process *š* (sort of like *shr* in English "shrimp") alternates with glottalized *ts'*. I knew from earlier experience that the semispeakers with imperfect learning had great difficulty with this glottalization and with the phonological difference that signaled these different grammatical forms of verbs. Semispeakers just didn't learn them accurately. I remembered that the verb root *pu:šu* "to squeeze, to milk" alternates with *pu:ts'u* "was squeezing" in the imperfective; so I asked him if he knew the word *pu:šu*, intending to follow that up with a question of how he would say "was squeezing" if he did, to see if he controlled the glottalization process that was an important part of the grammar for verbs. He, however, apparently understood me to be asking him to say the obscene local Spanish word *puxa*, pronounced [puša]) that means "female genitals," pronounced *pusa* in other parts of Guatemala and El Salvador. He said that yes, he knew that word but did I really want him to say it with a lady present, referring to Dr. Maxwell, who was with us? He had misunderstood it to be a question about an obscenity in Spanish rather than a question about a Guazacapán Xinka verb.

I was never able to determine whether he controlled the glottalization involved in verb alternations in the grammar, but that turned out to be moot. Though he did know quite a lot of the language, unfortunately he was unable to create new sentences that he had not memorized in the past or to tell stories.

In this context, it is worth mentioning that, unfortunately, women fieldworkers need to be especially aware of and cautious of men in the field who take a sexual interest in them. Mostly men I have worked with have been respectful and appropriate with the women who worked with us, but not always. I know of several bad cases of encounters by women in the field in which men behaved inappropriately, sometimes very aggressively with some truly unfortunate outcomes, though mostly not on projects that I worked on.

Fakers

Let me finish this discussion of finding language consultants and about kinds of consultants with a note about "fakers," would-be consultants who actually are not speakers of a language of interest but try to fake a language.

In fieldwork in Central America and Mexico scattered over several years, a few times I came upon individuals who attempted to fake a language, to fabricate what they hoped I would take to be an Indigenous language. New, previously unidentified languages are discovered on occasion, as, for example, in the case of Jumaytepeque Xinkan. So it is conceivable though not likely that some language not previously known given by some "consultant" could turn out to be a new language. Fortunately, the attempted fakings of a language that I have encountered have characteristics that make them very easy to distinguish from real languages.[5] A few cases of attempted fake languages that I experienced include what I will call:

> Fake "Pipil" of Comapa, Guatemala
> Fake "Pipil" of Panchimalco, El Salvador
> Unidentified "language" of La Trinitaria region, Chiapas, Mexico
> Mystery "language" of Las Cumbres, Chiapas, Mexico
> Mystery "language" of Guatemala.

Given the large number of potential speakers of various languages that I talked with over the years, this number of actual attempted language deceptions does not strike me as remarkable.

Among whatever motives there might be for why someone would try to forge a counterfeit language, two stand out. In some cases the faker was hoping to make money from his or her deception. Because I paid consultants for their work with me on their languages, some fakers showed up hoping to cash in on the funny gringo's strange language interest. The other main motive was personal status. In two instances particular individuals were recognized as the repository of local cultural and linguistic knowledge, a symbol of the town's heritage, and this reputation gave them a status in their communities that they clearly enjoyed.

For example, in Comapa, Department of Jutiapa, Guatemala (near the El Salvador border), Pipil (Nawat) used to be spoken. When I visited Comapa to find out whether there might still be any speakers, an elderly woman there enjoyed the position of being a symbol of Comapa's Indigenous heritage. Unfortunately, Pipil had ceased to be spoken there at least two generations before her time. She knew only four or five words of Pipil, learned as a girl from elders who remembered some words from the last speakers.

Together in a group, several town leaders took me to visit her with the expectation that she would through her language represent the heritage and pride of the community. To save face, she attempted to fake answers to my questions about how do you say such-and-such in Pipil. That she did not know the language and that she was attempting to invent answers became apparent almost immediately. I felt for her and definitely did not want to embarrass her, so I quietly suspended the interview and thanked her for allowing me to learn about her language, and paid her for her time. In the cases of sheer fraud that seemed to be based on hopes of payment, I just did not pay; I just politely told them that this was not the language I was looking for and so I could not pay for it.

Vocabulary fabrication seems to be the main thing fakers attempt to do, even if they are unable to keep it up for very long. The fakers soon ran out of steam, unable to continue producing new "words." They would start repeating "words" already given though saying that they had radically different meanings from the meanings offered earlier. They often cribbed from Spanish, sometimes offering archaic or rare Spanish words that they thought I, a foreigner, wouldn't know, or they gave essentially Spanish words but changed them somewhat so as not to be identical to Spanish. For example, when asked for the word for *lechuza* "barn owl," one faker gave me *avis* [áβis], a slightly modified version of Spanish *aves* "birds." As interviews went on, the fakers had greater difficulty keeping up the act, with coming up with additional created stuff. In all these attempted fakings of language, the material offered did not differ in pronunciation or structure from that of their main language, Spanish in these cases. The invented forms contained no non-Spanish phonetic material. A characteristic of all these fakers was that when they were asked again for something already elicited earlier in the session, they could almost never repeat what they had given earlier and rather gave something with no connection to what they had said before. The fabricated material never revealed anything of a grammatical nature, and none of the fakers was able to offer whole sentences or even phrases in the made-up language.

So, in all these cases it was very easy to detect the attempts to fake a language (see Campbell 2014).

Contact language

For working with language consultants, it is necessary to be able to communicate. Most fieldwork is conducted through a contact language with bilingual consultants. The contact language is usually the official language of the country or the dominant language of the region. In most of my work in Latin America the contact language I used with consultants was Spanish; it was English for most cases outside of Latin America.

Of course, it is very valuable and more efficient for the fieldworker to know the contact language well. However, limited communicative competence in the contact language does not make fieldwork impossible. There are long questionnaires with English and Spanish or Portuguese or French equivalents that one can use to begin investigation. One can without extensive knowledge of the contact language learn enough to arrange for consultants to give narratives that the fieldworker can record. It has frequently been the case that a fieldworker began with limited ability in the contact language but the very fact of being intensively immersed in the environment where that language is spoken and attempting to use it to do fieldwork sped up the language learning immensely, so that after not a long period of time the fieldworker was much more able to use the contact language in his or her ongoing fieldwork that he or she previously knew only poorly.

That mostly matches my own experience with Spanish. I had taken Spanish in high school (in truth learning little) and then at university (coming out far from being able to use the language for any real communication). When I began doing fieldwork in Guatemala, my ability in Spanish was limited, though as I did more fieldwork, I got much better at Spanish. When I started doing fieldwork using Spanish, I never would have suspected that eventually I would end up with academic appointments in Spanish departments, teaching undergraduate and graduate courses in Spanish linguistics. I was the head of Spanish at my university for a while, though my "training" in Spanish came mostly from doing fieldwork and living in Spanish-speaking countries, and not so much from university courses.

I have used Portuguese for elicitation in Brazil even though I did not know Portuguese well. I ended up needing Indonesian in work with two languages of the Pacific from Indonesia and former Indonesian territory, Bimanese in particular and also with Tetum, even though I knew in effect almost no Indonesian. I used it more for looking up in dictionaries things to say and to attempt to read things written in Indonesian about the languages, in particular about Bimanese, so I'd know more about things to ask the consultants about with respect to their languages—very slow going, very inefficient. It's far better to be able to use the contact language reasonably well.

There is also the famous monolingual method of elicitation, starting with no knowledge of the language of investigation at all and with no contact language, though extremely few linguists have ever actually used it and most of those who have used it have not done so to any significant degree. The idea is, in the beginning, to point at objects nearby—for example, a rock, stick, or leaf—and at parts of the body, and use animated motions, like, say, breaking a stick or dropping a rock, writing down all the responses. It's sometimes recommended that you say the names of these objects in your language to give the consultant the idea of what you are after, though that isn't really necessary.

Depending on the consultant's ability to guess what you are trying to get at and on the complexity of the language, a good linguist is able to learn quite a bit in a short period of time using this

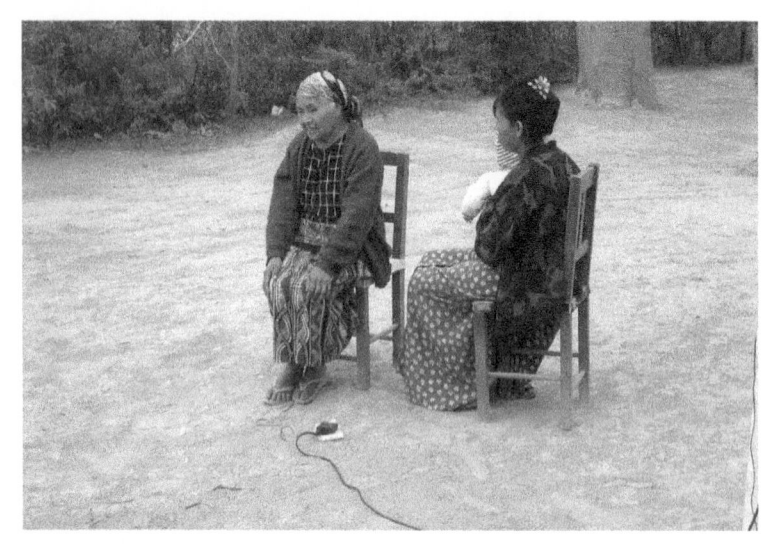

Figure 4.9 Fieldwork with Teresa Ramos and Josefa Ampú (doña Teresa does not know Spanish, but speaks Nivaclé and understands Chorote) (Misión La Paz, Salta Province, Argentina, 2004)

method, and hopefully can go on to learn how to form questions in the language and then move on to real monolingual elicitation and eventually to actual communication in the target language.

I have been in situations only twice where it was necessary to undertake monolingual elicitation. It was fun, and fortunately I had patient, cooperative consultants, willing to try to figure out what I was asking for with my animated motions. In both cases I knew a good bit about a related language so that I could get some idea from those other languages about whether the responses I was getting were on the right track for what I was hoping to get.

There are cases, though, where linguists have had to do monolingual fieldwork where no other option was available. For example, Carolina Aragon wrote a grammar of Akuntsú, a Tupían language of Brazil, based entirely on monolingual fieldwork (see Aragon 2014). The Akuntsú were massacred, with only six survivors in 1995; today only three women survive; the last man died in 2019. They were monolingual. Carolina was invited by Fundação Nacional do Índio (National Indian Foundation, FUNAI) to work with them. She lived with them in the bush, in her tent, pitched next to where they lived, and learned the language entirely by participating with them in their work and daily activities. Akuntsú is a very sad case, as this language will be lost with the death of the last of these survivors; it is not possible for them to have children. Carolina's documentation of the language, all done monolingually, is both important and impressive.[6]

Some scholars emphasize learning to communicate in the target language, the language upon which the linguist is doing fieldwork, and recommend fully avoiding interacting in a contact language. That's a great approach, though few fieldworkers actually end up doing that and it does usually require more time than working through a contact language. For many of the languages I have worked on, that approach would not have been practical or even possible. In many cases it would have been very unnatural for the consultants. Much of that work involved highly endangered languages, where the consultants themselves have the national language as their main means of communication. And in any case, there was limited use at best of many of those languages in the communities involved, meaning opportunities for me to hear the language and learn it, and then to use it were extremely limited. In these situations most language consultants would be uncomfortable attempting to speak the minority language with an outsider when nearly all their interactions with almost everybody were in the dominant language.

Doing fieldwork remotely?

In recent years it has become possible for fieldworkers to continue working with community members at great distances, via email, Skype, Zoom, texting, and various social media platforms. In most of the fieldwork I have done, if I wasn't present, communication wasn't possible, and even making long-distance contact was difficult, in many cases impossible. Several situations had no electricity, no telephone or internet access, some had no postal service. For several, contact from outside was possible only by asking a radio station whose broadcast range reached the region in question to air a message for people I worked with—for example, to let them know I planned to arrive on a certain date. Typically someone would hear the broadcasted message and tell the intended recipient about it.

In many cases the consultants I worked with were illiterate, making even use of a telephone challenging for them and anything involving the internet or technology impossible. Thus I have been both excited for and somewhat jealous of linguists who are able, after they have returned home from doing fieldwork, to connect remotely with consultants or friends in the community to ask questions, to clarify doubts about some point of analysis or the meaning of some word or sentence, and even to get new data and recordings. There is now a considerable amount of literature about use of mobile phones in fieldwork and in community involvement in documentation and revitalization efforts.

Situations obviously will vary enormously from language community to community with regard to their access to technology and ability to use it. Fieldworkers just need to do their best while they are there to arrange means of contacting and communicating with people in the community after they leave. This may involve purchasing cell phones for principal consultants or project team members in the community along with prepaid phone cards with calling time. It often involves training local people in how to use a cell phone, how to make or receive a Skype call or how to make Zoom connections, how to get an email address and to use it at, for example, publicly available internet shops, if they exist, and how to reach the fieldworker at his or her telephone or email, or by Skype or Zoom, or whatever.

There is much other excellent advice not rehearsed in this chapter that can be consulted about best practices for recording, archiving, and eliciting data in the field and for the best recording equipment and software programs;[7] and also about what we do and why we do it.[8]

Notes

1. Later, another reason for avoiding "informant" was added. The term seems to suggest inappropriately a sort of social hierarchy with the investigator seen as much more important than the language consultant in the working relationship, reminiscent of former interactions in colonial settings.
2. This work is reported in Campbell (1985).
3. The results of this research are reported in Campbell (1988).
4. There is another, different variety of Spanish spoken just south of New Orleans, now extremely endangered. It is called Isleño, after the Canary Islanders also settled there by the Spanish. *Isleño* means literally "islander."
5. I have heard of fakes in other parts of the world, languages created to deceive the investigator, that are reportedly much more elaborate and harder to detect. One example might be "Taensa," usually considered a hoax perpetrated in the 1880s by two French seminary students, Jean Parisot and A. Dejouy. They wrote a grammar and other materials said to be on Taensa, an otherwise unattested language of Louisiana. It was vehemently disputed among leading Americanists of the time, and there are still some opinions that it might be authentic.
6. For details, see Carolina Aragon's PhD dissertation, *A Grammar of Akuntsú, a Tupían Language* (2014), which I was fortunate to be the supervisor of.
7. For example, Bowern (2015), and Chelliah and de Reuse (2010), among others, and various websites, such as <https://www.eva.mpg.de/lingua/tools-at-lingboard/tools.php>, <http://www.endangeredlanguages.com/resources/>, <http://www.dynamicsoflanguage.edu.au/research/resources-for-linguistic-tools/>, <https://www.oxfordbibliographies.com/

view/document/obo-9780199772810/obo-9780199772810-0015.xml>, and <https://scholarspace.manoa.hawaii.edu/simple-search?location=10125%2F1221&query=resources> (all accessed July 11, 2021).
8. For example, the chapters of Rehg and Campbell (2018).

5

Perils, parasites, politics, and violence

Introduction

In this age of institutional review boards (IRBs) and research ethics committees (RECs), researchers hope to avoid the faintest suggestion of violence, conflict, risk, or political complications, not to mention potential harm to any participant associated with their research projects. Nevertheless, unanticipated things do come up and these kinds of problems often do confront fieldworkers. In this chapter I mention a few of my experiences that involve such difficulties, both by way of illustration and as cautionary tales. The most ubiquitous problems involved health and travel, but there were many others. Health issues related to food and drink are talked about in Chapter 6, and Chapter 7 deals with issues involving travel and living conditions.

Critters

Issues with animals blend into health issues, but let's begin with animals and then move on later to other kinds of troubles.

Fleas

Probably the most persistent problem in my fieldwork in Central America and Mexico was the fleas. You get them from dogs, household pets, domestic animals—it's wise not to pet or even touch any animal there. And you get them from people, in buses, riding in the back of trucks, in movie theaters, or almost anywhere where people are put in close proximity to one another. Fleas seem to be everywhere. Their bites swell and itch mercilessly. Often you end up scratching them so much that they bleed and can get infected, or at least can get blood on clothing and sheets and what not. My father, who went with me for one fieldwork season to El Salvador and Honduras, called them the "man-eating Central American flea." They are tricky because they seem able to avoid detection; they climb—usually imperceptibly—up inside clothing as far as they can get, until blocked by something, for instance a belt around the waist or tight seams somewhere in the clothing. They hide and are difficult to find, and shaking clothing usually doesn't dislodge them. They can stay there for days, continuing to bite over and over; when the item of clothing that they are in is not being worn, they just move from it onto other people or animals. Even when you can find them, they are hard to catch, and if you manage to catch them, they are hard to kill. The most common local method is to get the captured flea carefully on the back of one thumbnail and crush it vigorously and repeatedly with the edge of the other thumbnail. Spraying with insecticide also works.

A much-used method of dealing with them in areas where little else is available is to sprinkle DDT powder liberally around and under the bed and over and around the doorsill. Though DDT is dangerous to people and especially to the environment, it is still widely available in many parts of the world, though its agricultural use is banned in most developed countries. I discovered that it worked whenever I was staying for a while somewhere with a bed, but I had what seemed to me legitimate doubts about the wisdom of inhaling dust from DDT powder. In most places, if close to a store, insecticides can be bought and then whatever room or rooms the fieldworker is staying in can be sprayed. For example, Raid is available in many places. In Guatemala a much used and well-known brand is Baygon, introduced by Bayer, later sold to and distributed by SC Johnson, available in countries around the world and now even on Amazon.com.

A quick aside: once, way back in the sticks on a barely passable road in Guatemala, four kids sitting on a fence saw us, two gringo linguists with two Kaqchikel-speaking friends, driving along slowly due to the road conditions and they began shouting "bye, bye," as kids often did to foreigners. The smallest of them, maybe about five years old, wasn't sure what this was all about, and so he instead shouted "baygon, baygon," testimony to the ubiquitousness of this insecticide there.

When I was not staying in some fixed location but instead had to move often; for example, when I was doing survey work, sprinkling DDT powder or spraying rooms with Raid or Baygon wasn't usually an available option. Whenever I had enough space in my luggage, I brought lots of insect repellent with me from home, and I applied it liberally and often. In many places that kind of repellent is not available. It also helped when I was able to soak my trousers and socks and especially the mosquito net wherever one was needed in permethrin; that kept ticks and mosquitos away, too. Insect repellent and just avoiding the fleas wherever possible turned out to be the best options.

Fleas and some other insects seem attracted to biting some people more than others. It's said that people who have a vitamin B deficiency get bitten more than those who do not. Unfortunately, the medicines taken to kill off amoebas and to cure amoebic dysentery also kill off the intestinal fauna (micro-organisms) that help to produce vitamin B. This always seemed viciously unfair to me, since

I often had to take those amoeba-killing medicines, resulting in getting bitten even more often by fleas.

Fleas can carry diseases. For example, fleas are known for transmitting typhus, the plague, "cat scratch disease" (infection from *Bartonella*), even as intermediate hosts for tapeworm. Fortunately, most of the time being bitten by the menacing Central American fleas does not result in contracting these diseases, and I was lucky never to catch any of them.

In case it might not have been clear from what I just said, I truly hate these fleas—I recommend being prepared and doing everything possible to avoid them.

One very important lesson that I learned concerning fleas and mosquitos and many biting insects is to avoid passionately anything scented—no scented soap, deodorant, shampoo or hair conditioner, perfumes, lotions—nothing. Scented things on your skin or hair attract biters and blood suckers; using scented stuff is just asking for it! I learned to try to get an adequate supply of unscented soap, shampoo, and deodorant before leaving home and then used only them while in the field. These unscented things are impossible to find in most of the countries where I've done fieldwork.

As long as we are on fleas, I might as well mention a word or two about other biting insects.

Mosquitos

Mosquitos can be and are a huge problem for fieldworkers, since in many parts of the world they carry malaria, dengue, and scads of other diseases—mosquitos are ranked the world's most deadly animal, responsible for the deaths of more people annually than any other animal. Great care is to be exercised to avoid mosquito bites. Everything said about avoiding scented things goes double for mosquitos; long trousers and shirts or tops with long sleeves should be worn during hours when mosquitos are active; staying indoors and away from them during their active hours is highly recommended. Avoiding clothing with dark or bright colors is also important, since mosquitos and some other biting insects are attracted to these colors; white, beige, light yellow, light gray are better choices. And at night, mosquito nets in good order with small mesh are a must. I have been fortunate never to have gotten malaria, dengue, or a mosquito-borne disease, but a number of colleagues and students of mine have—not something to be taken lightly. There is more about malaria also in Chapter 6.

Ticks

I've also been fortunate enough to have had only a few tick bites over the years, though I got several in Brazil, and I've never gotten a tick-transmitted disease. Nevertheless, ticks are prevalent in many parts of the world, especially where there are cows and other large mammals, domestic and wild, and they can transmit a number of diseases. Protective clothing and liberal insect repellant are in order in areas where there are ticks; the best defense is just to avoid walking in fields and forests where there are tick-bearing animals. When ticks bite, they tend to bury their heads into the victim and suck blood, expanding their bodies greatly in size. One thing to avoid, emphatically, when trying to get them out is pulling them so that their heads come off, stuck inside your skin. That can cause nasty infections, not to mention associated discomforts. Health officials recommend also not touching with your bare hands a tick that may have lodged itself into your skin, as you can catch stuff from them that way, too.

There are tick-removing small implements you can buy. One is a tick key, a sort of small, pointed, loop-like device that is slid over the tick's body and then is pulled tightly underneath it, close to the skin, to remove the tick by pulling gently on it. I did on occasion use one of these, but didn't like it very much. A more commonly recommended one is pointed-edge, fine-tipped tweezers. A problem with these instruments is that it is still possible, though less frequent, to break the tick's head off and leave it stuck in your skin.

One trick that I have always liked and used a lot to get ticks off of dogs is to heat up the end of a pin or needle or the end of a paperclip with a match and press it against the tick's protruding backside. They tend to come backing out in a hurry, not leaving their heads embedded to cause nasty troubles.

Health advisory sites provide more reliable recommendations for tick removal. The Centers for Disease Control and Prevention (CDC) in the US, for example, say, "use fine-tipped tweezers to grasp the tick as close to the skin's surface as possible." They are against tick twisting or jerking; they say "pull upward with steady, even pressure. Don't twist or jerk the tick; this can cause the mouth-parts to break off and remain in the skin." Then, "after removing the tick, thoroughly clean the bite area and your hands with rubbing alcohol or soap and water." And, "never crush a tick with your fingers." Finally they have jolly instructions for what to do with the extracted tick or with one found before it needs to be extracted: "Dispose of a live tick by putting it in alcohol, placing it in a sealed bag/container, wrapping it tightly in tape, or flushing it down the toilet" (Centers for Disease Control and Prevention 2019). For some people, just throwing it into the fire gives welcome gratification—retribution does not always feel like a bad thing.

Scorpions

Scorpions tend not to be too common, but can be a serious danger for fieldworkers. There are many species of scorpions but the sting of none of them is pleasant and several are very serious, indeed even potentially deadly, although extremely rarely could the sting of even the most lethal species cause death to healthy human adults. In areas known to have scorpions, something sometimes seen in adventure movies really is in order: shake out boots/shoes before putting them

Figure 5.1   Scorpion (Misión La Paz, Salta Province, Argentina, 2008)

on. Shake out clothing, too, before wearing it. I also developed the habit of checking the bed and around the room for them before going to sleep whenever I was anywhere where scorpions were around.

I've experienced scorpions a number of times while doing fieldwork, though fortunately I was never stung by one. I did accidentally sit on one once, but that smashed it before it could sting me, so, as they say in Spanish, *menos mal* ("it could have been worse"). For example, in the Chaco in Argentina, scorpions would come into the house where I was staying, a former health center abandoned by Anglican missionaries. We would sweep them out when we saw them. In the morning occasionally we would find them climbing on the mosquito nets under which we slept. A good swat with a shoe or boot, once they were knocked off the mosquito net, usually took care of them and relieved with a sense of satisfaction any tension caused by their visitations.

Once in a small *pensión* in Flores, Petén, Guatemala, I discovered what to me was a really large number of scorpions on the walls of the room where I was staying. I ran out to find the owner of the *pensión* to say something along the lines of that I thought this was dangerous and that I wanted a different room, though her reply with a big smile was, "Oh yeah, they come in off the palm trees; they're everywhere, in all the rooms." So, back to the room, where I carefully knocked all the scorpions off all the walls, swatted 'em with a shoe, and inspected every cranny and visible crack in the room for any that might have gone undetected and were hiding, and then closed up all the windows in spite of the heat, and spent an uncomfortable night hoping no others had gotten in and that none had escaped my detection. I did not get stung.

Vinchuca and Chagas disease

The *vinchuca* (*Triatoma infestans*) of eighteen Latin American countries is called variously in English the assassin bug, the cone-nosed bug, the gaucho bedbug, the kissing bug, and winchuka or vinchuca. It is serious because it can transmit *Trypanosoma cruzi*, which causes Chagas disease (American trypanosomiasis). Worldwide six to seven million people are estimated to be infected by it; it is the cause of approximately 12,000 deaths annually, and considered a neglected tropical disease, though most countries now have a vigorous ongoing eradication and control program. This parasitic disease affects different individuals in different ways. In the early stages symptoms can be very mild or not even noticed. From ten to thirty years after becoming infected, 30–40 percent of individuals develop such serious symptoms as enlargement of heart ventricles, leading to heart failure, enlarged esophagus, or enlarged colon. There is no vaccine, though the disease can be cured by medicines if taken early.[1]

In the Chaco in Argentina the *vinchuca* bug lives in the cane walls and thatch roofs of the houses of the local people; this means that it could be quite perilous for foreign investigators and in fact for anyone to stay in those houses. The *vinchuca* bugs can get to be about an inch (2.5 centimeters) long, though the ones I saw were only about half that size. These bugs come out at night, while people are asleep. They

Recomendaciones para prevenirla:

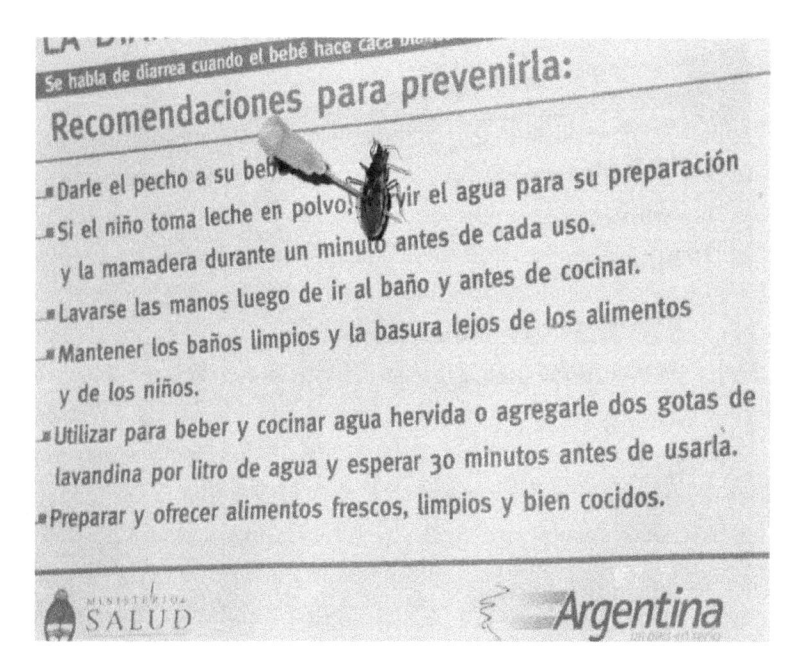

Se habla de diarrea cuando el bebé hace caca blanda

- Darle el pecho a su bebé
- Si el niño toma leche en polvo, hervir el agua para su preparación y la mamadera durante un minuto antes de cada uso.
- Lavarse las manos luego de ir al baño y antes de cocinar.
- Mantener los baños limpios y la basura lejos de los alimentos y de los niños.
- Utilizar para beber y cocinar agua hervida o agregarle dos gotas de lavandina por litro de agua y esperar 30 minutos antes de usarla.
- Preparar y ofrecer alimentos frescos, limpios y bien cocidos.

SALUD   Argentina

Figure 5.2   Vinchuca bug (Misión La Paz, Salta Province, Argentina, 2005)

bite people's faces, one reason why they are called "kissing bugs." After they bite and suck blood, they defecate near the bite wound, and scratching the bite site allows the *Trypanosoma cruzi* parasites in the feces to enter the host. Since I stayed in the Anglican missionaries' old abandoned health center, with adobe walls and corrugated tin roof, I was not bitten and did not get Chagas disease, at least not to my knowledge. However, I did encounter *vinchuca* bugs; on two separate occasions I saw them in the functioning health center!

It should be acknowledged that Argentina had a very aggressive and effective program to eliminate the *vinchuca* and control Chagas disease. Whenever the insect was discovered, teams would be sent to fumigate whole villages. Unfortunately, however, the *vinchucas* came in from Bolivia and Paraguay, just across the river, which meant new fumigations were frequently needed and it was impossible to control all of the insects all the time.

Snakes

Popular accounts in films, on television, in books, and all over the internet depict rainforests, often deserts, and especially swamps as teeming with aggressive poisonous snakes, just aching to attack and bite. In my experience in all these kinds of environments, you rarely see a snake, and when you do it is usually as it is hustling to get away from you as fast as it can. There are some species of snakes that do not flee in this way, some quite aggressive, but fortunately I never had to deal with any of them. Most of the time, these wilderness and remote areas are quite tranquil and pleasant; there are dangers, but they are not the horrifyingly dangerous places they are so often made out to be. Still, snakes can pose dangers, both for fieldworkers and for their language consultants and the community members where they work.

I've never been bitten by a snake, but a number of consultants who worked with me have been bitten, by venomous snakes. I have, though, had a few less-than-pleasant snake interactions doing fieldwork. In one case, in the Chaco in Argentina, a snake entered the house that our project team used for documenting languages; it came

Figure 5.3 Anaconda skin (with don Altín and Franco, Misión La Paz, Salta Province, Argentina, 2006)

under the door and crawled, fast, across the floor, crossing under a chair and over the heels of Megan, a graduate research assistant on the project. She let out a high-volume shriek. I initially was unsure whether her scream indicated something delightful or something awful. I chased the snake into a corner behind a couple of crates, moved the crates, and killed the snake with the end of a broom handle. I really don't like killing things, but in situations like this, I am like the local people we worked with. They are not like a lot of bunk lore suggests, that Indigenous people know intimately which snakes are venomous and which harmless—for the people I worked with, all snakes are considered probably poisonous and it seems that in their eyes the only good snake is a dead one. So, reluctantly I killed it, seemingly a better option than having a potentially deadly snake loose and lost somewhere in the house.

On another occasion, also in the Argentinian Chaco, I was sleeping in a sleeping bag on the floor and had to get up in the night to go relieve myself. I discovered that a coral snake was trying to crawl into my bed, fortunately obstructed from doing that by the mosquito net, tucked in all around where I slept. It was a cold night and possibly

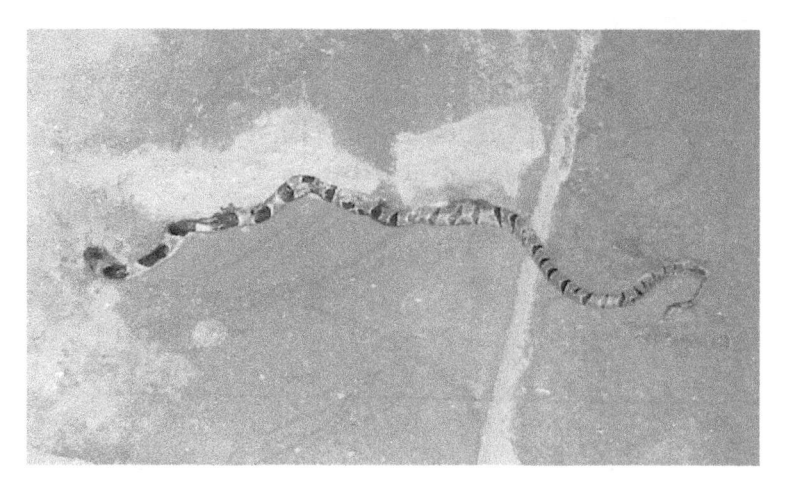

Figure 5.4 Snake that tried to visit me in the night (Misión La Paz, Salta Province, Argentina, 2013)

the snake was seeking warmth from my body, ick! I killed it, also with a broom handle, urinated, and went back to sleep. It didn't frighten me then, though I confess I hate snakes, hugely. However, the next day I kept wondering when the next one might try to join me at night, and that did indeed bother me, a lot.

Misión La Paz (henceforth MLP), where I worked in the Chaco, was a couple of inches higher in elevation than the surrounding areas. Each year the Pilcomayo River overruns its banks and floods the region, though MLP remains just slightly above the floodwater level. This means that lots of critters come to MLP to escape the floodwaters, snakes in particular. There seemed to be snake tracks in the dust everywhere. A local belief was that you should not step over a snake track left in the dirt but rather should walk around it, because if you do cross it, then the snake will follow you and maybe find you and bite you, or something else of a bad nature will befall you involving the snake.

Figure 5.5 Snake track (Misión La Paz, Salta Province, Argentina, 2007)

Figure 5.6 Snake skin (with Fernando Ángel, Misión La Paz, Salta Province, Argentina, 2013)

Figure 5.7 Coral snake (Misión La Paz, Salta Province, Argentina, 2004)

We often found skins that snakes had shed in many places—for example, under the house and once a very long one in our latrine.

There was a dead coral snake in the middle of the path when I first arrived to do fieldwork in MLP. Soldiers from the military post, just over a mile (2 kilometers) from the village, there to control traffic crossing the river from Paraguay, had killed the snake and left it there on the path, sort of local humor I guess, but an eye-opening introduction to the place.

Another time we arrived for the beginning of a fieldwork season just as Josefa's five-year-old son had been bitten by a *yarará*—Josefa was a consultant who worked with us for some time. The *yarará* (*Bothrops alternatus*) is the most dangerous of the snakes there, a poisonous viper species whose bite kills the weak and results in very long, painful recoveries for others. There was intense drama because of Josefa's son's being bitten, but fortunately they were able to get the boy to a health center in time in a town 20 miles (over 30 kilometers) away that had the right snake bite antivenom; he survived

Figure 5.8 Fernando Ángel recording (Misión La Paz, Salta Province, Argentina, 2008)

and recovered. Nearly all the people I worked with there had had terrifying snake encounters and many had been bitten.

Not surprisingly, snake bites were typically associated with tales of bad witches (*brujos*). For example, Fernando Ángel, a Nivaclé-speaking member of the language documentation team, had been bitten as a child by a rattlesnake. His father had died sometime not long before that. Fernando's family were convinced that his dead father was trying to capture Fernando's souls to bring Fernando to him. There it is believed that people have several souls, and that witches capture souls of others and these captured souls become auxiliaries that help the witches to capture other souls of other people. When a soul is captured, the person becomes ill, and if all the several souls are captured, that person dies. In Fernando's case it was determined that his dead father was sad and lonely, and so had sent the snake, his auxiliary, to capture Fernando's souls to bring Fernando

Figure 5.9 Asencio (Misión La Paz, Salta Province, Argentina, 2007)

to him to lessen his sadness. A shaman curer was contracted to intercede with Fernando's dead father to convince him to let his son live, telling Fernando's dead father that he had lived his life but his son had not yet had the opportunity to live his, so not to take Fernando and let him have the chance to live.

Asencio,[2] a Nivaclé consultant who also did artwork for our project, illustrations in the educational materials we produced for the community, had been bitten by a *yarará* the previous year and had been incapacitated for several months and was still not fully recovered. Franco, another member of the research team, harangued Asencio often about how if Asencio had only just gone to Franco's father, considered a powerful shaman/curer, he could have been cured much sooner and suffered much less.

A final "snake" experience that I will mention involved misidentification. This one happened when I was sleeping in a hut in Agua Azul, in Chiapas, Mexico. The hut there, as elsewhere in that part of the world, was a small house made of a frame of poles, a thatch roof, and walls of cane and reeds. The thatch roofs are the habitat of many insects, lizards, frogs, toads, sometimes small birds, mice, rats, and other small animals, and at night you hear them rustling around, larger ones foraging on smaller ones, and smaller ones scurrying through the thatch trying to escape being eaten. Snakes also move around in the thatch, preying on whatever they can catch. Late one night something large and heavy fell out of the roof smack-dab in the middle of my stomach—I was horrified, both by being awakened in that way and mostly because I was sure that it was a snake that had landed on me and that it was only a matter of moments before I would be bitten.

There was no electricity and my flashlight was deep in my backpack, so I leaped out of the sleeping bag and plastered myself against the wall and worked my way along it to where the candle was, and I lit it with a match. It turned out it was a toad! It was big, about 5 or 6 inches (12.5–15 centimeters) in both length and width. I believe it was a cane toad (*Rhinella marina*, that used to be called *Bufo marinus*). Cane toads are poisonous; they have poison glands and can harm or kill animals, dogs especially, that bite the toad's skin, but humans who haven't eaten them have not died from contact with them. I caught it and threw it out and went back to sleep, relieved to have avoided a snake bite, but still feeling jittery from the burst of adrenalin that being awakened in this way and the whole experience had given me.

Mostly in places where I worked there was no need to worry about or deal with snakes, but sometimes in some places, yes, they were around and caution was necessary; heads-up was definitely called for.

Dogs (and cats)

First, it should be said that dogs are probably a much more serious concern than snakes, scorpions, and other animals in most fieldwork situations. Second, I really like dogs, always have. Third, nevertheless the very concept of dog and dogs' characters differs widely from culture to culture, place to place, and not all dogs everywhere are likeable; sometimes some are just dangerous.

In many places dogs are not the pampered household pets showered with affection that they often are in North America and Europe. I've seen households' dogs horribly mistreated, routinely, in parts of Africa, Mexico, Central America, and South America—kicked hard, beaten with sticks, hit by rocks, and starved. Dogs treated like that don't typically end up with gentle characters. In some places the primary purpose for keeping or tolerating a dog is for hunting; for example, a good iguana-hunting dog is much prized in the Chaco in South America. In other places they are just tolerated as barking guardians, watchdogs, but treated badly, not fed much, and not liked much.

I soon learned that dogs needed to be avoided in most fieldwork situations, given that I did not want to get fleas, not to mention round worm, hookworm, tapeworm, and a host of bacterial and viral infections. However, dog bites and attacks were the biggest problem from dogs that I had to be careful of.

I was often rushed at and attacked by village dogs. They are especially vicious at night. In most of Central America and Mexico it's fairly easy to avoid getting bitten or attacked in such situations. Dogs there have had rocks thrown at them so often that throwing a rock will usually result in the dog slinking off. Sometimes it is enough just to stoop down as though you were picking up a rock and pretend to throw it, or even just pretend to throw something, no stooping needed. Carrying a big stick or club is also a good deterrent, and using it was sometimes necessary. Having a good flashlight to shine in aggressive dogs' eyes turned out also to be useful; it at least slows them down, long enough to take better aim with a rock or the big stick, or maybe to get away.

My worst dog experiences were in MLP in Argentina. The village has many dogs, some closely linked with particular households, others much more loosely associated with particular houses. They accost anyone who goes out at night in the village, usually in large, barking packs, and the longer a confrontation with them goes on, the larger the number of participating dogs becomes and the fiercer and more aggressive their behavior. The doctor whose task it was to visit MLP on occasion had access to good accommodation near the military post, just over a mile (2 kilometers) from the village, but he refused to stay there overnight, because he considered walking back at night from the health center in the village through the masses of menacing dogs too dangerous. Research assistants on our project did not go out at night, because of the dogs. I kept two long quarterstaff-like poles and always carried one with me, with a good flashlight, if I had to go anywhere at night, and I would hurry through town before the dogs could congregate in large numbers—I very often had to wield that staff to make particularly aggressive dogs leave me alone and to make the others hesitate, to allow me a small snippet of time in which to try to escape from the mob. Our student research assistants were terrified of them, with good reason—those packs of aggressive dogs were terrifying.

In short, a piece of useful advice is don't leave home without getting vaccinated for rabies, and avoid dogs.

And as with many other things, there were some special beliefs in MLP about dogs. Usually their barking would abate early enough at night that it was possible to sleep, though on a few occasions some dogs just incessantly barked through the night, making sleep very difficult. I wasn't happy about not being able to sleep one night because of the loud, incessant barking of one dog. Before I understood the local perspective on this dog's barking, I had determined that I needed to do something to try to keep this from continuing to happen. Fortunately, before asking the owner of the dog in question please to do something to quiet his dog down at night, I made the offhand comment to one of the language consultants that because of the night-long barking I had been unable to sleep and that I wished that the dog's owner had gone out to quiet it down. The consultant explained why no one had done anything to dissuade the dog. Someone there had died not long before and it was believed that the dog was barking because the man's soul (a spirit) was attempting to come back and that any human who might intervene in the barking was at risk of this man's soul damaging or capturing some of their own souls, and therefore, because of this fear, no one chastised the barking dog.

Cats in some ways are worse than dogs, though where I have done fieldwork cats are much rarer than dogs. Where I worked in Chiapas, Mexico, cats were prized to help protect grain and corn storage from rodents. However, cats were scarce there and I often heard people say they were looking for a cat because of difficulties they were having with rodents eating their stored corn. I never had any bad experiences with cats, but then I avoid them in the field. They carry fleas and many of the other parasites that dogs do. From both dogs and cats you can get various kinds of worms, salmonella, giardia (giardiasis), mites (scabies), etc., and additionally from cats and their fleas you can get cat scratch fever, also called cat scratch disease, caused by the bacterium *Bartonella henselae*. It typically involves a fever, swollen lymph nodes, and a sore (scab or pustule) at the place that got scratched.

My advice: never touch domestic animals, and wash your hands well if you should happen to; don't let them touch your clothes, either.

Monkeys

Most places don't even have monkeys and even where there are wild monkeys, often they avoid humans. However, there are a number of places where monkeys are accustomed to humans and have little fear, especially in south and southeast Asia. I said animals generally like me; apparently that does not hold for monkeys, for I was assaulted by monkeys on several occasions. Once, in India, I was changing film, before digital cameras, and the rattle of the paper from the film container attracted a troop of monkeys; they associated the sound of paper with food and the whole troop literally leaped on me, sticking their hands into all my pockets and hissing and screeching if I tried to free myself from them. Eventually, discovering no food, they left me alone, though declaring their discontentment with me by additional aggressive hissing and growling as they walked off.

Another time, in Indonesia, I was just sitting on a log resting in a forest that I was walking through when a large monkey climbed up my back and started ripping at my backpack—I had forgotten that I had had an apple in it earlier; the apple was no longer there, though apparently its smell persisted, and apparently the monkey wanted it—or maybe it just liked getting into people's backpacks. This one climbed on my head, and shrieked at me seemingly insanely; I was quite certain it was going to bite me viciously, but in the end I managed to persuade it that I was every bit as unhappy and aggressive as it was and that it had to leave.

On another occasion, I was walking through trees in Cambodia and I forgot that I had some bananas in my backpack that I had brought along for lunch. A troop of monkeys, a dominant male and some subordinates or adolescents and females, some with babies, attacked me. The dominant male climbed right up my leg and on up onto my backpack, holding onto my hair, and grasping one of my ears, trying to get into the backpack or perhaps trying to get me to drop it. In the end I managed to swing one arm out of the backpack's strap and slide the pack out along the other arm to catch it by a strap, holding it out at arm's length with my extended arm. The monkey ran right out to the end of my arm in pursuit of the bananas and backpack; I managed to shake the monkey loose from there, sending it to the ground, whereupon I charged it making a very loud noise with both arms stretched out wide to make me seem bigger and more threatening. It ran off and the troop followed.

So I was lucky not to have suffered monkey bites. Monkey bites can be pretty serious; monkeys can give rabies, herpes B, and a bunch of other diseases that they can pass to humans, and their bites can easily become infected.

I had always believed that most animals were afraid of humans and would run off if humans confronted them with noise and signs of aggression. This always seemed to work with aggressive dogs and cows and wild mammals of North America. However, I was wrong. In northern Ghana at a place where I was eating lunch on an outdoor table, a troop of baboons came, rushing at people to scare them away from their sandwiches so that they, the baboons, could eat them. I thought this was not right and so I confronted them. I stood and roared and rushed at them. This did have the effect of scattering several members of the troop; however, the big male baboon that was apparently highest in rank did not leave; in fact, he stood his ground and hissed and roared back at me. For several seconds it was a standoff and I was uncertain whether he was going to attack me or not. In the end he left, seemingly with his dignity and arrogance intact, tail held high.

I drew a moral form these experiences: it appears best not to rush baboons, and probably it is best not to confront any animals you are not fully familiar with.

Birds (and bats)

Birds and their droppings can carry over sixty different diseases, so, again, I learned that it is just best to avoid them. I never to my knowledge got any illnesses from birds, but they can complicate fieldwork in various other ways, too. Their noise is the most common problem. Alas, I have many recordings in which a rooster crowed right over the top of something in the language that I earnestly wanted to be able to hear accurately. Noise from chickens can make hearing language consultants' speech difficult and often messes up recordings. I might add that goats bleating and donkeys braying have the same frustrating impact on recordings, as a good number of my own reveal.

In the Chaco in Argentina, a persistent problem was the parrots—there are twenty-eight species of parrots in northern Argentina. One kind of parrot there (*catita* in Spanish, *ch'ech'e* in Nivacle, *kik'i* in Chorote) hung out in great numbers in trees around where we worked, making an incessant, annoying racket that made hearing the languages really hard and made recordings of the consultants' speech worthless. Sometimes the young guys who worked with us brought their slingshots and chased the parrots away with them. On a couple of occasions, they killed a few of the parrots . . . and later ate them. Well, I was sort of fond of those parrots—though I wanted to be fond of them with them at a much greater distance from us—so I hadn't hoped for their death, and I admit, I really hadn't expected them to be eaten or even be edible, though I guess it should not have come as a big surprise. The older people of the community there will eat almost anything that moves, and lots of non-moving plants that we would never have suspected of being edible, too.

A note to add to this is that in this region there are no stones—the Pilcomayo River adds additional silt deposits every year as it overruns its banks and floods the land, deposits so deep that there is no stone anywhere. The boys there make small balls about the size of a big marble out of clay and these clay balls (*kôtôsej* [katasex]) are the ammunition that they shoot in their slingshots. This lack of stones means also that stones are not available there for confronting the dogs, alas.

In Santo Domingo de Guzmán, El Salvador, when working with Pipil (Nawat), I had to contend with a different sort of disruptive noise associated with birds. In this case young boys were shouting loudly pretty much non-stop all throughout the daylight hours; it was very annoying because it made it very hard to hear

Figure 5.10 Clay slingshot balls (Misión La Paz, Salta Province, Argentina, 2007)

what language consultants were saying and made it impossible to make usable recordings. I asked town leaders if they couldn't ask the boys not to shout like that. They told me that in fact that was what the boys were supposed to do, that it was important and that they paid them to do it. The shouting was to drive birds away from the cornfields before harvest so that the birds wouldn't ruin the corn. The town leaders were very friendly as they told me this; to them it was a good joke that the gringo knew so little about growing corn that he would suggest such an unimaginable thing as trying to quiet the boys when a good harvest depended on their noise. Fortunately, this shouting lasted for only another week or so until the corn was harvested, and then I was able to continue my language work without that particular impediment.

There were some other ways in which certain kinds of birds were a concern in my fieldwork. All over the Americas and in many places around the world owls are omens of impending death or misfortune. I always think of the Nahuatl saying, from Mexico, whenever I see or hear an owl:

> In   tecolotl   cuica,   in   macehualli   miki
> /in   tekolōtl   kʷīka,   in   māsēwalli   miki/
> the owl   sing   the commoner die
> "When the owl sings, the Indian dies"

During one field season in MLP in Argentina, an owl was living in the tree in front of the house I slept in. I was very unhappy about that, since I did not want people there to associate me with the owl, or it with me, and think I was a witch bent on harming people. I tried often to drive it away, but it always eventually returned to the same tree. Fortunately, as far as I know, local people never associated that owl with me; that, nevertheless, did not mean that I did not

Figure 5.11   Owl (with Franco, Misión La Paz, Salta Province, Argentina, 2007)

suffer anxiety about possible consequences if they had made such an association because of that owl's persistent presence that year.

Bats, of course, are not birds, but I'll mention them here in this context just for convenience. From them, too, people can catch lots of horrid diseases, but I never had any difficulty of that sort. I did visit a good number of caves, but tried to avoid touching stuff where bats had been and even tried sometimes to avoid breathing in parts of caves where there were lots of bat droppings, or at least tied a bandana over my nose and mouth, unsure to this day whether that did any good or not. I did have a few bat encounters, though.

In Guazacapán, Guatemala, when I was working on that Xinkan language, I lived in a house in which a bat and I were in complementary distribution . . . not by my choice. It was a small one-room house with dirt floor and adobe walls; the bat would hang off the log roof beam throughout the daytime, when I was away working, and would be off at night, when I was there sleeping. I tried everything I could think of to convince that bat that it did not want to share that house with me, though I never succeeded. For example, I would come home in the middle of the day to chase it off with a broom, but it would just come back later. I wasn't concerned about any illness I might get; I was pretty sure my bat was no vampire; I was not afraid that it would bite me and that I'd get rabies or anything awful from it, as just sleeping seemed to be its thing. However bats, like owls, are also considered bad omens in lots of places, and I really didn't want people to associate me with that bat. That could have meant they might refuse to work with me . . . it was bad enough, as I later found out, that they thought I was a witch (shaman). I doubt that their belief had to do with this bat—people didn't know the bat was there—but I'm not sure about that, since in their account I could go off at night in my spirit, leaving my body sleeping . . . and it was at night that this bat was gone and I was there asleep.

Since people are often somewhat shocked if I mention the vampire bats, I'll add a small clarification about that. There are vampire

PERILS, PARASITES, POLITICS, AND VIOLENCE | 143

bats in all the places where I have worked in Mexico, Central America, and South America. These are not, however, the vampires of legend and popular culture, horrifying supernatural beings whose modern purpose is to titillate and entertain people so movie and television producers and some writers can hope to make piles of money. They are like the many other species of bats, except that there are three species of bats that have evolved to feed exclusively on blood, vampire bats. As an aside, there's a word for this, *hematophagy*, also sometimes spelled *haematophagy* or *hematophagia*, "the practice of feeding on blood"—I can just imagine everyday people trying to slip that one into casual conversation; it's based on Greek *haima* "blood" and *phagein* "to eat."

I saw vampire bats only a few times—they're nocturnal and I'm not—but I very often saw evidence of their handywork. You'd see the bite marks, the two puncture wounds often on the side of the

Figure 5.12 Dog with vampire bat bite (Misión La Paz, Salta Province, Argentina, 2007)

neck, upper part, on various animals, cows and dogs in particular. I assume that the upper neck got bit because it was harder for the animals to knock the feeding bat off from there with a foot or tail or to roll on the bat. Some animals would put up a tremendous fight whenever the vampires would try to bite them, rolling on them, kicking at them, etc., while others did nothing. The bats came back to those placid animals night after night, and often they got weaker and weaker and sometimes died as a result.

I went out once with a friend of mine at night to protect one of his cows that was getting repeatedly bitten and had grown weak. The idea was somehow to wait until the bat showed up and try to injure it without injuring the cow. It wasn't much of an event, though; the bat detected us and took off, abandoning the cow.

One last bird comment, this time of a more positive sort. In MLP, Argentina, several people have pet parrots, birds they raise

Figure 5.13 Lyle Campbell with Chorote-speaking parrot (Misión La Paz, Salta Province, Argentina, 2006)

from chicks. One of these parrots spoke Chorote and another spoke Nivaclé, two of the languages spoken there that our project was attempting to document. That is, these parrots had learned to say a number of words in these languages. I regret very much that I was never able to record either of these birds speaking those languages. Perhaps that may still happen one day.

Violence

Though I know fieldworkers who have suffered violent attacks, I personally have been reasonably lucky, though I saw the results of human violence on a number of occasions.

Once as I was walking downhill in a small town in Chiapas, Mexico, where I had been interviewing an elderly Zoque-speaking couple, someone threw a baseball-sized rock at me from further up the hillside; it missed me but made a horrible dent in the car I was walking past. Some kids once threw walnuts at me when I was standing in line in a town in Alta Verapaz, Guatemala, where Q'eqchi' is spoken.

However, violence wasn't far removed in several instances. I had left Chinautla in Guatemala where I was doing fieldwork on Poqomam one morning, and that afternoon there was a shootout in the town plaza involving the local police and a taxi driver with contraband weapons in the trunk of his car. It left several injured and the taxi driver dead.

On another occasion I was riding a bus back from Cobán in Alta Verapaz to Guatemala City when the bus was halted on the high mountain road where on the left side of the road the slope plunged down steeply for a very long way. The deep slope all along a long curve was fully visible, left bare by an enormous landslide. The bus was stopped on the long curve and because nothing obstructed the view on that side of the road, I and the other passengers sitting on that side of the bus watched as at least half a dozen bodies were retrieved from down the steep slope, slowly brought up and put on the bed of a truck up the road ahead of us and hauled off. In those days there were guerrillas in eastern Guatemala but that mostly did not affect Indigenous communities, and foreigners there were not yet very aware of the clashes.

Later, violence affected the whole country and was particularly devasting in numerous towns where Mayan languages are spoken. A friend of mine, a school teacher and brother of a main Q'eqchi' consultant, was killed by soldiers just because he hoped to improve the lives of the kids he taught. Any thoughts of change to the status quo were considered dangerous by some.

One of the Philippine priests working in Cobán, whom I knew, was killed because he preached liberation theology. The official version of his death was that his car ran off the road and that's how he died. No one accepted the official version; it seems the physical evidence did not support that. I went to Christmas Eve mass with Q'eqchi' friends not long before he was killed and he preached liberation theology that night. I was shocked, because I considered that a dangerous thing to do. Liberation theology links Christian theology with socio-economic concerns, often thought to have Marxist leanings, a reaction to the poverty and social injustice in much of Latin America. I had assumed that the politically sensitive nature of what he was preaching would be lost on my Q'eqchi' friends. However, when I asked them about it after the mass, they said that oh, yeah, they had been telling the young priest over and over for a long time that he should cool it, that what he was doing was dangerous—they had understood perfectly the political sensitivity and the risk, probably much better than I did. His killing later confirmed our fears about possible consequences in the worst way imaginable.

One of the men who had worked with us on Mayan language projects at the Proyecto Lingüístico Francisco Marroquín (PLFM) in Antigua, Guatemala, was murdered, since he was seen not as working towards community development as he saw it, but rather, because anyone interested in change was suspected of sympathizing with the left. For me that was the last straw, that people could end up killed possibly because they had worked with us on linguistic projects that could benefit communities. I did not return to work in Guatemala for several years after that, not until the civil war was long over.

From 2005 to 2008, we had a project one objective of which was to work with grassroots groups in El Salvador who were trying to revitalize Pipil (Nawat). I saw two men who were shot dead, a large reason for why I did not spend as much time in the country then as I had intended to. One was in a Volkswagen van along the side the road with the front door on the driver's side thrown open. The man was in the driver's seat sprawled back with arms splayed wide and head thrown back with his chin pointed up, in a pose that would almost suggest he was sleeping in his car, though this was belied by the several large bullet wounds in his chest and by lots of blood.

The other was along the main highway going from the capital, San Salvador, towards Sonsonate and the Pipil (Nawat) region of the country. The traffic was moving very slowly, just creeping along. A man had been killed and his body was just left on the edge of the road, facedown with several bullet wounds in his back. The police had drawn a chalk outline around the body, which gave the whole scene a sort of surreal feel, since the body hadn't yet been removed from the outline around it, like some poorly made TV police drama.

In another case a man of Pipil (Nawat) ethnicity but not a speaker of the language, who had worked with our group, was killed. He was the director of the Casa de Cultura (cultural center) in Pamchimalco, one of the former Pipil towns. Police reported that his murder had to do with personal matters and not because of association with us or with his work at the Casa de Cultura. Nevertheless, violence against associates is still violence.

El Salvador was the murder capital of the world then, and still has the highest homicide rate per capita of any nation anywhere, with 83 per 100,000 people (World Population Review 2021). The violent gangs controlled much; they demanded what they called *renta* ("rent"), extorted money, and routinely savagely killed someone to make a fearful example in order to keep others afraid, in line, and paying.

I made the mistake of mentioning some of this within the hearing of a fundraiser at my university and he almost immediately attempted to put out in a fundraising newsletter the claim that I "step over dead bodies to save endangered languages." This was mentioned in Chapter 1. I obviously did not want me nor my research to be characterized in this way, for many reasons, the IRB being the least of them. Fortunately, I was able to get this intended publicity stopped before it got very far.[3]

Violence can force fieldwork projects to be cancelled. I had obtained research funding for a reasonably ambitious project which included a component to document Tuzanteco, a Mayan language spoken in Tuzantán and nearby Belisario Domínguez, in Chiapas, Mexico, on the border with Guatemala. A graduate research assistant had prepared to do extensive fieldwork there and to write a grammar of the language for her dissertation based on the results of this part of the project. However, between when the grant for the project was approved and its official starting date, a massacre took place there. It involved rival gangs attempting to control the flow of Central American migrants crossing the border into Mexico trying to make it to the US, a very lucrative enterprise for the gangs. Given this violence and the continued conflicts there, clearly it was not possible for this graduate student to go forward with her planned fieldwork on Tuzanteco. In 2009 there were only five speakers of the language, really only one elderly man and woman that we were confident we could work with; today there may no longer be any native speakers of Tuzanteco.

So, alas, in summation, violence in fieldwork situations, while not characteristic of most fieldwork, can and does happen, often cropping up suddenly and unforeseen. Fieldworkers need to be alert and careful, for themselves and for those who work with them. It is not a few projects that have had to be abandoned or severely postponed due to violence of various sorts.

Politics

Most fieldworkers learn fast that we need to stay aloof from local politics. We also learn that often some people will try to entice us or force us to take sides in some political disagreement. Much has been written about intra-tribal, intra-group quarrels and disputes, factionalism, and rancor, and about inter-ethnic conflicts, and about the problems they can cause for linguistic research and language revitalization efforts. There is a large literature just on orthography wars alone. These things are not addressed here. I will, though, mention some other kinds of instances involving politics that have impacted my research.

I had gone to Santo Domingo de Guzmán, El Salvador, for several seasons to work with Pipil (Nawat), and I was well-known and accepted by the people of the town. During an election year the military party then in power announced that there were Cubans in the country fomenting communism and therefore any meeting of four or more people had to be watched (*vigilada*) officially. In truth there were no Cubans and no one going around fomenting communism; that was just an artifice to allow the government to clamp down on any who might oppose the ruling party. I was working with the two elder sisters of the mayor of the town and the daughter of one of them, and so we constituted a group of four people meeting together, in this case working in the mayor's house! So, don Lalo, the mayor, had two soldiers with machine guns from the regional *comandancia* (military headquarters) come to watch us as we worked each day, since we constituted a meeting of four people. I was really miffed at this; I protested to the mayor that he knew me, he knew all four of us, he and the whole town knew well who we were and what we were doing, and that our results could be useful to them, so why had he called armed soldiers down on us? His reply was that he wanted to show the ruling political party, his party, that he was so loyal that even his own sisters would not be exempted. I believe the more likely reason was that he wanted to put on a show for the governing party by telling them that he had a gringo in his town and so, "Hey, look at me, at what I'm doing to show solidarity with and foster the party." In the end these soldiers just hung around, lay out in the sun with their machineguns and rifles at their sides on the grass, mostly slept, and were just bored, and we proceeded with our business as usual, opposed to their presence though I was.

Later on, on actual election day, I made sure to discover that I had urgent business in the capital that had to be taken care of. Later, I got the report that during the siesta, mid-day break, members of the military had come, seized the ballot boxes, and stuffed them in plain sight in front of everyone. One of the Irish priests working in El Salvador told me that soldiers assigned to oversee the integrity of the election process did nothing, just stood there "with their 'tumbs' [thumbs][4] in their pockets" as the voting boxes were stuffed, an arrogant show of who was in charge and that there was absolutely nothing that townspeople or anyone could do about it. Not so long after this, the long, bloody Salvadoran civil war broke out.

An example of a different sort involves orthography as a political symbol. In Argentina the Anglican missionaries from Great Britain in their translation of the Bible to Wichí wrote "th" for Wichí's voiceless "l." This is a sound not found in English, like an "l" that is whispered, like blowing through an "l" sound. To the Anglicans, voiceless "l" sounded sort of like the "th" of English in words such as *thing*, *thought*, *thatch*, etc. and so they chose "th" to represent that Wichí sound. Because of the Falklands War in 1982 between the UK and Argentina, the Anglican missionaries had to leave Argentina, and some returned only many years later. One thing they did upon return was to gather many chiefs and leaders together from across the Wichí territory to discuss orthography reform. One result was the recommendation that "th" no longer be written to represent voiceless "l" and that "lh" be used instead.

Meanwhile, Acompañamiento Social de la Iglesia Anglicana en el Norte Argentino (ASOCIANA), the social arm of the Anglican church, got involved in land reform, return of land ownership to the Indigenous peoples of northern Argentina. For many years the Argentinian government had promised return of land title but nothing concrete ever came of it. ASOCIANA backed the plan called *título único* according to which there would be a single title to the lands, shared by all the Indigenous people involved. However, many opposed *título único*, wanting instead for each location to have its own title.

Those who supported ASOCIANA and *título único* were seen as also being supporters of the orthographic change from "th" to "lh" which ASOCIANA was implementing, while those who opposed *título único* also resisted this orthographic reform—opposition to "lh" in the orthography became equated with and a symbol of the political stance against the *título único* proposal. For opponents to *título único*, the Bible was written with "th" and anyone wanting to change that was considered politically, if not morally, suspicious.

The conflict was heated at times. Local Wichís on one or the other side of the *th–lh* debate repeatedly tried to enlist us, the linguists, into supporting either "th" or "lh," depending on which land-reform version they favored, as a way to attempt to gain further support for whichever side of the *título único* debate they came down on. We had to insist that we did not engage in politics or religion, that as outsiders we had to remain neutral and that we had no right to inject our opinions into what was a matter for them to decide. When pressed, we would just say, truthfully, that as for "th" vs. "lh" we didn't see it as a serious issue, since clearly all those who could read Wichí could read it just as well spelled with either "th" or "lh."

Who'd ever have guessed that such a small spelling difference could come to represent such monumental political differences and raise such strong feelings?

As it turned out, though, most of the Wichí materials produced by community members that we worked with did utilize "lh," done primarily by younger community members who seemed unconcerned with the orthographic hostilities and the associated politics, who probably had little experience trying to read the Bible or anything else written in Wichí.

It can be noted that finally, in April, 2020, the Inter-American Court of Human Rights (Corte Interamericana de Derechos Humanos) issued a ruling that supports *título único*, that Argentina must issue a collective title of property and must repair various problems involving water, food, healthy environment, and cultural identity for 132 Indigenous communities in the Chaco region of Salta Province. It remains now to be seen how or even if this will be implemented (Mac Kenzie 2020).

Another fieldwork experience involving politicians did not seem particularly perilous, but it did involve lots of guns. I had driven with Terrence (Terry) Kaufman to Lanquín, in remote northern Guatemala, in a beat-up twenty-year-old Plymouth, on horrible roads that really weren't passable in a car so low to the ground, though with careful and creative maneuvering, we made it. Our objective was to get consultants who spoke the unusual dialects of Q'eqchi' of this region to come work with us in Antigua. It was an election year and campaigning was going on. By sheer bad luck we arrived in Lanquín only shortly before the president, Carlos Arana Osorio, was to show up on an election campaign visit. We were told by town officials that they'd be happy to help us find the consultants we sought but that we'd have to wait until after the president's visit.

So, shortly thereafter, four military helicopters landed, one on each corner of the town's soccer field. Heavily armed soldiers burst out like a swarm of ants, or, you might say, possibly less kindly, like a cloud of cockroaches, and rapidly took up positions all over town, including in the bell tower of the church, a good vantage point for a soldier with a high-powered rifle. Then, some fifteen minutes or so after all the soldiers were in place, the president's helicopter arrived and landed in the center of the soccer field, and eventually out came the president, vice president, minister of defense, and the president's wife and adult unmarried daughter, plus the wife of the minister of defense.

On that day in all of Lanquín there were only two vehicles, a dump truck for work on the road and my old Plymouth. The visiting politicians climbed up into the dump truck, which drove along slowly with the male politicians standing up in the bed of the truck, waving. Without us even being asked, unceremoniously the three women were in effect shoved into the back seat of my car with the expectation that I would drive them to wherever they were supposed to be taken. This suddenly having these women pushed into my car was jolting, but I couldn't help feeling amused by the sheer irony of it—with the many armed soldiers and the elaborate, choreographed protection procedures for the president, while Terry and I could have been anyone, guerrillas or crazies or whatever. They had no way of knowing we would not maybe try to drive off with the women, hold them hostage, or harm them in some way.

If I had been involved in the decision about whether to place these women in my car, I would have had grave doubts about that. We obviously looked very foreign, as of course did the car. I was pretty clean-cut but Terry wore a beard, had long hair, and looked and dressed like a staunch hippy—even the marked difference in our appearance could have seemed perhaps reason enough for extra suspicion in our case.

As part of the occasion, the president and his entourage were taken to Lanquín Cave, an impressive cave not far out of town with a large opening out of which surged the turbulent Lanquín River, later made a national park. And of course, I was expected to drive the women there. At least the cave was interesting, so *menos mal* (it could have been worse). We told the women of our work with Indigenous people and their languages and asked them what they thought about the Indians and their languages in Guatemala, seeming an appropriate question since they were visiting an Indigenous town. The answer was more or less that they didn't really think about such things but that they supposed educational interests on behalf of those people might be OK.

We did eventually manage to arrange for Q'eqchi' consultants from there to return with us to Antigua, after the president et al. had departed.

A very different sort of incident involving politics (mentioned in Chapter 4), a sad one, involved health and death. It did not affect me directly, but did affect communities where I worked. At the time measles was a terrible problem and many children were dying from it. Measles is usually not fatal to otherwise healthy children, but in Guatemala at the time in the mostly Indigenous towns and villages, many children suffered from severe malnutrition and were afflicted with multiple internal parasites, including various types of intestinal worms. In their typically weakened condition, measles was fatal to many of them. Vaccinations to immunize against measles were available and at the time volunteers from aid organizations were giving free inoculations in communities there. Unfortunately, this became a disastrous political issue.

Leftist guerrillas undertook a vicious propaganda campaign denouncing the foreigners from the aid organizations who were giving the injections, saying that it was all an American deception, a plot to sterilize the women! Apparently it was not necessary to explain why American and European aid organization volunteers would want the women sterilized. Probably their thinking was that anything that could divert any possible positive feelings away from the foreigners, whom they associated with the politics of the right, anything that could contribute to curtailing foreign influence, was a good thing. Their propaganda was sufficiently scary and confusing that it stopped many from allowing their children to be vaccinated. This resulted in the needless deaths from measles of a large number of children—it broke my heart; it still breaks my heart when I think about it, years later.

Drugs and alcohol

I'll add just a small, quick word about drugs and alcohol. This is not about anyone taking illegal drugs in the field—I'd like to think that no sane linguist would be stupid enough to do that, given the risks of imprisonment and worse and the problems it can cause in the communities where fieldwork is done. However, alas, it wouldn't be hard to cite a number of true horror stories of what has happened to some fieldworkers in some places because of drugs. Here instead I concentrate on issues that involve the communities where fieldwork was done. Drugs can have and have had an impact on some places, making it impossible for fieldwork to be done there now. There are many languages that need to be described that are spoken in areas of heavy marihuana, coca, or poppy cultivation. These zones are not safe and some fieldworkers have been harmed, others have been driven out at gunpoint.

In my own fieldwork I have had no significant difficulties from drugs or drug growers or drug runners, but I have experienced annoyances. On numerous occasions in several countries, shady-looking guys have slunk up to me in shady ways to solicit that I buy drugs from them. I have in each case just said "no" and that was the end of it. This happened more rarely in remote places, but often enough to make me unhappy that drugs are circulating even in places inhabited by Indigenous people who worked with me.

One language consultant in northern Argentina told tales of when he was only 16 years old being recruited to carry drugs from a small Indigenous hamlet to towns around the region on a motorbike.

Apparently he was supposed to look so young and innocent on just a motorbike that he would not be suspected.

The military stationed at MLP in Argentina sent out constant patrols to control for drugs in this region so remote and inhospitable that no one would expect traffic or movement of anything or anyone. On occasion these military police captured men floating large bundles of coca across the Pilcomayo River from Bolivia or Paraguay into the remotest reaches of northern Argentina, where hardly anyone lives except a few widely and thinly scattered Indigenous people.

Like people across the Andes, many people in northern Argentina chew coca, a very widespread practice. In Argentina selling coca is illegal but it is mostly openly tolerated—small shops in the larger towns, such as Tartagal and Salta, put out signs on the street that say "Coca is sold here today."

The chewing of coca leaves acts as a mild stimulant, not like taking heavily narcotic cocaine, derived from coca leaves. Incidentally,

Figure 5.14 Coca sign: "There is coca and lime (bicarbonate of soda)" (Tartagal, Salta Province, Argentina, 2013)

Figure 5.15   Coca leaves for sale (Tartagal, Salta Province, Argentina, 2007)

Wikipedia advises not to confuse coca with Coca-Cola or cocoa . . . ha ha! Chewing coca helps suppress hunger, thirst, pain, and fatigue, and it helps with the effects of altitude sickness, not a problem in the regions of northern Argentina where most of the Indigenous people live, because the altitude is low; MLP is at about 870 feet (265 meters) above sea level.[5] Most of the Indigenous men who can afford it chew coca in the region, but because of the very crushing poverty there, few actually do chew it, at least not regularly.

I detest the smell of coca being chewed and the spitting involved; I made it a point to try to work only with consultants who were not big on coca chewing. The coca leaves by themselves smell fine, but for chewing it is mixed with an alkaline component, typically lye from burned limestone, and formed into a ball that is held in the cheek, where its effect is absorbed between the teeth and the gums. The saliva-soaked quid stinks; I hate it. Coca in the mouth also distorts pronunciation, an obstacle for fieldwork.

About tobacco, most of the Indigenous men and women I have worked with in Central America and South America aren't really smokers, but many definitely will smoke a cigarette if it is offered to them, especially the men. That is, as with coca leaves, the poverty prevents them from being serious smokers, though many would be if they could afford to be.

Alcohol

Possibly alcohol is usually a less serious problem for fieldwork than illegal drugs, but it is often a bigger nuisance. The biggest bother is from drunks. It seems often drunks' attention is attracted almost like a magnet to any foreigner or outsider in sight. Drunk men sometimes latch onto you and can be very difficult to get away from. Most are just annoying but not aggressive, though some can become belligerent. From frequent advice I received and personal experiences, I learned it was best to make absolutely no eye contact with them and to not speak to nor respond to anything a pestering drunk says. In the open it is usually possible to just walk away and solve the problem that way. It's especially unfortunate to be latched onto by a pestering drunk on a bus where it is not possible to get away from them easily. Unfortunately, local buses did seem often to have a drunk, sometimes multiple drunks, among the passengers, some of them passed out and asleep, but others who seemed too often to find a way to get to where I was sitting or standing, despite how packed the buses were, to be really annoying. The drunk men seemed even more likely to try to bother foreign women, very distressing for some of the female research assistants working on some of the language projects.

A serious difficulty that confronted me on a number of occasions was when language consultants I relied on got drunk. Sadly, some consultants when they were paid would go out and get so badly drunk that they would not show up to continue the fieldwork; in some cases, they never came back at all.

Other linguists advised me that it is not wise to pay language consultants for work they do until either the project is finished or, with longer, continuing projects, to pay them only at intervals, say once a month or once a week. I came to appreciate the soundness of this advice firsthand, more often than I care to confess, where a consultant took the money they had earned, got drunk on it, and end up not being able to work, and in the worst cases the consultants just never returned.

The issue of illegal alcohol also came up in some of my fieldwork experiences. When I was working in Guatemala, there were many roadblocks along highways where military police stopped cars and buses and searched them, saying they were looking for illegal moonshine, homemade liquor called *guaro* in Spanish. Actually, it was generally assumed that they were really trying to control the flow of illegal arms to guerrillas with maybe some alcohol and drug control as a useful side effect. I and other foreigners doing research there got very used to being stopped by very young, only partially literate soldiers who held machine guns or military rifles on us while they searched our car or luggage or the bus we were riding on or whatever. We got so used to most larger businesses and every bank having armed guards with machine guns or rifles that they became like part of the woodwork, so commonplace and familiar as to be essentially unnoticeable. They'd only be called back to active attention when some new North American or European would arrive and freak out about all the guns and soldiers everywhere.

I never thought illegal liquor was a big deal there, and in any case it had no impact on my work. I did, however, get to know one man who did make *guaro*; he traveled around with whomever he could hitch a ride with to deliver the stuff around the area, with two large plastic drums full of *guaro* encased in large burlap sacks, disguised to look like sacks of corn. I don't think he ever got caught, though with all the patrols I'm not sure.

Theft

Theft was and is a huge problem. I lost little to theft in my fieldwork, though I had lots of run-ins with thieves. However, students, colleagues, and local people working with us did suffer numerous robberies. Over time I learned strategies to protect against various kinds of thefts and cheating scams. Whenever I was around groups of people, I always put my wallet in my front pocket and kept a hand over it, with a thumb looped into the top of the pocket. I used money belts in which I could fold up bills of larger denomination; others used money pouches worn under a shirt or blouse, interior pockets that zipped, etc. Backpacks or bags of any kind were carried in front, never on the back or out of sight. Some thieves were really good at slicing open the bottom of a backpack or the bottom of a back pocket without the victim being aware of it. One of my students traveling in the back of a truck lost everything this way. Being robbed by pickpockets on buses and subways is rampant—it's best just to avoid traveling on them if possible or to not have anything worth stealing with you.

I didn't wear a wristwatch where there were many people around; thieves were known just to run by and rip watches off of wrists, sometimes taking some hide along with the watchband, or to tear off any jewelry women wore, even ripping earrings right out of ears. No money or anything of value should be flashed around or even allowed to be visible in public, including cameras, binoculars, laptops, or smartphones—anything like that.

Thieves had numerous slick tactics. For instance, one would create a distraction or just suddenly stop in front of you—for example, pretending to tie a shoe—while another "accidentally" bumped into you from behind, robbing you in the process. One scam in Mexico was to boost a skinny small child up to very narrow bathroom windows on second floors of hotels or *pensiones* and have the child enter and steal the patrons' pants (trousers) or anything else loose and easy to get away with, with hopes that the pockets would contain the victims' wallets. No one suspected that anyone could enter through such small openings at such heights in those buildings.

Nothing could be left in cars, no matter how well locked. Once in Honduras, my father and I were sleeping in the back of his pickup truck with our passports in the glove compartment, locked in the cab. Thieves were able to force open a small side window without us noticing and take the passports. Since my name is similar to my father's and my father's passport was newer than mine, the thieves apparently thought mine was just an old, expired one of his and so threw mine down in the dirt but took his. The process at the US embassy to report this theft and get papers to allow us to continue on our way was an ordeal. Apparently we were being suspected of selling my father's passport. Finally, after quite a long time of this, in desperation and exasperation I blew up and forcefully insisted of the embassy personnel that they stop harassing us and assist us, as we were the ones wronged here and that all this was just not right and too distressing. That seemed to work.

Some scams are so blatant as to be done right before your eyes. For example, it is quite frequent for people working in shops to give you back the wrong amount of change after purchases—this short-changing "mistake" is always to their benefit. Foreigners often don't notice and if they do, it is easy for the perpetrators just to pretend it was an accident and just say "Sorry." A less common trick is just to put less of what you paid for in the bag or container you will carry away, or not put what you had bought in the bag at all but put in something else instead. A sort of related scam at some service stations is to not clear the amount of the previous sale from the gasoline pump so that an unobservant customer ends up being cheated into paying not only for the fuel actually delivered to his or her gas tank but also for the amount of the fuel of the previous customer. It pays to keep a sharp eye out in such encounters. Sometimes some taxi drivers take riders with luggage to their hotels or destinations and then just drive off when the client exits the taxi, hoping that the contents of the baggage that they drive off with will be worth more than the fare for the taxi ride. I never suffered from mugging at knifepoint or gunpoint, nor carjacking, nor bus-hijacking, but these things were pretty common in some places, and lots of people I knew and worked with did experience these kinds of robberies.

Conclusion

In this chapter I have talked about an array of fieldwork problems, from violence, animals, and parasites, to political complications and the like, exemplified by incidents in my own fieldwork. However, the number of things touched on here barely scratches the surface of the problems of this sort that can be encountered in fieldwork in various parts of the world. The major conclusion that I take away from experiences with these difficulties is that it is important to attempt to be prepared before the fieldwork begins, to find out as much as possible about known kinds of scams and frauds and dangers, about local political issues, about possible diseases, and in general about everything that can compromise or impede the work, in order to be able to try to avoid them. The webpages of the US State Department and comparable agencies in other countries typically provide travel advisories, ranging from current unusual kinds of thefts, frauds, and scams to watch alerts for local outbreaks of diseases, ongoing armed conflicts, etc. It is very helpful to consult them, even though, of course, they lack information about other sorts of problems that can be encountered.

We can become aware of and prepared to deal with many of these sorts of obstacles and complications; however, there will no doubt always be others that cannot be anticipated until they actually happen. That is, while we can speak generally about several categories of problems to be cautious about, there are nevertheless many things about which we cannot generalize. Some would say, come what may, it's all part of the adventure. I'd say instead, forewarned is forearmed ... it's better to be prepared, to the extent that that is possible!

Notes

1. See, for example, the information provided by the World Health Organization (2021).
2. Nearly everyone spells this when used as a first name as "Ascencio" and many assume "Asencio" is misspelled; nevertheless, there are cases where it is spelled "Asencio," as in this instance.
3. On a different occasion, another publicity person for the university wrote a piece for the local newspaper in which she called me a "hero" several times, saying that I was single-handedly "saving languages." Fortunately, I think very few saw it. I was appalled by this use of "hero" in connection with the linguistic work that I did, and me "saving" languages and doing it all by myself is hardly a proper way to talk about collaboration with community members to help them with language revitalization efforts. I was certainly no hero, not in the classical sense of "hero" anyway. That meaning was a "warrior or protector who lived and died in the pursuit of honor, typically a semi-divine and extraordinarily gifted person, held in the highest esteem and considered of supreme importance." The word has been so overused that its modern meaning has devolved to little more than that of "a good guy (male or female)," maybe with a sense of "someone admired for their acts or good qualities." Its meaning has been so eroded with overuse that it is at best now a weak approbation, and worse, it has become such a cliché as to be embarrassing. In any case, "hero" and single-handedly "saving languages" was just inappropriate in this context.
4. Phonetically, that was pronounced [tʰʊmz] "thumbs."
5. In the Spanish of northern Argentina, the verb for to chew coca is *coquear*: *coquea* "he/she chews coca, is chewing coca."

6

Eating, drinking, and matters of health

Introduction

Tales of fieldwork are often full of accounts of eating weird, outlandish things and suffering exotic illnesses. In reality, though, much fieldwork involves neither, and it is not an image of fieldwork that should be fanned. Rather, staying healthy in the field is important, and when health issues arise, very often they have to do with something the fieldworker ate or drank. In this chapter I report some personal experiences involving food and health, coupled with something of an ulterior motive of hoping to allow others to benefit from my mistakes and to take precautions.

Eating and drinking

Talk about fieldwork often involves macho-like accounts of eating various bizarre foods and also of suffering from weird and mysterious health complications. Some advice often given to fieldworkers goes along the lines that you should eat or drink anything offered to you, no matter how suspicious or disgusting it may seem, so that you don't offend the people offering it, so you'll fit in and be accepted better. About that, let me say this as directly and forcefully as I can: Horseshit! This is horribly wrong and dangerous advice.

A great many things you might eat in fieldwork situations can make you extremely sick, and can even kill you. It is just foolish to eat or drink something in an unguarded or cavalier moment that can make you so ill that it forces you to abandon your fieldwork or causes serious delays, not to mention consequences for your health. It is beyond foolish if, for example, eating or drinking something unusual results in squandering thousands of dollars spent to get you there and equipped to do fieldwork that you have to abandon due to compromised health. If the funding is taxpayer money from federal agencies or from donations to non-profit benevolent organizations, the needless loss can raise the ire of some and bring forth tears of lament from others—funding is scarce. Even worse, it is just irresponsible if an illness due to unguarded eating or drinking causes abandonment of a fieldwork project with the last speakers of an endangered language, where that language may receive no documentation before it becomes too late.

No one is under any obligation to eat or drink anything they don't want to or do not trust not to make them sick. Everyone everywhere understands when you say something makes you sick or that you are allergic to something. It is always OK to decline, but that can be made easier usually with a smile and a genuine thanks for what is offered.

OK, it is true that in some settings a fieldworker may end up eating some exotic stuff, though we need to be careful. I've been offered and have eaten, or at least tasted, all of the following: ants, alligator (caiman), grasshoppers, grubs, iguana, monkey, peccary, tapir, turtle, and horse, and donkey in salami, and probably some other things I don't recall right now or didn't know of at the time. The first times I ate alligator (actually caiman) and iguana, both tasted exactly the same—like *pipían* sauce, very spicy, because that's

Figure 6.1 Cooking our dinner in Misión La Paz (Salta Province, Argentina, 2008)

how they were prepared. Later on I got a sense of what they tasted like *sans* sauce. Tapir was served as ground meat; I thought it was just old hamburger from beef until I was told later what it was. The monkey meat that I ate a few times was over-cooked, deep-fried; the meat was fried so hard that care was needed not to spear my throat on the wooden-splinter-like pieces that broke off of the meat when I bit it, tough chewing for sure. Notice that all of these things were eaten hot, so less risk—see the recommendations below.

Eating these things is not part of most people's fieldwork experience, and others end up eating other exotic things. The point is fieldworkers need to do their best not to get sick, and to be aware of how easy it is to get sick. I'll mention a couple of cases in point.

Once I was working with Poqomam in eastern Guatemala and I had only a few days left to finish the goals of the fieldwork there, so I did not want to leave before I had completed it. However, I had gotten a bad case of amoebic dysentery. *Entamoeba histolytica* seemed to love me and I got it seemingly often, requiring cures that were quite hard on intestines—it is necessary to kill both the parasites and the cysts that they leave in the intestines. Because I delayed getting it attended to on that occasion, I got severe intestinal cramps, and the longer I left it untreated, the more severe the cramps became. I finally finished the fieldwork there and headed out to see a medical doctor in Guatemala City, a drive of a few hours. The severe cramps were coming at an interval of every five to ten minutes, and I was forced to pull my rented Volkswagen Beetle to the side of the road to wait for each cramp to pass before continuing on my way. When I finally arrived, I walked into the doctor's office and precipitously passed out, collapsed on the floor right in front of a waiting room full of patients. Needless to say, I did not have to wait long to be seen, though that is far from a recommended way to get in to see a doctor fast.

That was foolish; from it I learned always to carry with me medicine for the cramps and to attack the amoebas, and to be more careful.

Usually I carried a medical book with me that had been prepared for missionaries; later I carried *Where There Is No Doctor* (Warner 2015). These books were very good at describing symptoms and recommending medications. I discovered that not all doctors in Central America were particularly good, though some were excellent, and worse, when I got back to the US and got examined, hardly any doctors there were good at recognizing tropical parasites. I went through series of laboratory examinations several different times only to come up with answers that were already known to me from past experience and from my book of medical advice that I carried with me. No one should treat themselves, but I soon learned that I wasn't likely to get the help I needed from the doctors, at least not timely help. Because medicines can be bought over the counter without prescriptions in most Latin American countries, I just carried dosages along with me of whatever my medical book and past experiences recommended for treating amoebic dysentery, and I took the pills when the symptoms indicated that they were needed. I learned which ones alleviated the cramps and which would kill the intestinal parasites and their cysts. So, I could continue working in the field without disruption and losing a lot of time.

I do not necessarily recommend this approach to others, but it worked for me. It could have been dangerous if something non-bacterial, non-amoebic had been involved, but after enough times of unhelpful, costly, time-consuming laboratory testing, it was pretty clear that what I was doing was what the medical personnel whom I would have seen would prescribe in any case and it addressed the problem without creating worse ones. Though self-treatment is not recommended, for anyone who will be for any extended period of time in an area without access to doctors, health facilities, or medicines, it is definitely a good idea to take along reliable information about ailments and treatments in such contexts, and appropriate medicines for the most likely ones.

On various occasions I got other illnesses. Once in Sololá, Guatemala, where I was working with Kaqchikel (a Mayan language), I got food poisoning—apparently it was from some spoiled pork I had eaten, not knowing it was bad because the hot sauce it was cooked in demolished any taste that was not the sauce. I was staying in a small *pensión*, with no one around whom I knew and no one to help me. Really rapidly I lost seemingly all the fluid in my body, lots that I hadn't suspected was there, eliminated in watery diarrhea. I spent long bouts in the loo, mostly in fear of passing out if I stood up and in fear that if I left, I'd just have to come right back but might be too weak or too faint to be able to make it from the bed to the toilet. I hallucinated off and on for two or three days, having out-of-body experiences, where I felt that I was floating a meter or two above my body looking down, watching the poor miserable, wretched thing. High fever can cause that sort of reaction.

I had managed to get a boy at the *pensión* to go buy me some bottles of Coca-Cola. A Peace Corps doctor I knew there recommended

Coca-Cola for stomach troubles—the bubbles from the carbonation were like Alka-Seltzer for placating a nauseous stomach, the Coke syrup helped to soothe things, the sugar provided energy, and I guess the caffeine kept me from feeling as weak and energyless as I really was. Whatever the real value of Coca-Cola in such a situation, it did help me endure what seemed unsurvivable, and most certainly helped with the problem of extreme dehydration from the severe diarrhea.

I did not eat pork again after that for two or three years and then not again in Latin America for some years beyond that. I do eat pork again now, but always with a watchful eye, checking it out before consuming it.

I also got several other illnesses from protozoa that attack the gastro-intestinal tract; I'm not sure what all of them were. I got giardia (giardiasis, from *Giardia lamblia*) a few times. It involved a sudden explosive, acute, stinking diarrhea with cramps and the dreadful sulfuric belching that the Peace Corps volunteers called the "purple burps." I got salmonella a few times, with bad nausea, severe abdominal cramps, nasty diarrhea, headache, chills, and fever. I was diagnosed as having typhoid fever more than once. Salmonella wasn't talked about as much then and in any case I was uncertain of what the difference between typhoid and salmonella was. I get that there are some non-typhoidal kinds of salmonella, though apparently all of them can cause serious illness, maybe just not all of them resulting in typhoid fever.

I always had up-to-date typhoid vaccinations, but it is only around 70 percent effective for the first year or so, and only 50 percent after three years—I hate to think of what I might have caught or how bad it might have been had I not had those vaccinations at all.

Other instances of illnesses could be recounted, but suffice it to indicate by sharing these that health problems in fieldwork can be extremely dangerous. My motto, acquired the hard way: Be careful! Be prepared!

Some health precautions

I'll recite here some of the general advice usually given for how to try to avoid getting sick from eating and drinking in settings of the sort where much fieldwork takes place—I followed this advice more closely than most devout believers follow their Bible or other holy books, and I'm sure it saved me untold miseries; nevertheless, I still got sick far too often—I learned the value of this advice in episodes I'd have preferred to have missed:

- Avoid being close to sick people.
- Develop a fanatic hand-washing habit—with soap.
- Do not use shared towels.
- Try not to touch your face, especially not your eyes, nose, or mouth.
- Do not drink from a bottle, glass, or cup that someone else has drunk from.
- Don't drink the water. Don't drink it unless it is boiled or purified and you are certain of that. Bottled water, soda pop, and hot drinks if boiled are OK. Hot coffee, tea, and hot chocolate are OK. Most places in the world these days except very remote ones have safe bottled water. You have to take care with the seals on bottles of water, however; in some of the poorest places, bottles are refilled with polluted water and sold as though it were safe, purified water. The water-filtering bottles sold, for example, by sporting goods suppliers for purifying water in places where safe water is not available work reasonably well, eliminating most bacteria. In most situations, though, they are not necessary.
- No ice, and no popsicles either. While you may be told that it is safe, from purified water, and often it is, you should not trust that.
- Eat only hot cooked food, no room-temperature food; eat only fruits that you can peel yourself or that are cooked and hot.

- No salad! Salad seems to be the downfall of many who find it difficult to resist an appetizing appearing salad, especially after not having had any for some time. You can eat only salad that you yourself prepare from lettuce and vegetables soaked in iodine (to kill parasites). In fieldwork it is often not possible to do this. It's just better to forget salads and rely exclusively on hot, cooked vegetables. Eat salad and die!
- Avoid street food—even the best of it is highly risky.
- Do not eat food cooked in old grease or cooking oil. Often street vendors and some restaurants reuse the same old oil for a long time without changing it. Food prepared in it can make you very sick—or worse. Bacteria develop, feeding on food particles left in the oil, with growth of botulism (*Clostridium botulinum*), which causes food poisoning, potentially fatal. Lots of travelers and fieldworkers have been laid miserably low by eating food cooked in such oils, yours truly included. Best advice: if you're not sure, don't eat it.
- Do not use unpasteurized milk or dairy products. Raw milk from cows, sheep, goats, or horses can carry really dangerous bacteria—for example, *Salmonella, E. coli, Listeria,* and *Campylobacter*—and you can get tuberculosis from unpasteurized cow's milk. This means avoiding not only milk itself but also ice cream, yoghurt, and cheeses, if you are uncertain whether they have been made from pasteurized milk.
- Eat nothing with raw eggs, and not soft-cooked or runny ones, either. Uncooked eggs are salmonella havens, and that's not all one can get from them.

However, the advice also includes "Don't panic if you get diarrhea or headache." Treatment is recommended when needed, but most of the time these are temporary things that go away soon on their own. In many parts of the world almost all new arrivals get *turista*—traveler's diarrhea—after a week or so in country. It has a number of colorful names, depending on where you get it—called *Montezuma's revenge*, *Aztec two-step*, *Delhi belly*, *Spanish tummy*, or just *the trots* or *runs*, among a host of other names.

It starts with abrupt onset of diarrhea and an urgent feeling of need to be near, or better on, a toilet, with abdominal cramps, nausea, fever, and often vomiting. It can cause severe dehydration. It is usually not serious in that it resolves itself in a few days and leaves no long-term effects. Usually no specific treatment is needed and it will run its course, though the BRAT diet is recommended: bananas, rice, applesauce, toast, with lots of liquids—for example, tea, Coca-Cola, or bottled or purified water. This diet is not a cure, but eases the symptoms and keeps you from losing all strength and getting too dehydrated. I found that keeping something bland in my stomach like bread or tortillas or rice during attacks of *turista* helped to keep the feeling of nausea down and helped ease intestinal cramps.

The recommendations also say that if symptoms persist or become very severe, you may need medication. There are a number of readily available things for diarrhea—loperamide (e.g. Imodium), bismuth subsalicylate (e.g. Kaopectate, Pepto-Bismol)—though they only address symptoms and are not cures. Bismuth subsalicylate (e.g. Pepto-Bismol) is sometimes recommended, not just for soothing the stomach during a bout of *turista*, but also as a prophylactic; if taken with or slightly before meals, it can reduce the chance of getting the malady. Antibiotics are not recommended except when symptoms persist or become serious.

In some locations syringes with needles are not available or are sometimes reused without proper sterilization. For those reasons, it is often recommended that travelers in such places take their own syringes and needles with them. They are easy to buy; however, for crossing national borders, because of serious issues surrounding illegal drugs, it's best to take along a letter from a doctor explaining why they are needed and that they were prescribed by the doctor. I have traveled with syringes and needles several times, but have never needed them and never had any police, immigration, customs, or other official ever raise a question about them. I suspect I was just lucky in that regard.

Related to this, each time when we went to Misión La Paz for fieldwork, we took a couple of hundred syringes with their needles, bought in country, in a town with one of the bigger pharmacies. Although Argentina has a very good rural health system, very often the local health center, run by a nurse, had no syringes or needles. On some occasions, syringes would arrive but without the needles to go with them; other times the needles but not the syringes were sent; sometimes all that was supplied were needles whose gauge was wrong and so could not be used. We donated the syringes and needles to the local health center, as well as nebulizers, blood pressure monitors, and other medical supplies each time we went, one way we could help the community. There was no particular motive for doing this, other than that it was needed and we could do it, and we wanted to help. It was not part of some premeditated decision following the dictates of some ethical code about payback to communities for allowing us to document their languages, though it would have been fitting for that.

About precautions, I came to be a firm believer in the advice to go to a travel clinic, get the best advice possible, and do this well in advance before traveling. The advice to check the World Health Organization (WHO) and the Centers for Disease Control and Prevention (CDC) also turned out to be extremely useful. Their websites provide valuable information about health conditions and issues to be aware of in countries to be visited as part of the fieldwork.

Though I resented the weight that a medical kit added to and the space it took up in my luggage, eventually I learned from bad experience and took on board the advice always to travel with one. Various websites tell what the medical kit should contain. While I rarely needed anything other than the occasional band-aid or disinfectant, the medical kit proved invaluable time and again for various accidents and maladies that affected language consultants, graduate research assistants, and community members where I was engaged in language research projects.

I learned that in Latin American countries, it was often helpful to consult local pharmacists. They were not always able to help, but often they were very knowledgeable. Pharmacists in more remote locations often had excellent understanding of the illnesses people of the region got, and they typically knew the best medicines to recommend for these and other things. I did, though, also maintain the stance that I needed to be careful with and sensible about any medical advice I received, from anyone. I always carefully read the information on contraindications and possible side effects that come with medicines.

Malaria and HIV/AIDS

I never got malaria, but several people I worked with did get it. Fieldworkers in areas with malaria often have stories to tell about reactions to anti-malarial drugs, of which there are many kinds and not everyone is able to take all of them. I have been prescribed various of them on different occasions—I never liked any of them much. In India I took doxycycline. It's an antibiotic, so not desirable. It increases sun sensitivity so I had to avoid exposure to the sun, kind of hard to do effectively when moving around often on foot. I suffered from a side effect that was not listed with the contraindications—a respiratory complication. I got a bad cough while there and I thought I had caught a bad cold that just wouldn't go away; it lasted for over six weeks while I was taking doxycycline for malaria prevention. Only when a medical doctor friend in Germany, where I went after India, checked on it were we able to discover official acknowledgement of the possible respiratory problems from taking this drug. Needless to say, I was not happy about this. I learned to pay very careful attention to any medications and to attempt to find out information even beyond what came with medicines concerning possible complications associated with them.

I was prescribed mefloquine several times for malaria prevention. It is not to be used by anyone with psychiatric conditions or a seizure disorder, and not recommended for those with some heart issues. "Mef," as it was affectionately called by some users, used to be the preferred malaria prevention for many people, though there were always those warnings about possible psychotic complications . . . talk about the risk of jumping off a bridge while on mef, about disturbing nightmares, hallucinations, etc. I personally never noticed any effect on me other than shortly after taking the tablet each week I could remember parts of my dreams, where otherwise, without mef, I almost never remembered anything that I dreamed, assuming that I did dream. Mefloquine, though, along with several others, sometimes made me feel irritable after I took it.

I'll just mention HIV/AIDS briefly. It was never a serious consideration in most places where I worked and traveled, except in Africa. In Africa it was and is extremely serious. The prevalence of HIV/AIDS in several African countries exceeds 10 percent of the population, and according to some reports in some countries it exceeds 30 percent, though with substantial decline in rates of new HIV infections—and it is often asserted that the rates are underreported. This monumental impact on individuals and communities can have devasting consequences for the vitality and survival of small languages, and can severely complicate efforts towards language documentation and revitalization in these locations.

One thing I noticed in Ghana, Burkina Faso, and Mali is that I was almost always the oldest person I encountered. I assumed the general absence of old people, especially men, must at least in part have something to do with the prevalence of AIDS. On some occasions I did meet someone who appeared very old to me, like my grandfather's age, only to discover later that in reality they were considerably younger than I was.

In my work in Latin America, only in MLP, in northern Argentina, did the issue ever arise directly. A French tourist had visited Santa Victoria Este, a town about 20 miles (over 30 kilometers) from MLP, a few years earlier and had given AIDS to a Wichí woman there. From that event, HIV/AIDS had entered the population and several cases were discovered in the region. In spite of this, the consultants we worked with in MLP insisted that it was only a white man's (*criollo*) disease and that they, as *paisanos* (Indigenous people), could not catch it and were in no danger. That was truly unfortunate, since traditionally there was a fair amount of culturally permitted premarital promiscuity, still the case today. Their risk of contagion is fairly high despite these unfortunate, misguided denials. This never complicated our language work there, though our attempts to convince the young men who worked with us on the project that theirs was not a safe attitude about the disease were not well received.

Children and fieldwork

As for taking small children into the field, I personally have always thought that the risks to health and other dangers are enough to make this not advisable in many places. Sometimes having a child along can give a fieldworker an in with the community that might be more difficult to establish for a person on their own. People in most places like children, and are curious about foreign kids, and fieldworkers accompanied by children don't seem as dangerous or suspicious as childless adults.

My children were with me one year in El Salvador. It mostly went OK, though my kids got really tired of all the adults running their hands through their blond hair—they would take off running with their head down if they saw anyone approaching who looked like a potential hair-groper or petter.

The worst that happened is that one of my children—who doesn't mind me telling about this here so long as his name isn't mentioned—got a large egg-sized and egg-shaped abscess in the very middle of the top of his head; he was about five at the time. There was a serious scare when medical doctors there initially thought it might be anthrax, though that, thank goodness, proved to be a wrong diagnosis. The doctors were never able to figure out what it was. Eventually it healed, but left a very nasty scar which fortunately is not visible under his hair. It was never suggested that he caught this somehow from someone running their fingers through his hair, and I've never believed that to be the cause, but I would also not rule it out as an involved factor.

It is sometimes thought that a fieldwork experience will be educational for children, learning other languages, experiencing other cultures—I believed that when I took my own children with me to El Salvador. Probably it is often true that fieldwork can have these sorts of positive benefits for children—but it is not as true as we might want to think. Children obviously pick up languages fast and effortlessly, but unfortunately recent research shows that they forget a language almost equally fast and very completely if they don't have sustained contact with it.[1] My children fit that. They soon forgot the Spanish they learned after returning from living in El Salvador. That is, the educational value for pre-adolescent children may be much more limited than might be imagined.

In short, taking children to the field can have some advantages in some fieldwork situations, but it can also often be a huge risk, especially to their health. And, in practical terms—not the most important considerations when your child's health is at issue—the time required to deal with children's health problems or other complications involving them can result in loss of much time or even in having to abandon the project in order to obtain necessary medical treatment for a child.

Help for maintaining well-being in the field

Fortunately, there are many readily accessible publications and websites that provide reliable information and advice about maintaining well-being and about ailments and treatments in contexts where doctors and medicines may not be readily available. A much used and particularly valuable one is:

> Warner, David. 2015. *Where There Is No Doctor.* Berkeley: Hesperian Foundation. It is available online at <https://hesperian.org/books-and-resources>.

Another much consulted one is:

> Centers for Disease Control and Prevention and Gary W. Brunette. 2020. *CDC Yellow Book 2020: Health Information for International Travel.* Oxford: Oxford University Press. It is updated and published each two years.

A Google search for "health advice for travelers" or "traveler's health books" brings up dozens of websites and publications.

Note

1. O'Grady (2018) reports on this kind of language attrition in children.

7

Surviving fieldwork: Travel and living in the field

Introduction

Fieldwork usually involves travel, sometimes quite a lot of travel, and often staying in accommodations that are far from ideal. Some might be lucky enough to stay in a pleasant motel or with a nice family, with modern comforts, in or near their field site, maybe even in the fieldworker's own hometown or village or reservation or reserve for those doing fieldwork on their own native or heritage language. For others, especially typical academics, fieldwork usually involves at least some long-distance travel to and from the location of the language that is the object of the fieldwork, and staying in often taxing accommodations. In this chapter the intention is to share some tips for travel and living in the field derived from repeated vexing experiences. I report some coping strategies that come from these personal experiences—many of them learned the hard way—that may be of use to others who do fieldwork, or even for anyone traveling or working in difficult or out-of-the-way places. Of course, not everything reported and suggested here may have any relevance for everyone and it definitely does not work in all situations or locations. Also, sadly, some of what is talked about here may seem just downright unpleasant.

Travel

Travel is often enjoyable and enlightening, but at the same time travel in less developed countries and in remote regions is usually difficult and can be perilous as well. Some of the fieldwork projects I worked on involved lots of local travel—for example, for surveying dialects or seeking possible speakers of languages where it was not known whether any speakers remained or where they might be found if there were any. I have done many kinds of travel for fieldwork, lots and lots of travel actually. I've traveled many times by bus, boat, bush plane, car, dugout canoe, horse, mule, and on foot. What follows reflects some of that travel.

Buses

Local buses in Central America and Mexico tend to be Bluebird buses, the same as the school buses seen all over North America. The gear ratio for these buses tends to be set very low in those countries, good for climbing mountains, which are everywhere in Guatemala and abundant in other places there. Even in their highest gear these buses cannot get up to very high speeds, though plenty fast enough to be dangerous. Though it was often necessary to ride local buses, I avoided them wherever and whenever possible.

The overcrowding in these buses is notorious. They get two to four extra passengers on each bench beyond what would be thought possible, usually also with people standing in the aisles—many, many people standing there. The fleas one can catch on these buses were mentioned earlier. Passengers are typically jammed really tightly together. The American idea of trying to keep some distance between passengers is totally unknown and absent. For example, in

Central America even if you are the only one seated on a bench, the next passenger to enter is likely to slide in right up next to you, so close you are touching. This, not surprisingly, has caused some misunderstandings when, for example, a local woman has slid up next to a foreign guy who was not aware of local spacing norms, when there would be enough space on the bench so that this sliding-up-next-to custom would not seem to be necessary from his culturally uninformed perspective.

The space between rows of seats is typically so small that there is no hope of the average-sized gringo fitting in. This results in sitting painfully with knees jammed against the back of the seat in front of you or hoping somehow to be able to sit with your legs angled to the side though that is usually not possible, at least not possible without significant inconvenience to those sitting near you, who also have little space for their legs. I learned always to do my best to get a seat on an aisle or even better in the first row in the bus so that with luck I could aim my knees out into the aisle a bit rather than having them paralyzed from being wedged torturously against the seat in front of me.

I learned definitely to try to board buses early and get a seat if possible. Standing in crowded aisles for a very long time with the bus tossing you around as it goes over rough roads and around tight curves is no picnic.

Theft on the buses is also notorious. Everyone, even the poorest people, get robbed by pickpockets on buses. Also, entire buses get hijacked, especially on certain routes, where everyone on the bus is robbed of anything and everything worth having. I was never robbed on a bus; I always took precautions mentioned in the last chapter; however, several graduate students and language consultants working on projects with me were robbed on different occasions.

What I hate most about local buses is the behavior of macho bus drivers, particularly in Guatemala. I was often on buses where drivers attempted to show how macho they were by racing other drivers up and down mountains, attempting to pass on blind curves—dangerous as hell, and pretty scary, too—with seeming total disregard for the lives of the hundred or so passengers onboard. Drivers also competed with the drivers of the many other buses on the same route, racing each other to get to passengers waiting at the next bus stop first, to make money from the fares that those passengers would pay. There were crashes with cars, trucks, motorcycles, and other buses, and occasionally buses ended up going over steep drop-offs into deep ravines, killing many of the passengers.

Buses often break down there, which is well-known, and troublesome for the delays and inconveniences that this causes. In one case, in Guatemala, a bus had died and would not restart so the driver lit a match to see whether there was still fuel in the gas tank. The burned-out carcass of that bus remained there for several years as a testament to the driver's wisdom and as a sad reminder of the many who were killed that day. The local buses are always slow, always uncomfortable, often unreliable, and dangerous.

Cars

I also traveled by car frequently. For some projects I was fortunate enough to have sufficient research funds to rent a car in country to help the research. A few times I was able to get a panel van from the university motor pool for projects. I also was offered use of a jeep both in Chiapas, Mexico, and again sometimes in Guatemala from organizations involved with Indigenous peoples or their cultures. And many times I drove my own vehicle from the US to fieldwork sites in Central America and Mexico. I would take off in my Volkswagen van or a university panel truck and drive pretty much straight through, just pulling over somewhere at night to sleep in the car until daylight, and then push on again. Once, somewhere in Texas, where I had pulled onto a side road to sleep the night in my Volkswagen van, a local sheriff and his deputy woke me up. There had apparently been cattle rustling in the area and they checked me out to see if I was not there to steal some cows. I could make it all the way in just a few long days of hard driving—from California, Missouri, or upstate New York. That would not be possible today; it is utterly unsafe now to drive through Mexico or Central America in that way.

I, like nearly everyone else, managed to get stuck crossing rivers and streams and mudholes from time to time. This was pretty common; it was usually possible to get a local farmer to help pull me out with a team of oxen or wait for another truck or jeep to come along to hook onto my vehicle and help pull it out. Not a big deal. However, I did learn one cool trick about how to cross rivers in cars or trucks. Local drivers taught me that if you loosen the fan belt or take it off so that the fan won't rotate blowing water up onto the sparkplugs, you can cross rivers so long as the water isn't so deep that it comes up to the spark plugs. You also covered the distributor cap with a plastic bag to help in case of any splashing. Many modern cars no longer have these components; I have no idea what would happen to them trying to cross these rivers.

I visited Chicomuselo, in the far south of Chiapas, Mexico, several times, and for that it was necessary to cross a fairly big river, where when the water level was normal the water was deep enough that it entered the car and got up to around mid-calf depth while I was sitting in the front seat, but with the fan belt trick, it was possible to drive on across. I went to Chicomuselo several times in search of possible speakers of Chicomuceltec, a Mayan language once spoken in Chicomuselo but no longer spoken by the time I went there. I found only a few elderly people who could remember a few words learned when they were children, but no real speakers.

One year, by sheer accident the day that I had chosen to leave Chicomuselo to drive back turned out to be the last day it was possible to leave, though I did not know that at the time. The last of the various coffee-hauling trucks and logging trucks were all leaving that day. The river was very high and the trucks were being towed across by what was a sort of tow-truck-like giant tractor; it had four enormous tires, about 10 feet (3 meters) high and 4 feet (1.2 meters) wide, with a very thick crane that had a cable hanging down from it. The tractor drivers agreed to tow my small vehicle across. This was truly exciting in several of the worst sorts of ways. My pickup was bouncing up and down, swinging back and forth in the current, and worst of all it was tilting back and forth seeming to be determined to capsize in midstream. The water came in and reached to the level of the windows, that is, roughly to my armpits while I was sitting there. The pickup and I did make it out, alive, in spite of doubts I had had about that at the time.

It was really fortunate that by sheer happenstance I had decided to leave that day, since otherwise my car would have been stranded there by the high water for a long time. I would not have been stuck there; if necessary, I would have been able to leave on foot, with the car left behind. Downstream a ways there was a hanging footbridge. I had crossed it on other occasions, when the river was too high to enter by car and also just to show people traveling with me something interesting. It was high over a deep canyon that the river ran through, where the river was narrowest. It was used by men carrying coffee sacks on their backs to get them across the river during times when the trucks couldn't cross the river. The bridge was constructed of cables and ropes with single planks about 8 inches (20 centimeters) wide to walk on, laid end to end on the ropes supporting them. The bouncing of this hanging bridge with men running across it with large, heavy coffee sacks on their backs was both intimidating and impressive.

Speaking of bridges, when I went to Montaña de la Flor in Honduras to learn about and work with Tol (a.k.a. Jicaque), there was a road, but used only rarely, by the Summer Institute of Linguistics (SIL) missionaries stationed there. There were two bridges on that road spanning two different ravines, which I found distressing in the extreme. These bridges consisted of two parallel tree trunks across which saplings of 3 or 4 inches (8–10 centimeters) in diameter where placed, loose, not attached in any way. I was assured that these bridges could be driven across and that the saplings would not shift enough to allow the car to fall through, though from their appearance I doubted this. Still, I did drive across them, quite fast actually per instructions I was given, feeling the saplings shifting and giving way under the van as I quickly passed over them. Had the panel van fallen through, the bottom of the ravines below the bridges would have been only roughly 20–30 feet (7–10 meters) below, but more than sufficiently deep to mean that the vehicle would probably never be retrieved, not to mention probable damage the fall would cause to its driver, me.

Tol is a fascinating language. Its speakers had run away in the 1860s to escape from the sarsaparilla exploiters, crossed the mountains, and formed a new community removed from and hidden from outsiders. Not for nearly a hundred years were they in contact with the outside world again. They were very uncomfortable with outsiders, since they easily caught illnesses against which they had little immunity. Though they worked with me, they were not happy to have me there and I left after only a few days, but I was able to get a considerable amount of information on the language's vocabulary and structure, a really interesting language.

Car problems seemed constant, perhaps not unexpected, given the distances and the road conditions. A vexatious and frequent problem was fuel filters getting clogged because of all the dust and dirt from unpaved roads and also because of the contaminants often already in the gasoline that was pumped into the cars at service stations. I got good at spotting bad car behavior due to gasoline filter problems, because it happened to me so many times. This was especially frequent with rental cars. A trick that was easier to execute in some cases than in others was just to remove the fuel filter altogether, not always possible on some cars. Clogged gasoline filters seemed to have a wicked sense of when to leave you and your car stranded in the most inconvenient of places. I'm not sure how serious a problem this would be for many modern cars, where the fuel filter is located inside the gasoline tank and the fuel pump is equipped with a fuel strainer, replaced when the entire fuel pump assembly has to be changed. It could be really nasty.

For a couple of field seasons I took a Chevrolet panel truck from my university's anthropology department, where lots of archaeological research was conducted and the vehicles were of great use for that. Having a panel truck identified with archaeology came in very handy once in Belize. I was driving through Mexico and Belize to Guatemala with graduate assistants. We arrived in Belize City late on a Friday afternoon and found all the hotels fully booked—it turned out that most hotels there then only rented rooms by the hour on weekends, for kinds of liaisons about which nothing further need be said—and it appeared we would be left without any accommodation at all. However, one hotel proprietor took pity on us and rented us one room for the four of us because he had seen the logo painted on the door of the panel truck that said "Archaeology"; he said that because he liked archaeology a lot he would rent us a room even though he could have made more renting it to others by the hour.

Way back on a very remote road in El Salvador, as I was driving up a steep hill, the gas tank just up and fell off this panel truck. A local farmer who was plowing his field with a team of oxen happened to be in sight of this breakdown. He noticed how I struggled unsuccessfully to raise and reattach the tank and he came over to help. With a lot of grunting and strenuous experimentation, we managed to rig up a way with rocks and fence posts lying alongside the road to lever the gas tank up and reattach it, supported by ropes that I had with me with which we tied it and held it in place. I used duct tape—never leave home without duct tape—to attach the rubber gas line to the gas tank. I managed to get the panel truck started again by coasting downhill, and then I drove very slowly and carefully back to the nearest town where repair was possible, about 25 miles (40 kilometers) away, where they cleaned the tank, repaired a small hole in it, and reattached it more properly.

All seemed good until the return drive back to the US. Weirdly, a metal tube on the gas tank that connected to the rubber-hose gas line that fed the carburetor had gotten a small crack in it when it had fallen off the car or while it was being repaired and reattached, and whenever the gas tank got below about half full, it would start sucking air and the motor just died, though I understood this only much later. This happened a number of times. Each time I'd just wait an hour or two until an Ángeles Verdes (Green Angels) pickup would come along. They belong to a Mexican government-funded fleet of mechanics who offer free assistance to drivers on highways. They would help me get to the nearest repair shop, always ultimately by putting some gasoline in the tank from cans that they carried with them. Each time the backyard mechanics in these small roadside repair shops would find something that they thought was the cause of the problem and they would change it or fix it, and I'd be off once more, happy until the gas tank got below half full, and then it would all start over again. In total, thanks to this problem, six different "repairs" were performed along the way—no one ever figured out what was going on, and it didn't occur to me until near the end that it had to do with how full the gas tank was.

Finally, when I arrived in Texas and the car stopped again, I managed to get it to an official Chevrolet garage in Corpus Christi, and after I told them the symptoms and the many things that had been changed or "fixed" along the way, mechanics got it up on the rack and after a long investigation discovered the small crack in the metal tube at the top of the gas tank, and fixed it.

This is just one car incident, but one that cost me a lot of time and money, and illustrates the sorts of things that can confront fieldworkers traveling by car.

In another incident a taillight and brake light of my Volkswagen van got broken out by vandals in Mexico. It wasn't possible to get it repaired where I was doing fieldwork, so, since such things were not given great importance there, I just drove it around that way until it was time to return to the US. For that, I bought a flashlight, several batteries, and some red fingernail polish; I painted the lens of the flashlight red with the nail polish; I attached it to the rear of the van with duct tape—never leave home without duct tape—turned it on after dark, and managed to drive all the way back to New York state without being stopped by police for not having a taillight. Of course, it didn't signal braking, but there wasn't a lot of braking needed on major interstate highways across the US. I was able to get it repaired when I got home, of course.

It goes without saying that driving in Latin America can be dangerous. In Mexico and Central America many drive at night with their lights turned off—new headlights cost money. Drivers sometimes do extremely dangerous things, like suddenly turning left across several lanes from the far righthand lane without signaling, barely being missed by oncoming traffic, or considering stop signs and red lights as only mild suggestions that apply mostly only to other drivers.

Possibly the most annoying thing about driving in these countries is the traffic police always demanding what are called bribes but are just flat-out extortion. In Mexico in particular, traffic cops randomly stop drivers and ask for "bribes." In Spanish it's called a *mordida*, literally a "bite"; the traffic police are called *tiburones* "sharks," not to their faces, because of these "bites" that they take. They especially gravitate towards stopping more expensive-looking cars and cars with foreign license plates or whose drivers appear to be foreign. It usually starts with a policeperson stopping you and informing you that you have committed an "infraction." The infraction is usually cooked up. I have been told, for example, that I entered the pedestrian crosswalk after the light had turned red when my car was still considerably outside of the crosswalk and had never entered it at all, and that I had made an illegal turn when in fact I had driven only straight ahead making no turns, to mention just a couple of examples. After the supposed infraction is named, you are told that you can settle this here on the spot by paying the equivalent of $5 or $10 or $20, or that they can take you and your various papers, your driver's license, registration, etc., down to headquarters where you will pay a much larger fine and it will take several days to process, requiring extra days for you to get your documents back before you'll be able to drive again.

Most local drivers just paid the nuisance bribes so they could be on their way. Eventually, when I was in Mexico City, I got so fed up with being sought out so often for "bribes" that when they stopped me and explained the options of paying on the spot or going to headquarters, I told them very politely that I very much wanted to do everything properly and so, yes, let's go to headquarters and get this taken care of. Well, apparently that had never happened to them; they were perplexed and didn't know how to deal with it. Usually they would just leave me pulled over to the side of the road and go off to tell someone else about some "infraction" they had committed, and then come back to me to suggest again that we just take care of it here, and I again would say that I really wanted to do it properly and so let's go to headquarters. Eventually, after stopping other drivers, they would come to me and say that for this time they would just give me a warning and let me go. This cost me some time, but I felt that the satisfaction of defeating the frustration of paying those "bribes" more than sufficiently compensated for the lost time.

A couple of final notes about fieldwork travel involving automobiles. One is about availability of fuel. For a few years, travel to do fieldwork in Argentina was extremely complicated. Because of the amount of equipment and supplies we had to take with us because it was a large, long-term project, it was necessary to drive from Buenos Aires to our Chaco language project in Misión La Paz (henceforth

MLP), almost exactly 1,250 miles (2,000 kilometers). We made the trip many times, two long days of driving, passing many hundreds of large trucks each way, both going out and on the return trip. The government was controlling petroleum prices in hopes of not exacerbating the country's economic crisis, while petroleum companies wanted what they felt to be fairer prices and so withheld fuel to pressure the government to relax price restrictions. Sometimes there would be no gasoline or diesel available at gas stations for hundreds of kilometers and then even when it was available, often the maximum one could buy was only a few liters at a time. Most often it was gasoline that was not available, sometimes it was diesel, sometimes there was neither.

The upshot of this was that we had to figure out before setting off whether it was diesel or gasoline that was most in shortage at a particular time and then we rented a pickup that ran on gasoline or alternatively on diesel, according to what was most available at that time. We always carried a couple large *bidones*, plastic gasoline drums, full of fuel with us for those stretches where no fuel was available.

Finally, in travel, one must allow for delays from obstructions of various sorts. I have ended up waiting for many hours for roads to reopen in cases of landslides and rockslides. Washed-out bridges have often necessitated tricky crossings through water or driving sometimes very long distances to find alternative routes. Most frustrating are the roadblocks by *piqueteros* ("picketers"), protesters calling attention to their various particular political and social issues or demands. These happen in many places, though they are especially frequent and refined in Argentina. Sometimes major highways are blocked for many hours at a time.

On one occasion, we, along with hundreds of others, were stopped on the main highway in northern Argentina that goes to the Bolivian border by Wichí *piqueteros* who were protesting the hiring and firing practices of a local petroleum refinery that happened to

Figure 7.1 *Piqueteros* roadblock (main highway north of Tartagal, Salta Province, Argentina, 2007)

be located at the side of that highway. After waiting quite a long time, I got to talking with the military police (the *gendarmes*) present at the head of the blockade who were there just to make sure nothing bad erupted, not there to resolve anything or to get the blockade suspended. I asked them if they knew a particular military officer who had been stationed in MLP that we had gotten to know and liked. They did know him and were happy to talk about him, and then they asked the Wichí *piqueteros* who were the organizers of this roadblock if they might let us through, since we were going only a short distance further on that highway before turning off at the junction of the highway with the road out to MLP, and they did let us through. It pays to know people, though approaching the police is not always wise. The point, though, is to be prepared for delays, for unexpected things, and for things not always to work as planned.

Horses and mules

In looking for possible remaining speakers of languages that may or may not have recently become dormant, on many occasions I ended up hiring a horse or a mule to get to remote areas with no roads, often in mountains with rough terrain. I rode lots of horses growing up—not mules though—so this was no big deal for me.

There was, though, one great disappointment riding horses there. The horses I rode growing up were tamed and trained with care, with the kind of respect for the horse dictated by the Code of the West. However, the horses and mules I dealt with in Mexico and Central America had been broken cruelly, their spirits crushed in the process. They responded poorly or not at all unless spurred or whipped forcefully. I found it really hard to do that, and it hurt my heart each time it proved necessary just to get an animal to go anywhere.

I'll mention just a couple of cases to give a flavor of how this hunting for speakers on horseback went. As mentioned above, I went to Chicomuselo, in southern Chiapas, Mexico, near the Guatemalan border, to search for possible speakers of Chicomuceltec. I rode a horse to the small villages in the surrounding area, visiting every place where people mentioned that they thought there might be speakers of some Indigenous language. I confess that I was not as prepared for this as I should have been. I left Chicomuselo in hot country with light clothing but rode up into the mountains to visit the villages, where it was much cooler, really cold at night. I ended up sleeping on rough-hewn benches in the local schools—freezing and being bitten mercilessly by the abundant fleas that gleefully inhabited these schools. "School" probably calls forth misleading images in this case. They were small, one-room shacks with dirt floors and thatch roofs. The walls were of irregularly sawn boards with a couple of inches of open space between each board and the one next to it.

Figure 7.2 Fieldwork with Mam while seeking Chicomuceltec (Lyle Campbell with Mam-speaking immigrants, Paso Hondo, Chiapas, Mexico, 1986)

Chicomuceltec is a Mayan language that is all but unknown except for two short wordlists collected by German visitors in the late 1800s. The language is especially interesting to Mayanists because, though it was spoken near the bulk of the other Mayan languages in Guatemala and southern Mexico, it is closely related to Huastec that is spoken over 620 miles (1,000 kilometers) away to the north, in Veracruz and San Luis Potosí. How the two came to be located where they are, so separated from one another geographically and yet closely related, is an unresolved question. In the end I found many speakers of Mam, recent immigrants from Guatemala, living in these small villages or households, but no one with any knowledge of Chicomuceltec.

Something that struck me about the incongruity of it all was that on several occasions when I was riding along out in the bush far from any town or source of electricity, I would hear off in the distance the latest hit songs wafting through the air. Typically I'd eventually come upon a small house compound of cane walls and thatch roof where a transistor radio would be blaring away. In those days everyone in the most remote locations had a transistor radio that worked on batteries. Today's equivalent is to discover cell phones in similarly remote and unexpected locations with no electricity and little evidence of other technology.

As an aside, it was while riding through thick brush in a very remote area out from Chicomuselo that it occurred to me one day that I had a birthday coming up soon. I checked and it turned out that I had missed my birthday by some several days.

In another case I was visiting former Lenca towns and villages in Honduras, several of them high in the mountains, hoping to find surviving speakers of Honduran Lenca. After walking part of the way up into the high mountains, to one of the villages reported to have had speakers of the language, I rented a mule and continued the climb and the search for possible speakers. In Opatoro I ended up sleeping in the local jail, which at that moment had no one locked up in it. Again, saying it was a "jail" probably suggests misleading images. It was a small, one-room building, with a low sod roof and solid log walls. It had no windows but the door let in light. The upper half of the door had something approximating bars, made of vertical wooden poles about 4 inches (10 centimeters) in diameter. Again, in this jail I slept on a wooden bench, froze all night, and suffered from fleas nourishing themselves on my blood. No one in Opatoro, however, had any knowledge of the language.

From there the mule and I continued on in the mountains to Guajiquiro. I stayed there for three days, but the village was suffering from a famine and there was basically no food; in any case, I would have felt guilty about eating any of the little food that there was, needed by those who lived there. So, for those three days, I had only

Coca-Cola, which was trekked in on mule back, and one plate of beans, given to me by the family of the telegrapher who was guiding me and who introduced me to people there.

Once again I found no speakers of the language in Guajiquiro, though one elderly woman remembered a couple of words she had learned as a girl. In the end I left the mule there to be returned to its owner by the telegrapher's family, and the telegrapher and I ran, really ran hard, the entire way down the mountain, arriving after dark to where I had left my van. From running down the mountain in tennis shoes, what others call "sneakers," and accidentally kicking my toes against rocks, especially after it got dark, I lost several toenails on each foot.

That should suffice for horse and mule stories, except to say that often it was not possible to rent horses, since they tended to be quite small, considerably smaller than the typical riding horse in the US and unable to carry my weight for long distances and long periods of time on strenuous trails. I was 6 feet (1.82 meters) tall and weighed 200 pounds (over 90 kilograms), much heavier than most local people. Thus, I sometimes ended up walking farther and more often than I would have preferred if a horse could have been rented that could bear my weight.

Dugout canoes and boats

A few times in Guatemala I was out in a *cayuco*, a dugout canoe, going to local villages along large lakes in order to do fieldwork, when storms came up and put us in peril. In each case the procedure was the same: I was asked by the *cayuco* owner who was doing the paddling to sit out on the prow of the dugout as near the front as possible so that my weight would keep the bow of the dugout from being thrown too high and keeling us over as the wind-driven waves hit us—the *cayuco* was aimed so as to take the waves straight on, not from the side. So I sat there, straddling the front of the *cayuco*, legs dangling down, being pelted by heavy rain, as it bucked in the waves, with me holding on for dear life.

It was not so bad on Lake Atitlán, since we paddled along relatively near the shore. I was investigating Kaqchikel dialects around the east side of the lake. After short bouts of contending with the storm, we were able to make our way to shore where I could just be deposited while the *cayuco* owner waited out the storm there. There was a path around the lake, higher up on the walls of the volcanic cone in which Lake Atitlán lies; if the storms appeared to be going to last too long, I was able to walk back in just a couple of hours, generally a pleasant walk, though not so in the pounding rain.

It was more serious on Lake Petén, which is much wider and so the *cayucos* there went straight across the center of the lake rather than skirting the shore as they did on Lake Atitlán, which would have made for a hugely longer journey. Fighting against the wind and rain and the heavy, wind-driven waves made for very slow progress, at times even lack of any progress. I was returning to Flores from doing fieldwork with Itza', a critically endangered Mayan language, in San José Petén where Itza' is spoken. It is over 3 miles (about 5 kilometers) by boat directly across the lake, and in those days going to San José by *cayuco* was the only practical option though today tourism has increased immensely and now there are motorized boats one can take and it is possible to drive there by road.

At the opposite end of the boating extremes were the large motor launches in Nicaragua out through the mangrove swamps to Bluefields, on the Atlantic side, a jumping-off place to get to speakers of Rama (a Chibchan language), of Sumu (a Misumalpan language), and of Mísquito (also Misumalpan), a much larger language of the Pacific side of Nicaragua. These boats zoomed along at fast speeds with loud noise to match. On one trip, a rifle-toting upper-class Nicaraguan, who seemed much assured of his own importance, shot at anything that moved on either side of the boat as we careened along through the mangrove-lined channels. As you might guess,

I was not in favor of this activity—no one in my opinion should find sport in shooting at animals and birds for no good reason and not even knowing most of the time whether the shots hit anything. Showing off, as seemed to be the biggest part of his motive, was in my estimation poor justification for such behavior.

Planes

Flying can be particularly trying, especially in less developed parts of the world. My advice, based on hard experience, is always be at the airport early and board the plane as early as possible. This is because sometimes mistakes are made—for example, with two passengers assigned to the same seat. The one in the seat first is usually the one allowed to remain; the other can end up with considerable inconvenience, often losing that particular flight and being much delayed. Also, space in the overhead bins gets taken up by the first passengers to board the plane, often leaving no space there for the bags of those who enter after them. For example, flying in Latin America around Christmas time can find many people squabbling and vying for overhead bin space for the many extra Christmas gift packages they are trying to bring onto the plane. When flights are cancelled and passengers are transferred to other flights, as happens sometimes, it is those near the check-in counter who are accommodated first, and when the available seats on other flights and other airlines are gone, those who came to the counter later are left waiting for much later flights, often until the next day or even longer.

On an Aeromexico flight to return home I and some other passengers noticed that the jet engine just outside our window was shooting out flames; we notified an airline attendant, who assured us that that was just normal, but a short time later, somewhere over Texas, the plane abruptly turned around and returned to Mexico City. I remained near the ticket counter while most others took the airline's voucher and went off to eat while waiting for alternative flight arrangements. The few of us near the ticket counter were given seats on a flight from a different airline leaving not long after our re-arrival in Mexico City, while those who had gone to eat ended up not being accommodated until the following day.

Occasionally corruption can hamper travel. Once in Tuxtla Gutiérrez in Chiapas, Mexico, a local politician paid the airline employees working the gate a bribe which resulted in my assigned seat, confirmed long in advance of the flight, being given to him and me being out of luck and bumped from the flight. There was only one flight each day, and fog prevented flights for the next three days—I lost a lot of time and suffered much frustration because of this.

However, it was even deeper-level corruption that ultimately was behind the fog problem that prevented me from flying then. The airport had always been down in the valley, much nearer to the town of Tuxtla Gutiérrez, but a new official airport was built very far from town at a far higher elevation, where frequent fog was known to be a problem. The reason for building it in this impractical location, where weather conditions were known to be often less than favorable, was assumed to be because the land where the new airport was built belonged to the brother of an influential politician, and the sale of the land for the airport had, so the story goes, made a lot of money for both the seller and his politician brother. I asked more than once why, if planes could take off and land at other airports in the fog, they could not do that there. I was given some answer that I did not fully understand but was assured that it was indeed the case that they could not depart in the fog at that airport at that time.

I once had a confirmed flight and paid-for ticket on an airline that turned out not to exist, and had not existed for at least three years. The university travel agent had been too efficient in this case. Upon arrival in country expecting a short connecting flight, I discovered chaos in trying to work out how actually to get to where I was going. A problem was that there were apparently several small airlines, mostly charters, that had similar-sounding names. After considerable delay and distress and cost, I was able to arrange an alternative flight. I also once had a confirmed ticket for a ferry, though this ferry was under repair and hadn't run for several months. No one had told me this. I had arrived at the airport late the night before and slept on some cardboard in a corner, expecting to go to the ferry terminal to take the ferry very early the next morning. Since there just was no ferry service then, in the end I managed to get a seat on a flight in a local plane that was not too expensive, and arrived days sooner than the ferry would have.

Among the worst flying experiences I had was a trip from Helsinki, Finland, to Guatemala City. I was to arrive in Guatemala to run a linguistic field school in Cobán, in Alta Verapaz, for the summer. I was in Helsinki as part of a sabbatical. An SAS flight from Helsinki connected with a supposed direct flight from Brussels to Guatemala on Belgium's Sabina airline. The "direct" flight turned out to have a stopover and plane change in Montreal and again in Mexico City. However, due to who knows what, the connecting plane that was supposed to go from Mexico to Guatemala never arrived. We passengers were never told anything. First we waited five hours in the airport, then were put up in an inexpensive hotel, and then waited the night and all the next day with no word. Finally we were put on a TACA flight, an airline from El Salvador, headed for Guatemala City. However, due to excess weight from the extra passengers and luggage, the TACA flight was not able to lift off in Mexico City's high altitude, so, after another long wait, the plane syphoned out half of its fuel, departed, flew to Acapulco, at sea level, refueled there, and then flew to Guatemala City, arriving nearly three days later than promised.

Several other airlines had had flights from Mexico City to Guatemala during the time that we waited, and by international aviation agreements Sabina was supposed to get us on the next available aircraft that could accommodate us. However, instead, Sabina was negotiating with different airlines to get the best deal so they would lose the least amount of money caused by them having to give up these passengers—this process took a long time—and TACA agreed to be the cheapest. Though the workshop organizers in Guatemala had been at the airport to pick me up and take me to Cobán for the field school, they had to leave long before I arrived and I had to take a bus, thus arriving yet another day later than originally planned. Sabina was not even apologetic. Sabina became the first major European airline to file for bankruptcy—good riddance!

In general for flying, I always like aisle seats, to be able to get up to go to the restroom without bothering other passengers and to be able to move around occasionally on long flights. Some prefer window seats, and the window can be good for sleeping on a plane to avoid people bumping you and waking you up as they move in the aisles. Window seats, however, are often colder than other seats.

Extremely important: I never leave home without earplugs—they are essential for coping with the noise of crying infants and rowdy children on planes, and on land also for dogs barking at night and for noisy occupants of hotels and *pensiones* or loud noise coming from the street.

On foot

Often the fieldwork that I undertook involved walking and hiking. Here I'll mention just a couple of cautions about hiking to get to where you want to go.

In attempting to get to Tacuba, El Salvador, where Pipil (Nawat) was reportedly spoken, I made it to the intersection of the main highway and the dirt road out to Tacuba, over 7 miles (about 12 kilometers) away. I had no idea if any local bus might go there or when that would be if it did. I reasoned that 7 miles was not so far, and so decided I would walk, hoping that a truck or car would come by that I could hitch a ride with, or that a bus would show up that I could hail. I learned the hard way about Kipling's mad dogs and Englishmen in the midday sun—I got sun stroke. I didn't die; I didn't even know it could be dangerous. I learned only much later of the more than six hundred deaths each year from sun stroke/heat stroke in the US, with the numbers on the increase in more recent years. In my case the result was a severe splitting headache and some disorientation, and then sensitivity for several years after that to sun on my head, rapidly bringing on headaches. No vehicle came along until I was at the entrance to Tacuba.

There were, it turned out, a very few elderly speakers of the language there and I was able to work with them, though I felt physically unfit for it, still disoriented on the following day.

One of the speakers there was a very old woman who was seriously ill in bed—I don't know what illness she suffered from; it might have been tuberculosis—clearly in distress and not always coherent. In spite of this, the mayor of the town, who had personally taken me to her house, was shouting at her to answer his questions about the language. For him it was, I believe, a matter of civic pride, with her as a symbol of the town's Indigenous heritage. For me, it was just a terrible experience, since clearly, at least in my mind, we had no right to be disturbing her in her condition, possibly even contributing to worsening it. I did manage to get us out of there, suggesting it would be better to return when she was better. I was able to work with other elders there to collect the information I needed for the dialect survey and for determining the vitality status of the language in that location.

I mentioned above losing toenails from running down the mountain from Guajiquiro in Honduras in tennis shoes (sneakers). Actually, I lost toenails a number of times after long hikes and I often ended up with blisters and damaged toenails from walking or hiking in difficult terrain to seek speakers of languages. I was young and foolish; I now know better about proper footgear and taking care of feet in hiking.

I wish I had learned sooner not be so foolish—for example, about defying the sun and neglecting my feet—and that I had just been better prepared.

Crossing borders and visa matters

In this context of travel, some mention of border crossings and visa issues might be in order. Crossing international borders in a vehicle can be especially trying. Immigration and customs officials in Mexico and Central America were very often on the lookout for what unofficial fees they could demand.

I have ended up at times driving many miles from one border crossing to another just to get away from a self-important border official demanding too much for a bribe or making matters too difficult. Once when I crossed from Guatemala into Honduras, the Honduran immigration officer was drunk and in that state stamped the Honduran entry visa right across the photo of my face on the main page of my passport—for some years after that until I got a new passport, I had the privilege of explaining to all border officials everywhere the circumstances of how my passport picture came to have this errant, suspicious Honduran visa stamped over it.

Let me add here a word about visas and permissions in general. It should go without saying, but let me underscore it in any case, that in many parts of the world it is necessary to get the proper visas and official permissions to be able to do the planned fieldwork. Sad stories of serious complications involving visas and official permissions are seemingly endless. In some places, especially in some parts of the Pacific, sometimes visas cannot be obtained at all and then at other times in the same place they are given readily. The Solomon Islands are notorious for uncertainties about whether visas will be given or not. Venezuela allows no American anthropologists or linguists to do research there, at all. In India there are several regions which are often restricted and unavailable for such research, and in China, foreigners are not allowed to do research in many regions, especially on the Tibetan Plateau, where there are many languages in need of documentation. The bureaucracy in Brazil has typically been notoriously complex for non-citizens of Brazil to obtain permission to work with Indigenous peoples there, and the inclusion of Brazilians to collaborate on such projects is typically required.

In general, the main advice that I would offer about visas is: (1) learn as much as possible about the requirements and process in advance ... and be sure not to forget that obtaining a visa can be quite expensive for some places; (2) apply way in advance and allow for delays and obstacles in uncertain cases; and (3) try to make contingency plans in case the visa is denied or delayed beyond when you have time available for the planned research.

Living in the field

Obviously conditions vary greatly from place to place. Here I report some personal tricks of the trade that I discovered or experienced involving shelter, hygiene, and food while doing fieldwork.

Hygiene

Running water is not always available. Even where in principle there was supposed to be running water, the water could often be off for some hours during the day, or for some days during the week, or the water just went off with no indication of when it might be restored. For that reason, many houses in Mexico and Central America have water tanks on their roofs, for times when the water is off. In those places getting used to not being able to count on water being available just became a way of life. In some other places there was no running water at all. In some there was only a communal well from which people carried jugs or buckets of water to their homes. In others the only water was from a river or stream, often polluted, also carried in buckets or jugs.

In MLP in Argentina, there was a large water tower to which water was pumped and from there it went out to several faucets sticking up out of the ground, scattered around the village, from which residents got their water. Later, small government-sponsored houses were built that had running water in them. There is a military post to guard the bridge at the border there with Paraguay. In early field sessions in MLP, water was available only when the military remembered to turn on the pump, and on a number of occasions they just forgot to do that.

On one occasion the hoses from the pump to the water tower burst and the whole town was without water for some time. When we arrived, we managed to fix the hoses with duct tape—never leave home without duct tape.

For my last two field seasons in MLP, I had to carry water from a spigot some hundred yards (meters) away. I got very efficient at cleaning dishes and at bathing while using very little water. I found that with a bit of soap, a sponge, and just a mug or two of water, I could get myself completely clean and feel comfortable. This was much more efficient and satisfying than it may sound. For hair, usually a second mug of water was needed, some of it to get my hair wet and to shampoo it, with the rest of the mug's water for rinsing. With conditioner, I'd use another mug of water for rinsing it out. Those with more hair might need more water than I did. Still, bathing and even shampooing hair requires much less water than most people think. In fact, most of the time you can get your body perfectly clean with just fresh water, no soap needed or just used on armpits and nether regions. Using soap sparingly saves both water and soap. Obviously where water was freely available, these sorts of tactics for keeping clean while conserving water were happily forgotten.

More about bathing

The Hitchhiker's Guide to the Galaxy was right—a towel can be a great boon to the traveler. A towel can serve, for example, as an extra bed covering for sleeping on cold nights, for covering shoulders or legs on cold days, for wrapping up and protecting delicate, fragile things such as recording equipment, for carrying things, and for drying oneself, among other uses. However, you do not need a large towel for bathing—you can get dry perfectly well on a small towel, or even just a dry wash cloth, and towels take up space that matters where it is necessary to be careful with bulk and weight in travel bags. Actually, if you have no towel, you can still manage fine. You can dry yourself with a T-shirt or other items of clothing, even cotton socks. In fact, in spite of any possible revulsions, some prefer already worn clothing for this since it gets you perfectly dry without depleting your supply of available clean clothes. Of course, really dirty already worn clothing might not be as appealing for this.

I very highly recommend something that I eventually discovered: scrape as much water off your body as possible with your hands before drying off with a towel or something else. That is, you can run your open hand, between your thumb and fingers for example, over your body, flinging the water off from your arms and legs, face and head, and so on. Whether a towel or some article of clothing is used for drying off, in tropical climes there is good reason to avoid, to the extent possible, getting this towel or clothing any wetter than necessary. Wet towels do not dry well and often sour and smell skunky fast. You can get relatively dry this way; you can even get fully dry by just waiting a few minutes after doing this before dressing. After flinging the water off from you in this way, you can use the towel or its surrogate to finish drying off, and because much less moisture remains for it to soak up in drying this way, it dries faster. This leaves you without the skunky-smelling towels associated with bathing in these parts of the world, so you don't have to launder them as often;

that may save lugging so much water for washing clothes in situations where fetching water is necessary, and you don't have to carry a wet towel along if you have to continue traveling.

Often even where water is available for showering or bathing in a tub, there is no hot water. I grew up with no hot water in the house and so I don't really mind cold showers. They can be bracing, also exhilarating; it's not that difficult to get used to them, I think. However, the prospect of a completely cold shower was apparently traumatic for some of the student research assistants on some projects. I never found good solutions for them, but here are a few things that can sort of help a little bit.

In Cobán, in Alta Verapaz, Guatemala, on a Q'eqchi' project, a couple of students discovered that if they left a garden hose on the roof of the house full of water, stopped off at the end, until mid to late afternoon, the sun would heat the water in the hose enough for them to get one short shower with warm water.

On some projects some participants brought along "sun shower bags" (solar camp shower bags), just black plastic bag-like things that are left out in the sun to heat up the water in them and then they are hung up so the water comes out of a small hose for a shower. A five-gallon sun shower bag lasts about 2½ minutes. The down sides of this are that they only work if in fact you have sun to heat up the water; you typically have to take time out of your day to shower in the afternoon—there usually won't have been enough sun yet to heat them in the morning, which is when I like to shower, not wasting time later in the day that I'd rather use for work; and they take up space where avoiding bulk and extra weight can be important for travel.

If you have electricity or good solar panels, in many countries you can buy small hot water wands, immersion heaters. They come in various sizes, shapes, and costs, but typically the ones available in smaller, more remote towns in developing countries are poorly made and the wires break easily. They are small, wand-like elements composed of an electrical cord and usually a small plastic handle and a metal element that is a few inches long. The metal part is inserted in a cup of water which it heats when plugged in. They are not efficient for heating larger quantities of water. Still, if you are bathing with a sponge and just a cup or two of water, having a cup of warm water can be quite pleasant. Also, the hot water wand is valuable for the purposes for which it was primarily designed, for heating water for coffee, tea, or hot chocolate, or to aid cooking when you don't have good cooking facilities.

Hair care

In the context of bathing and hygiene, let me throw in a couple more words about hair care. A comb and a backup comb ought to be taken along. If you lose your comb(s), sometimes you can do as locals do. For example, in Argentina and Paraguay traditionally the stiff hairs of anteaters' tails bundled tightly together were used to brush or comb hair. Some carve wooden combs. If you have a brush for clothing or any other purpose, it may work on your hair; even a toothbrush can work, though for anyone with much hair, a toothbrush is not likely to be efficient, and in any case, people have difficulty getting past the idea of using a used toothbrush on their hair, and worse, of brushing teeth after a toothbrush has been used on hair, even if it has been thoroughly cleaned. I found that I can approximate combed hair reasonably well just by getting my hair damp and running my fingers through it over and over in the directions that I want my hair to lie, the fingers functioning somewhat like the teeth of the missing comb. I'm told that people with abundant or long hair believe it unlikely that this would work for them, and they are probably right, though they generally say this before they have tried it. Obviously it's better just not to break or lose your comb, and if you do, to have a backup available.

There is something to be said for short hair in the field—it's much easier to take care of and more importantly, short hair is less

Figure 7.3 Combing hair with bundled hair of an anteater's tail (don Altín, Misión La Paz, Salta Province, Argentina, 2007)

likely than long hair to end up with lice. Lice are a significant problem in many places and it is often recommended, especially for those who have longer hair, that they cover their hair with a hat or scarf when they are in places where they could catch lice. I personally have never gotten lice in the field or elsewhere, but I know fieldworkers who have.

Fieldworkers usually take a small mirror along with them. If you lose your mirror or do not have one and there is no place nearby where you can get a replacement, you can possibly compensate by finding a reflective surface, for example, a window pane, or the screen of your laptop when it is turned off.

It's obviously best not to lose your toothbrush nor to lose or run out of toothpaste. I found that having a backup toothbrush is a must. If you do lose your toothbrush, there may be no really good substitute. It is possible to rub your teeth vigorously with your fingers and some toothpaste . . . or soap; this is far from ideal, but better than nothing. Indigenous peoples in various places clean their teeth with bundles of small twigs or soft ends of sticks, or they chew particular kinds of wood or bark to clean teeth. If your toothpaste gets lost or runs out, there is always soap—yeah, right, yuck! Well, it works; the taste is not so bad if you have scentless soap. You can usually get the bad taste out of your mouth with lots of rinsing. I have, alas, had to resort to soap for cleaning teeth in a number of situations—you get used to it . . . sort of.

Toilet

I've never liked comedians who go in for toilet humor, and I don't really like bringing the topic up here. But it is relevant in this context, so I'll mention a couple of things, discomforting though they may be. All who have traveled in developing countries know that toilets in public restrooms can be dreadful and disgusting; even in the US sometimes we encounter public toilets of this sort.

I'll mention a couple of tips, courtesy of some of my own bad experiences—and hopefully you won't find it necessary to resort to them. Often there is no water in these disgusting restrooms. Although there may be no running water in a restroom or the toilet is broken, nevertheless there often is still water in the toilet's tank. You can lift off the lid and wash your hands in the water inside the tank, if you really need to clean them. Typically this water is clean, so it's more the idea of it than the water itself that is off-putting.

Worse, public restrooms typically have no toilet paper—it's a good idea to carry a small amount or some tissues with you at all times. In extreme need you can take the left-behind cardboard cylinder that was the center of the used-up roll of toilet paper, usually still there even when all the toilet paper is completely gone, and tear it open. It usually is light cardboard made of layers of paper and you can strip layers apart, rub the layers of paper back and forth in your hands like washing clothes to soften them, and then use them as toilet paper. A single cardboard center doesn't provide a lot of paper, but enough to be helpful in cases of extreme need.

We had no indoor plumbing when I was a child, only an outhouse, and for toilet paper we used pages torn out of Sears, Roebuck & Co. or Montgomery Ward catalogues—not an unusual practice for many people in rural areas back then. Because of this, using improvised toilet paper from the cardboard cylinder left over from an empty roll of toilet paper seems to me less drastic and more reasonable than it might to others who did not grow up with such exquisite experiences.

In most fieldwork situations I've usually had access to modern Western toilets, though on various occasions all that was available was an outhouse, occasionally just an open latrine, and in a few places just the bush. I'll just blurt out here that it is wise to make sure that the food you eat is not prepared or served near an outhouse. It's very unhealthy and a sure appetite killer to see flies shuttling back and forth between the open holes of an outhouse and your lunch or dinner. Your health can depend on this precaution.

Also, if you do have to go in the bush, bury it—it can contribute to disease, not to mention being just generally unpleasant.

Climate and weather conditions

I'll refrain from commenting on hammocks, tents, *pensiones*, hotels, and a raft of other things involving accommodations and local living in fieldwork. Some mention, however, of local weather and climate should be made. Being aware of the damage that can be caused by local weather can be the difference between successful and failed fieldwork. Local conditions can raise havoc with equipment as well as with health. Mold, dust, and insects can be devasting. Knowing

Figure 7.4 Puppy investigating the recorder (Misión La Paz, Salta Province, Argentina, 2007)

how to protect computer and recording equipment and other gear in the rainy season or in monsoons is crucial—too much moisture and mold can cause things to fail. Insects in the equipment can wreck things. And food, of course, is especially vulnerable and especially in need of sealable containers or multiple zip-lock bags to protect it from vermin and other pests in many parts of the world.

Dust and damp

In fieldwork in the Chaco in Argentina, dust was almost indescribably difficult to deal with, along with climate problems in general. Each year, the Pilcomayo River floods over its banks and washes out roads, stranding communities. The waters subside and the roads get repaired in April; our fieldwork always took place between May and late July, winter there, summer in the northern hemisphere. In winter there, there are two weather systems that cycle from one to the other about once each three weeks. When the wind comes from the south, it brings very cold weather, with cold mist, and temperatures that can go below freezing at night. When the weather system shifts to wind from the north, it gets hot, to around 100º Fahrenheit (38º Celsius), but with strong, non-stop winds that carry vast amounts of dust along with them. It seems as though the whole land is in the air moving horizontally at a very fast clip. This constant, excessive wind-blown dust causes massively vexing problems. Recording equipment and computers even in three layers of zip-locked plastic bags still end up with dust in them. The dust damaged so much equipment that we always had to plan for backups, a problem because of the additional expense to buy extra equipment and its weight and bulk for transporting it.

A problem of another sort was the excessive noise when the wind blows. The sound of the wind itself and the flapping of things on the roof and the noise of tree branches banging into and scraping on each other made it impossible to record speakers and very difficult to hear well enough to transcribe, though good headphones helped with that.

Not only did we have to contend with damage from dust and with the noise, we had to be prepared with clothing and sleeping bags for both cold and hot weather, once again making for extra weight and bulk while traveling. It has gotten as cold as 29ºF (-4ºC) and as hot as 102ºF (39ºC) in July, when we were engaged in fieldwork there. We were not able to work there during summers (winter in the northern hemisphere), since the daily high temperature ranges around 104ºF (40ºC), with a record high of 116ºF (46.6ºC)! It has the unparalleled distinction of being the hottest region of all of Argentina. Local members of the research team who worked transcribing and translating texts during their summer months wrapped towels around their hands so they could write without the sweat ruining their notebooks and destroying what they wrote.

In other places it was the constant damp and mold during the rainy season that caused problems. I've lost cameras, binoculars, recorders and recording equipment, flashlights, shoes, and some clothing due to dampness and mold. The coping strategies for humidity and dampness are certainly not original with me, though I did learn from several instances of ruined things how important precautions for dealing with dampness are. The most important strategy is just to try to keep things out of the rain and to dry things off immediately if they do get wet or damp.

For travel by canoe or boat, it's good to have dry bags for important equipment such as computers, recorders, and cameras. Alas, traveling with several dry bags adds to the weight and bulk that you need to transport, and to costs. A good idea in general is to have lots of waterproof sealable plastic bags or air-tight containers for storing food and protecting papers, books, etc. In humid climates, putting rice in with equipment and things that must stay dry can help.

Humidity and dampness tend to speed up alkaline battery corrosion so an important caution is to keep a careful eye out for this, since equipment can be ruined if corroded batteries are left in too long. If batteries do leak and corrode equipment but not to the point of total ruin, it is possible to clean the corrosion from the device using a toothbrush or cotton swabs dipped in vinegar or lemon juice. Although the acid in the vinegar or juice can dissolve the corrosion that is in the particular item in question, it is of course better to remove batteries from electronic devices before that happens and store them separately when not in use.

I'm told that there are websites with tips about makeup in humid climates; not something I've personally ever thought to look into. It's probably not something of high concern to most fieldworkers, though perhaps some may be heartened to know that such advice is available.

Culture shock

A different matter, though one important to living in the field and to well-being, is culture shock. Much has been written about it, and that can be consulted on the internet, so I need say little here, though some mention of it should be made.

Culture shock is the feeling of confusion, disorientation, and often anxiety that can affect people who find themselves living in an alien culture or environment. It affects different people in different ways. Many experience no culture shock at all, while others are impacted so severely that they cannot cope and must leave—some freak out totally. It can involve longing for familiar things and feeling hostile to what feels unfamiliar, being irritated with or hostile towards people, and not infrequently having symptoms of paranoia.

I've been surprised by and sometimes put off by unexpected things in the cultures and environments that I have experienced, but I've never personally suffered directly from culture shock. However, I have experienced it vicariously through observing it in some of the students who have worked on fieldwork projects with me. There is no sure-fire cure or prevention. You can do your best to be prepared for the unexpected differences you will encounter as you interact with people in a totally different culture and environment by reading as much as you can about the culture, geography, history, climate and environment, etc. in advance. However, you should also avoid building up unrealistic expectations of what you will see and experience there, so that you are not thrown off guard when things turn out to be different from what you imagined or expected. Far too often students develop very rosy, romantic, positive notions of what they will experience and then feel deceived or disappointed when those unrealistic expectations do not materialize, and they can find that distressing.

Various sorts of things can contribute to and trigger culture shock, things such as coping with a strange culture you don't fully understand, the language barrier, making mistakes by doing things considered inappropriate in the local culture, loneliness and homesickness, being robbed or cheated, interactions with local people that are not agreeable, difficult living conditions, crushing poverty, and so on. Some linguists have reported that feelings of inadequacy stemming from difficulties they have with analysis of the fieldwork language and from a sense of lack of sufficient progress in their work have contributed to culture shock.

The trigger that led to one student's severe culture shock on a project in Guatemala was the constant, somewhat aggressive, uninvited and unwanted attention from men. It is very unfortunate that in some places local men have gotten the idea from movies and television that all North American and European women are promiscuous and so readily available for and agreeable to having sex. Sometimes, though not often, men with this belief can become angry and aggressive when their amorous overtures are not accepted.

Fortunately, for most people culture shock is not long lasting. Where possible, it is helpful just to get away from the situation for a while and then return to the fieldwork in a better frame of mind.

Religion, expected behavior, cultural norms

Usually the difference between the religion of the people where the work is done and the fieldworker's own religion or lack of religion is not significant. In fact, outsiders are typically just expected to be different and so no one bothers much about whether a fieldworker is religious or about what his or her religion may be. It can be more significant to the fieldwork, however, when there are expectations about appropriate behavior that stem from the religion of the people in the community. Misunderstandings can arise, even serious ones, and it is important to be on the lookout for expectations about behavior that might not be easy to be aware of.

In much of the Pacific, people go to church on Sunday; for them the Sabbath is strictly observed and no work is permitted, and often also no recreation. Some fieldworkers just go along with everyone else to attend the church services, considering it an anthropological experience and a chance to be with the local people and to observe the language in a different setting. In some communities that attendance may be expected, though usually it is possible just to stay out of sight. Some linguists are very unhappy about not being able to work or engage in any visible recreation on Sundays, while others are glad for the opportunity in private to catch up on entering data, to prepare for upcoming sessions with consultants, or to check data or complete transcriptions and attempt to make progress in analysis of the language's structure, or to do other chores that otherwise might cut into time that could be spent with consultants working on the language, washing clothes being a common one.

In most places at least some people will be curious about a fieldworker's religion. I always found that in most instances it was best just to avoid the topic when possible and when asked directly, to seem to give an accommodating answer but without saying much. Most researchers find that it is OK to mention the heritage religion of their family, even if they, the fieldworker, may not practice it themselves.

The fieldworker's religious identity can be serious in some situations. For example, in Indigenous towns in Guatemala and Chiapas, Mexico, Jews (*los judíos*) are seen generally as semi-supernatural malevolent beings, as devils, monkeys, a black man, demons, a soldier, and Spaniards—stemming ultimately from representations of Jews as murderers of Christ during Holy Week in Passion plays. Jewish fieldworkers and researchers there find, because of this, that to call themselves Jews can be misunderstood with negative consequences. Some find it more convenient instead to identify themselves as the equivalent of "Israelites" or "Hebrews" or something else that seems appropriate but with less complicated consequences.

In a few instances in parts of the Pacific, in Papua New Guinea in particular, some graduate students with Jewish, Muslim, Roman Catholic, and non-religious backgrounds have gone so far as to decide to change their research language and focus area just to escape the kind of Christianity there that seems to them to pervade everything in ways they find overwhelming and stifling. That is understandable but unfortunate, given that many languages spoken in the Pacific region are quite endangered and need documentation.

People's curiosity about your religion and judgments they may make about you and how you should behave extend also to your marital status and social relationships. For couples going to do fieldwork together, much depends on the circumstances where the fieldwork is done and on the nature of the relationship.

Unmarried couples in some places merit no comment or notice whereas in others they are simply not tolerated at all. Some couples approach this complication in different ways. Some assume that their relationship is equivalent to local marriage and so feel it is OK just to say that they are married. Some others just outright lie about it, saying they are married when they don't think their relationship is really like a marriage. Where this may apply, those fieldworkers definitely should be aware of the potential problem and decide in advance how they will deal with it. I personally favor total honesty, but it's not my place to make recommendations about this.

Openly gay relationships raise no objection at all in some locations, but they would certainly cause problems for successful fieldwork in many other places, even for the safety of the fieldworker in extreme cases. For fieldworkers to whom this may apply, again, it's not for me to offer advice about how to handle such matters, though again, I believe that those fieldworkers should do their best to be aware of problems that could arise and plan in advance for how to avoid them if at all possible.

I think I understood from the very beginning that it is important to attempt to avoid behaviors that are considered unacceptable by the standards of the local religion or religions. For example, modesty in dress for women may be expected and wearing shorts or short skirts or sleeveless tops may be considered so inappropriate as to threaten a woman's chance to continue her fieldwork—not something I had to deal with directly myself, but it was an issue in a couple of cases when some friction came about over how female students working on language documentation projects were dressing.

It was clear to me from the beginning that it was necessary to try to figure out the things one is expected not to do or is expected to do out of respect—often these things have religious connections, though not always. Hundreds of examples could be given—tourist guidebooks even sometimes have sections on what's inappropriate behavior in some cultures. For example, fieldworkers and others need to learn fast if there are any cultural expectations about people that one should avoid having contact with, for example, a man with young women, or with an unmarried woman, or with a married woman, and vice versa, women with a chief or shaman, menstruating women with men in general, etc.

In many places drinking alcohol is a sure way to attract the censure of the local people, and in others smoking tobacco is seen as very bad. However, in others, it can be just the opposite. Fiestas, ritual holidays, in Indigenous towns of Guatemala and Chiapas, Mexico, involve massive amounts of ritual drinking, and cigarettes in some places are excellent offerings at shrines and excellent gifts for people. It is important to learn where and when head covering is required, as in some churches or mosques, and where it is not allowed, and where shoes must be removed. We need to learn about matters of reverence and respect. For example, in parts of Polynesian one doesn't sit on a table, one does not touch another person's head, one does not sit on the floor with one's feet pointed at someone else. In much of Latin America one does not throw or toss objects to another person, rather respect requires objects to be delivered by handing them directly to the person intended. In Arab countries and Muslim-influenced areas one does not offer anything with the left hand—it's disrespectful, insulting; the left hand is used to wash oneself after defecating or urinating.

Learning what is culturally appropriate extends also to what we are allowed to record and what we can do with recordings. In a number of societies certain songs and certain stories are owned by particular individuals or families or clans, and others may not be allowed to hear them or alternatively they may be allowed to hear them but they are not allowed to sing them or tell them themselves. Recording such things requires appropriate permissions and it is necessary to have clear understanding about whether that includes permission to play these for other people and whether they are allowed to be archived, or whether they can be archived but only if they are embargoed to certain people, say, to everyone except members of the family.

In some North American cultures certain songs can only be sung during the winter or alternatively during the summer; certain tales are winter tales, others summer tales. It can be extremely harmful to a relationship that a fieldworker has developed or hopes to develop with community members and to the whole project if somehow he or she fails to understand this or just forgets and ends up playing a recording of one of these things at the wrong time of year. Similarly, in many places, certain songs can only be sung at funerals or a certain style of oratory is only allowed at funerals. If recordings have been made of any of this sort of material that is restricted in the culture to particular seasons or to certain ceremonial occasions, it is very important that handling of these recordings is done in ways approved by the people involved and does not cause problems for the fieldwork, for the fieldworker, or especially for the language community.

It is also important that fieldworkers learn to recognize and then be tolerant of, or at least to be able to deal with, aspects of cultures that clash with their own in sometimes frustrating ways. Many examples could be cited. In the Chaco in South America the view of private property and obligations to share can complicate fieldwork in ways that can take some getting used to. In the culture of several

Figure 7.5 Cooking fish (Misión La Paz, Salta Province, Argentina, 2007)

ethnic groups there, if you have food, you are expected to be willing to share it, first with any family members and then with anyone else from the community who asks. Money is considered like an extension of food, so anyone who comes by any money can expect others who find out about it to ask for it to be shared.

The degree to which fieldworkers in those communities are expected also to share depends on how long they have worked there, how much they are accepted in the community, and the kinds of relationships they establish with people there. In the Chaco various local people who had worked with us or just knew us well often would show up at dinner time and as expected we would share our food with them. Some of them would have liked for us to share money, too, but we made it clear that the money wasn't ours, but rather belonged to the university or the granting agencies and could only be spent on designated things for every one of which we were required to have a receipt.

This practice of sharing makes good sense for a small-scale hunting and gathering society, where sharing of scarce resources can aid the survival of the group and its members when procuring resources is tough. The down side was that people tended to eat everything they had as fast as they could so that they could benefit from it or enjoy it themselves before it was all eaten up by others, and there was little incentive to procure foodstuffs or grow anything, knowing that most of the benefits of one's labor would just end up being eaten by others.

There are numerous words in the languages associated with sharing and with the prohibition against being stingy or not sharing. A few of many examples from Nivaclé are:

ja-juktsen "I am stingy, I do not want to give/loan/share as I am expected to what you ask me for because I want/need it for my own use right now"
ja-jut='ay "I loan it to you, I give it to you"
ja-kle='in "I am not shared with, they don't invite me to share" (I am angry because I was not invited to share)
ja-shiyan "I am stingy, I don't want to give, I impede"
ja-tis "I share, I give, I pay"
ja-washan "I am not stingy, I am generous, I give/permit (in response to a request to borrow something)"; and
ni-nwashan "he/she impedes, does not permit something to be borrowed, is stingy"
ja-watk'asatesh "I share it in pieces, I share pieces of it"
kuyej "stingy, envious."

The notion of private ownership is also much looser in the Chaco than in Western society generally. People do own things like tools etc., but it is generally expected that it's OK to ask to borrow anything and that there is a sort of obligation to loan it unless there is some really compelling reason not to. "Ownership" of a thing, an animal, or a place is more a matter of ongoing use, not exclusive possession, and any evidence that one is trying to establish or exercise exclusive rights to the use of these things is considered anti-social. Possession might be seen more as a process or ongoing activity than as a fixed state. This is reflected in the languages, too; for example, as in Nivaclé *shtajuyjata* "we keep it for our work, we use it" (with its implication that because we need it and are using it, we are not willing to let it be borrowed).

Moreover, ownership within families is also fluid, sometime frustratingly so to outsiders. Basically, any family member can appropriate anything from any other family member that strikes their fancy or that they feel like they need or want badly. For example, one of our oldest consultants in the Chaco language documentation project had done a large favor for the brother of one of the linguists and so to thank him and to compensate him for his work, the brother bought him a very nice black hat that our consultant had admired, an impressive hat and a touching gesture on the part of the brother. However, our consultant's oldest son decided the hat was his and our consultant never even got to wear it. This was annoying to the brother and to the outsiders that observed it, since the oldest son was an alcoholic who was abusive to his family and was not well-liked, and so deserved nothing in outsiders' eyes, least of all this hat not meant for him. The heartfelt gesture of thanks and compensation seemed to be wasted.

Borrowing was often associated with not returning possessions for a long time unless the owner requested them back with a reason for why they were needed. In our case it was hoped that we would be willing to loan some things, though not necessarily expected, since we were outsiders and since it was made clear that all equipment belonged not to us but to the university and must be used for the purposes intended, only.

These notions of sharing and borrowing were at times trying—it was annoying constantly to be asked for things—but in the end both we and community members learned what we could expect and tolerate from one another.

What to take along

Some materials for courses on field methods or language documentation and some websites have sample lists of what you might consider taking with you as you prepare for your fieldwork. However, fieldwork situations vary hugely from one another so that what might be good or even necessary for one may be impractical or even bad for another. What you can take with you obviously depends on several factors, on the funds you have for equipment, where you are going, how you will get there, how long you will stay, what the objectives of the research are, climate and physical conditions, and so on. Fieldworkers typically want to take more than is really needed, and feel that they need more than they are able to take. In the end what can be taken is the result of a dialectic between the items desired to have along and the ability to get them there.

I'll give here the list we used for fieldwork trips to work in the Chaco. It has both what we recommended to graduate research assistants who worked on the project and what we reminded ourselves not to forget. In this case we were limited in part by what baggage we could take with us on flights from the US, and in part by ground transportation in Argentina. We usually rented a pickup truck and drove it the 2,000 kilometers from Buenos Aires to the Pilcomayo River, in order to be able to take all of what we needed. We separated items on the list into what we would need to get in the US and take with us and what we could buy in country. It is good not to take in airplane luggage things that can easily be obtained in country, sometimes for even cheaper. Here's our list.

documents
- passport
- driver's license
- travel insurance
- university ID

- letter from university, other letters of introduction[1]
- photocopies of passport, of other documents, of credit cards, etc.: these should be kept in two different places, in both checked and carry-on luggage.

funds
Sufficient funds are needed for paying consultants, and for in-country expenses. This can require some awareness and planning. In some places, even in larger towns and cities, ATMs don't exist or are unreliable, banks will not cash checks, not even traveler's checks, dollars cannot be changed, or only bills of less than $50 are accepted for exchange, etc. In Argentina government workers mob the ATMs on payday; their salaries are paid into accounts they can access only via ATMs. This means that all the ATMs in some places are often empty with no cash, and worse, if you try more than three of them, the credit card company cancels your card, and it can be extremely difficult to get it reinstated, especially where communications are limited.

money pouch or money belt

duct tape
Never leave home without duct tape. Minimally it may be needed, badly, to repair luggage and bags that get damaged during travel. Duct tape is not available in many countries. We recommend finding out in advance and if there is any doubt, be sure to take it along.

laptop
Though it would be good to have also a backup laptop, cost and extra weight and bulk usually make that difficult or impossible. Laptops can get some bad treatment in the field, so it is important

to try to protect them as best as possible—with a tough, protective carrying case, and bags to keep them dry from rain or rivers and protected from dust. Various forms of backup—for example, thumb drives and external hard drives—need to be taken, and everything needs to be backed up constantly and very frequently.

recording equipment
Recorder, video camera, microphone(s), cables, several memory cards for recorders and cameras, protective carrying case, and backup recorders if possible. There are websites and publications that provide advice about best practices for recording and about the best recording equipment to have.[2]

papers and books relevant to the planned research
Materials about the language(s), culture, geography, questionnaires, dictionary of the contact language, etc. It saves much weight and space if you can get electronic versions or can scan these and load them to your laptop or other electronic reading device before leaving.

dark glasses and backup glasses if you have prescription lenses

backpack
A good daypack. Some find the following features useful: padded back, padded shoulder straps; waist, chest, and side straps that are adjustable, to stabilize objects and distribute weight; suspended mesh back panel to allow air to flow between the bag and your back; waterproof or with a waterproof cover; lockable zippers; multiple pockets, pouches, and compartments, to make things easy to find and to access, and again to distribute the weight of objects; a good water bottle pocket; padded laptop

sleeve or laptop compartment; and a light color that does not attract biting insects or the extra heat from the sun that dark colors attract.

sleeping bag
One appropriate for the local climate and for whatever its extremes in range of temperature may be.

camping mattress or pad
Therm-a-Rest sleeping pads are great. I have on occasion ended up sleeping on a hard floor, sometimes on flattened cardboard, sometimes with nearly all my clothing under me to attempt to soften things; these experiences make it seem all the more important to try to take along something softer to sleep on.

mosquito net
Matrimonial size is often better than single; it gives more space, and more options for what can be done with it and for how it can be hung up or attached. It needs to have a fine mesh, fine enough to keep even very small insects out. If they are available, the ones already treated with permethrin are good. It is also possible to buy permethrin and soak the mosquito net, and also socks and pants (trousers), in it. Permethrin is sometimes available at camping and sporting goods stores.

earplugs
I say never leave home without them; they are needed to block out the sound of crying children on airplanes and the many kinds of noises that can make sleep difficult in fieldwork situations.

Leatherman or Swiss Army Knife
Or something comparable, for cutting and tools. Most of us took one of each, as backup, and also as gifts for people when

we left. If air travel is involved on a US-based carrier, of course, these sorts of knives cannot be taken on board in carry-on bags but must instead be in checked baggage. It should be borne in mind that regulations about carrying objects with blades vary depending on the country, as well as by airline and airport.

alarm clock
The one on a cell phone is OK if you have a reliable means to recharge it.

flashlights (torches)
At least two, one for a backup. They may be needed a lot where there is no electricity and are generally handy elsewhere; ones with replaceable or rechargeable batteries are best.

various supplies
Often many of these can be gotten after arrival in country, though not all, certainly not in all countries:

- Memory sticks and memory cards: several, for computers, recorders, cameras, etc.
- Portable hard drives: at least two with substantial memory are needed; everything needs multiple backups.
- Batteries: depending upon whether electricity is available and on the kind of use they'll have, lots of batteries for equipment and devices may be needed. It is helpful to have rechargeable batteries and a battery recharger, and better to have multiple rechargers. Recharging works only where there is electricity, a generator, or solar panels—most places have access to some electricity in one of these forms, though in some places this means taking solar panels or a generator along. Fuel for a generator can also be a complication; it is not available at all in some places.

- Electric currency converters: US (in our case) to local, also local to US. These can often be bought in country, though it is best not to have to rely on finding them there. Sometimes these converters are poorly manufactured and so can break easily or malfunction; for that reason, it is important to have several of them as backups and in case several devices need to plug in at the same time.
- Surge protector: electric current can fluctuate or surge wildly in many locations; this can harm or even ruin equipment. It may be possible to get a surge protector or something equivalent in country, adequate for the sort of electrical current there.
- Notebooks: notebooks with hard binding and covers are best.
- Pens, pencils, and erasers.
- Clipboard: a clipboard turns out to be more valuable than might be suspected, since in many situations there may be no table to work on; and the clipboard has other nifty uses—as a tray to eat on or serve from, for example; I've also seen them used to whack unwanted insects and small animals.
- Zip-lock plastic bags: plastic bags of various sizes are usually needed, lots of them, including extra-large zip-lock bags. The largest ones are probably not easy to find in country.
- A few nails or hooks and thumbtacks (drawing pins): for hanging mosquito nets and for small repairs.

fleece or jacket, fleece vest
Needed minimally for the airplane—often long flights can be painfully cold. In the Chaco in Argentina it can be below freezing at night, and it can be cold in the daytime too; enough layers to cope are needed.

windbreaker

umbrella

hat
For sun, rain, wind. Some will want to wear a hat or scarf to help protect against lice.

hiking boots/sturdy shoes
It's good to have also another pair of shoes, in case you get one pair wet or damaged and need something else to wear either as the wet ones dry or as backups. It's good not to have to wear heavy shoes all the time. In many places a pair of good sandals is great for when you don't need the boots or other shoes.

flip-flops
To keep from getting foot funguses and other undesirable things when you shower; useful for wearing around indoors, too.

clothing
It's best if it's easy to wash, quick to dry, and not bulky to pack:

- T-shirts
- socks: five pairs or more
- underwear: five or more
- pants (trousers): at least two pairs
- shorts: depending on climate and insects, and local mores.

towel (see above)

soap (scentless)

shampoo and conditioner (scentless)
You can use soap for shampoo, too. Conditioner is not readily available in some locations, though shampoo tends to be.

sponge (for bathing)

sunscreen
Sunscreen is not available everywhere, and in some places it is very expensive.

insect repellent
Different sorts are available. I prefer the sticks that you rub on all your exposed areas; they are easy to carry, effective, and make less of a mess than sprays and liquids. Repellents with around 30 percent DEET or more are most effective and are highly recommended.

small scissors, tweezers, nail clippers
Some may want these; however, nails can also be trimmed by scissors or knife. At least these items tend to be small.

medicines
- cold medicines: these are much needed, since after long flights and associating with many sick people in a place with new, unfamiliar microbes, fieldworkers very often get colds. Language consultants also often get colds, and having cold remedies also for them can be useful for several reasons
- pain-relief medicines
- diarrhea medicine
- medicines for intestinal cramps, e.g. hyoscine butylbromide
- antibiotic cream: to prevent or treat skin infections
- antibiotics: it is good to have antibiotics available, but to be used only where really needed. Sometimes they are absolutely necessary; life can depend on having them.

band-aids

medical kit

hand sanitizer
Not always required, but useful; washing hands thoroughly with soap is a more effective alternative.

rubbing alcohol
Get in country; for sterilizing and disinfecting.

skin cream or petroleum jelly
Cracked heel often develops in fieldwork; it is good to have something like cracked-heel cream or other cream or lotion to help prevent it or to treat it. Petroleum jelly is good for that, too.

your music
For example, on your laptop or cell phone.

books for recreational reading
Electronic books are easiest to transport.

freeze-dried foods
Optional, not needed. Local food or food bought in country can become monotonous, even when not scarce; sometimes to have some variety, freeze-dried food brought with you from abroad can be quite pleasant.

chocolate pudding mixes
Also optional, not needed. These are often not available in country; they can be extremely welcome on occasion to break the monotony of the sort of food typically available.

Here's our list of supplies to get in Argentina.

- bleach
- bottled water
- buckets: the number needed depends on the number of people involved and whether there was running water available or not; usually at least three buckets will be needed
- canned vegetables
- cans of tomato sauce
- canned peaches
- cereal
- cookies (of several sorts)
- cooking oil (olive oil)
- crackers (of various sorts)
- granola bars
- grated cheese
- insecticide spray: Raid, Baygon, or the like; several cans
- instant coffee, tea, maybe a powdered drink like Tang: Tang or something of its sort is usually available in country; people who turn their noses up at Tang at home often find it wonderful in the field as a hot drink when you are sick or just cold, or when you don't want caffeine, and in many places Tang comes in several flavors, not just orange
- canned juices
- lightbulbs
- matches, lighters
- powdered hot chocolate drink
- noodles
- padlocks
- paper towels
- polenta
- powdered milk: of all the brands available, I found Nido to

be the one with the least bad taste; I don't like the taste of any of them, though in general they are OK for cooking
- processed packaged cheeses (for where there is no refrigeration)
- salami (because it lasts well without refrigeration)
- salt, pepper, garlic powder
- soap—dish soap, laundry soap, hand soap; laundry powder is easiest to deal with and readily available for washing clothes
- soups
- sugar
- tinned "pâté" (canned deviled meat spreads)
- yerba mate (maté) (for the consultants).

Here's our list of supplies for the community health center.

- gauze
- nebulizers (always two, one for backup)
- thermometers (seven)
- blood pressure monitor
- syringes and needles (50–100 of each, both short and long needles)
- several medicines, including quantities of analgesics such as ibuprofen and acetaminophen, much needed and much sought after
- combs for lice
- we also took Sharpies, colored pencils and markers, and maps for the schools. Sometimes these colored pencils were used in our project also for illustrating language materials created for the community and for the schools.

This is something of a Cinderella list. For the Chaco fieldwork, we had time, sufficient research funding, and access to a good vehicle, and so we could take these things with us, both things that were truly needed and a few things that just made otherwise difficult living circumstances a little more bearable.

The opposite extreme for me was during some of the dialect survey fieldwork I did in Guatemala and El Salvador, where I carried with me no more than I was able to fit into a single *morral*, a woven shoulder bag for carrying things. I could get into it essentials such as questionnaire, tape recorder, tapes, batteries, clipboard, pens and pencils, dark glasses, a couple of T-shirts, underwear, socks, and little else. I arranged with a *pensión* in Guatemala City to allow me to store my luggage there while I was out doing survey work. In it I kept the rest of my clothes, batteries, tapes, a few books, an extra pair of shoes, etc., which I could access when I came back to town each two weeks or so to take care of mail, to get more money from the bank, to communicate with the rest of the world back home, and to get a good meal or two and usually catch a movie.

Notes

1. These letters are described in Chapter 4.
2. A few examples that can be consulted are: Rice and Thieberger (2018), Endangered Languages Archive at <https://blogs.soas.ac.uk/elar/category/documentation-software-tools> (accessed June 28, 2021), and "Language documentation tools and methods," *Wikipedia*, <https://en.wikipedia.org/wiki/Language_documentation_tools_and_methods> (accessed June 28, 2021).

8

What next?: What is needed in endangered language research?

Introduction

In this chapter I address in general the expectations and demands of language documentation with its need for fieldwork as we move into the future. My personal future work is, I think, easy to see—it will be, *inshallah*, much like a continuation of the present. I have the recordings and documentation of several languages and the results of quite a lot of fieldwork to get processed and archived. I have databases, including vocabularies and dictionaries, to get online and made accessible to scholars, communities of speakers of the languages involved, and the public. I need to analyze and publish more of the results of the fieldwork on several languages. I will do my best to get copies of all these things into the hands of those whose languages are involved, and will help them with programs to make the materials useful for language revitalization where possible. I also intend to examine the results for implications they have for linguistic typology and for what they can contribute to understanding of the history of the languages and of the people who speak them. But this chapter is not about my plans; rather, it's about the status of languages themselves and the need for future fieldwork.

Historical backdrop

Let's begin by putting some things into historical context. Understanding the past and how we got to where we are now will help clarify the current state of the field, the status of the world's languages, and will point in the direction of what needs to be done in the future.

Endangered languages and early American linguists

There has been concern for describing endangered languages from the beginning in American linguistics. Franz Boas (1858–1942), founder of American linguistics and of American anthropology, emphasized the urgency of describing American Indian languages and cultures before they disappeared. The theme of "the vanishing Redman" had already been around for a long time in Boas's day.[1] Boas himself provided the last and in several cases the only significant data on a number of languages that no longer have speakers and have ceased to be spoken: Cathlamet, Chemakum, Lower Chinook, Pentlach, Pochuteco, and Tsetsaut. He instilled this sense of urgency for fieldwork into his students, the need to collect accurate information while it was still possible.

Boas had to contend with and correct many outrageous and erroneous misconceptions propounded by armchair mavens of his day. For example, it was much repeated that certain South American Indians—sometimes specified as the Puris—could not communicate in the dark, since their language was so "primitive" that they had to use gestures, which could not be seen in the dark, to indicate notions such as "here" and "there" or "yesterday" and "tomorrow"—supposedly pointing before or behind themselves for conveying these concepts. The languages of "savages" were considered "primitive," claimed to be characterized by absence of true language, poverty of vocabulary, lack of grammar, and simpleness in structure. They were alternatively asserted on the one hand to lack abstract, generic terms and on the other hand to have only generic words, lacking specific terms. It was repeatedly claimed that the sounds of "primitive" languages could vary wildly and unpredictably; they were said to be so imprecise that learning such languages was all but impossible, that change in "primitive" languages could proceed so fast that grandparents and grandchildren could not understand one another, and a common belief was that only European languages, languages of "civilization," were fully adequate.

None of these claims has any basis in reality. Descriptions of so-called "primitive" or "exotic" languages attempted to force them into traditional European grammatical categories, inherited from Greek and Latin grammar, missing or misconstruing many distinctions important in the languages being described.

Today it is understood that there are no "primitive" languages. All languages are fully adequate for the communicative needs of the societies that speak them; no language is better or worse than any other for these purposes. Linguists today support and insist on "linguistic relativity," that languages can differ on their own terms and should not be judged based on what is thought appropriate in some other language. As Edward Sapir put it:

> The gift of speech and a well ordered language are characteristic of every known group of human beings . . . The truth of the matter is that language is an essentially perfect means of expression and communication among every known people. (Sapir 1933: 155)

In face of the many bad claims about little-known languages, Boas believed it was important to avoid preconceptions and instead to describe each language based on information derived internally from analysis of the language itself and not imposed on it from the outside. For Boas the sorts of errors common in his day needed to be avoided and this meant avoiding generalizing and instead seeking accurate information on the languages, described in their own terms. Boas, however, also maintained the concept of "inner form" from Wilhelm von Humboldt (1767–1835) and other German thinkers, seeing languages as conditioning the worldview of their speakers, a psychological approach. For Boas and his followers the adequacy of a description of a particular language could be judged by determining to what extent it reflected what native speakers knew of their language, a mentalistic orientation.

Leonard Bloomfield (1887–1949), a founder of American structuralist linguistics, followed the Boasian prohibition against generalization but opposed mentalism. Heavily influenced by behaviorist psychology, Bloomfield rejected any role for "mind." This meant that he and the American structuralists could not evaluate their language descriptions based on any understanding of human language in general, following Boas in avoiding generalizing or theorizing about language; and by denying "mind" (mentalism), they could not judge a description against native speakers' knowledge of the structure of their language. All that remained available to them was method, the "discovery procedures" against which Noam Chomsky later argued so effectively, limited largely to the search for contrast and complementary distribution in the data recorded by linguists. Given this state of affairs, it is not surprising that Chomsky's (1957, 1964) ideas brought about a revolution in linguistics.[2]

Mainstream linguistics came to be dominated by Chomsky's views. Chomsky brought back mentalism; the goal of a grammar for him is to account for the native speaker's "competence," defined as what a native speaker knows tacitly of his or her language. And, in opposition to both the Boasians and Bloomfieldians, Chomsky brought generalizing about language into linguistics, with the goal of attempting to determine what languages hold in common and to establish a rich theory of human language, universal grammar, to explain that. Rejecting both the anti-mentalism of the Bloomfieldians and the anti-theorizing of the Boasians and Bloomfieldians resulted in a radical reorientation of the field.

It is often lamented that Chomsky's influence, with its excessive zeal for theorizing about language, had an adverse effect on language documentation. There is no denying that the attention of many linguists was diverted from language description and from concern for endangered languages, but language documentation and work on endangered languages did not cease. For example, roughly half of all the presidents of the Linguistic Society of America since 1957 have done fieldwork and have engaged in language documentation, as, of course, have many other linguists.

Language death

In the 1970s–80s concern emerged for "language death," not just for describing languages before it was too late but also for what happens to the structure of languages as they move towards dormancy, for what causes that, and for what processes they go through.[3] Today, as with the word "extinct" when applied to languages, linguists typically try to avoid speaking of "death" of a language and say instead "dormant," and rather than "dying" language say "endangered language." In this context, Martha Muntzel and I wrote about different kinds of "language death" (the impact of language endangerment in different situations on the structure of the endangered language) based on our fieldwork experiences with several critically endangered languages, a work that came to be much cited (Campbell and Muntzel 1989).

Endangered language research and language documentation

Many believe that Michael Krauss's contribution at the Linguistic Society of America symposium on Endangered Languages in 1991 and the 1992 publication in *Language* based on that symposium was the catalyst that drew linguists' attention to the crisis of language endangerment and launched modern concern for documenting and revitalizing endangered languages (Hale et al. 1992). Krauss was not alone, though. There was Johannes Bechert's ([1987] 1990) short paper at the 14th International Congress of Linguists in East Berlin; Joshua Fishman (1990, 1991) wrote about reversing language shift; and there was the plenary panel on sociolinguistics of language endangerment at the 15th International Congress of Linguists in Ottawa in 1992, the presentations for which were published in advance of the Congress's meeting in Robert Robins and Eugenius Uhlenbeck (1991).

Language documentation

With recognition of the endangered languages crisis came renewed dedication to language documentation and then sustained concern for language revitalization; some prefer to call it language reclamation. Views differ about how language documentation is defined, and practiced.

Many followed Nikolaus Himmelmann (1998, 2006). Himmelmann contrasted language description and language documentation, saying that language documentation "aims at the record of the linguistic practices and traditions of a speech community," and that "language documentation may be characterized as radically expanded text collection" (1998: 9–10, 2). Himmelmann defined language documentation "as a field of linguistic inquiry and practice in its own right which is primarily concerned with the compilation and preservation of linguistic primary data and interfaces between primary data and various types of analyses based on these data"; he viewed "a language documentation" as "a lasting, multi-purpose record of a language" (2006: 1). Similar declarations from various other linguists followed. With statements like these, it was not surprising that some linguists, as Himmelmann himself noted, misinterpreted that approach to mean:

- Documentary linguistics is all about technology and (digital) archiving.
- Documentary linguistics is just concerned with (mindlessly) collecting heaps of data without any concern for analysis and structure.
- Documentary linguistics is actually opposed to analysis.

(Himmelmann 2012: 187)

Himmelmann's declaration of documentary linguistics as a new subfield of linguistics distinct from language description was followed by many, though not by all by any means; numerous others rejected its narrowness of scope and effort. Some questioned if it represented anything appreciably different from earlier descriptive and documentation practices, whether the new technological tools, archiving, metadata, etc. should be seen as just a natural evolution of the kind of language documentation that had been important in linguistics from Boas onward.

Some argued that its disproportionate emphasis on technology and recording was detrimental, encouraging projects whose only goal was essentially text recording, neglecting fuller description, analysis, production of a grammar or dictionary, or materials useful to the communities' revitalization efforts. Many linguists hold firm to the belief that language documentation and language description should not be separated. They follow the Boasian tradition, where language documentation includes production of a grammar, a dictionary, and texts or recordings representing a large range of genres. For example, Rhodes and Campbell hold that adequate documentation of a language requires:

(1) A text corpus of appropriate size and cultural breadth, representing a wide range of genres.

(2) The description of the grammar or development of extensive grammatical materials, based on an adequate analysis of the language, and a lexicon (dictionary). [See also Rehg 2007.]
(3) Materials in a form that can reasonably be expected to be accessible to future generations of the language community as well as to those with academic and other interests.

(Rhodes and Campbell 2018: 108)

Later, Himmelmann backed off from his earlier rigid separation of documentation and description from one another, explaining that there is broad agreement, but with differences of emphasis, and that the two cannot "be separated in actual practice" (2012: 188). Most linguists agree that documentation can and probably should include a grammar and a dictionary, in addition to a rich corpus of recordings, though some place greater emphasis on recording of texts representing many genres and on the technology for recording and archiving, while others give more prominence to description, to the analysis which includes a grammar and dictionary. This is reflected in the definition of language documentation recommended by Campbell and Rehg in *The Oxford Handbook of Endangered Languages*:

> Adequate language documentation has as its goal the creation, annotation, preservation, and dissemination of transparent records of a language where that record is understood explicitly to include language analysis and the production of a grammar and a dictionary, along with a rich corpus of recordings adequately archived. (Campbell and Rehg 2018: 12)

Language documentation and linguistic theory

The view that there is a distinction between language documentation and linguistic description or analysis in some ways parallels the belief held by a good number of linguists that language documentation and linguistic theory are hostile to one another. This is not an accurate nor practical view. Language documentation can and does contribute to linguistic theory. It has brought many formerly unknown linguistic traits to the attention of linguists—some examples were seen in Chapter 3—and these discoveries have impacted theoretical claims about human language in general, in some cases allowing new generalizations to be made and in others causing proposed generalizations to be modified or abandoned.[4]

It is commonly advised in language documentation that descriptions should be as accessible as possible to a wide audience of users, including members of the communities whose languages are described. This is understood to mean avoiding description in terms of formal theoretical frameworks whose notations and technical jargon limit accessibility. Some advocate making descriptions as theory-neutral as possible to make them as accessible as possible. However, this does not preclude taking advantage of theoretical insights. Linguistic theory can provide insights into and explanations for the things we encounter in the languages on which we do fieldwork; they can make us aware of what to expect and of how different constructions typically interact with others. A primary value of linguistic theory for language documentation is that it helps us to know what questions to ask, what to look for, and what to watch out for. Campbell and Rehg recommend that:

(1) The products of language documentation should be as accessible as possible and therefore not encumbered by terminology and theoretical frameworks that only the technically trained can follow.
(2) Findings in language documentation research can and should be written up for publications aimed at and accessible to the broad audiences, most of whom will not have the training to understand formal linguistic theories.
(3) Where the findings are able to contribute to theoretical issues, it is best to write them up and publish them in

> professional journals whose audiences have the technical background to appreciate them. They might also be given in the more general, accessible descriptions in an appendix that address important theoretical issues, or presented in footnotes.
>
> (Campbell and Rehg 2018: 13)

A common interpretation has been that with the Chomskyan revolution, descriptivists were considered second-class linguists and so language description was avoided and only theoretical research was prized. There is truth to this view; however, it is not entirely accurate. When I was a PhD student at UCLA, the curriculum was heavily theory oriented; however, many of the students were nevertheless not deterred from doing language documentation, and lots of descriptive dissertations on American Indian and African languages continued to came out of the UCLA program during those theory-heavy years. Moreover, lots of that descriptive work also helped inform theoretical discussions.

It is just not accurate to separate linguists into fieldworkers/documentary linguists vs. theoreticians, those who follow formal approaches. Many well-known formal linguists are also fieldworkers and have participated in language documentation, and many who do fieldwork and language documentation have been committed to and have contributed also to aspects of formal theory. Putting a wedge between theorists and fieldworkers/documentary linguists does linguistics no service. For some linguists, theoretical motives are what drive their concern for documentation of endangered languages—they document endangered languages in order to discover more about the full range of what is possible and impossible in human languages, in order to pursue the goal of linguistic theory of understanding universal grammar. Others have other motives, often more connected with needs of language communities than with linguistic theory. They want to foster language maintenance, language revitalization, reversal of language shift, and in general to help with pedagogical materials, language nests, master–apprentice programs, and family language learning and speaking guides, and to call attention to the language endangerment crisis and its impact on Indigenous peoples.

Language endangerment in broader perspective

It is difficult to overstate the seriousness and severity of the endangered languages crisis. For the future, much fieldwork, much more than is currently being done, needs to be dedicated to the endangered languages of the world—that is the punch line of this chapter.

As mentioned in Chapter 1, according to the *Catalogue of Endangered Languages* currently some 3,113 of the world's c.6,851 living languages are endangered—45 percent of existing languages—with 437 of them critically endangered.[5] All the languages of 91 of the world's c.398 distinct language families are dormant (formerly referred to as "extinct"); that's 23 percent of the linguistic diversity of the world, calculated in terms of language families. To repeat from Chapter 1, essentially a quarter of the linguistic diversity of the world has been lost forever. Language loss has accelerated at an alarming rate in recent years and many languages are being lost right now.

Causes of language endangerment

The following is a representative list of causes that can contribute to why languages become endangered. Obviously more than one cause can apply to a given language:

1. **Economic factors.** Some people consider these to be the most important: lack of economic opportunity, rapid economic transformation, ongoing industrialization, shifts in work patterns,

migration and migrant labor, resource depletion, forced changes in subsistence patterns, communication with outside regions, resettlement, destruction of habitat, globalization, etc.

2. **Political, geographical, demographic, and sociocultural factors.** Discrimination, repression, ethnic cleansing and genocide, official language policies, population displacement, population dispersal, rapid population collapse, marriage patterns, birth rates, access to education, refugee status, ethnic identity, the role of language in religion, religious proselytizing, military service, violations of linguistic and other human rights, number and concentration of speakers, extent and distribution of the language, low socioeconomic status of speakers, lack of revitalization or revival efforts, lack of standardization, the extent of acculturation, lack of social cohesion among speakers, lack of physical proximity among speakers, armed conflict and war, nuclear accidents, slavery, famine, disease/epidemics/pandemics, natural disasters such as earthquakes, volcanic eruptions, hurricanes, floods, tsunamis, sea level rise, and climate change in general, etc.

Much has been written in news reports about the impact of COVID-19 on Indigenous peoples and endangered languages. One example is, "'There are no words': as coronavirus kills Indigenous elders, endangered languages face extinction," in the *Washington Post* (McCoy and Traiano 2020). In another example, Jack Healy (2021) reported in the *New York Times* that "the virus has killed American Indians at especially high rates, robbing tribes of precious bonds and repositories of language and tradition." We await in horror news of the number of languages whose last speakers have died due to coronavirus infections. The news is already quite clear that several have been dealt severe blows by loss of some of the few remaining speakers.

The damage, though, isn't restricted just to the deaths of speakers of these highly vulnerable languages. COVID-19 has resulted in the suspension of much face-to-face learning in language revitalization programs. In many cases language reclamation efforts have just not continued during the COVID crisis. It has also caused most of the fieldwork projects I know of to be postponed, some cancelled. Researchers have been unable to travel to fieldwork locations, because of travel restrictions due to COVID-19, and because of health concerns for themselves and especially for the elders where they would work. Some granting agencies have retracted funding because the fieldwork could not be pursued. Graduate students' studies have been disrupted, delaying their preparation for the fieldwork they plan to undertake.

Given the loss of life and the continued threat of loss of life in the communities where the world's most at-risk languages are spoken, the endangered language crisis, already alarming in the extreme before this pandemic, has now been magnified significantly. The urgency is now much higher.

2a. **Lack of institutional support.** Absence of institutional support may lead to speakers shifting away from minority languages. Institutional support is represented in the roles of the languages in education, government, churches, the media, recreational activities (sports events, popular culture, music, etc.), military service, the judicial system, etc. Other causal factors include lack of official recognition of the language, lack of or very limited degree of autonomy and self-determination, etc.

2b. **Language use and language choice.** Influences from language contact, code-switching, different kinds of multilingualism, language instruction, lack of recognition of linguistic and other human rights, the nature of language transmission in the community, limited literacy in the minority language, restricted degree of competence in the minority language, etc.

3. **Subjective attitudes (motivations).** Attitude is considered by many people to be the most deterministic factor in language

loss. Groups have been known to maintain their minority language in face of overwhelming odds because of language pride and strong positive attitudes about their language and its role in their identity and culture, while others have given up their language seemingly with little provocation other than lack of a positive attitude towards the language.

Attitude includes a number of factors: attitudes of the speakers towards the languages under threat and towards the official national language(s) and dominant languages that surround them; attitudes of members of mainstream society towards minorities and their languages; the symbolic value of the dominant language, as a symbol, for example, of nation, civilization, progress, the future, affluence, upward mobility, etc., vs. the symbolic association of the endangered language with, for example, the past, poverty, lack of opportunity, backwardness, etc.; the relative prestige of the language, as a cultural symbol, symbolically connected with notions of being international and urban vs. local and rural; the stigmatization of a local language; low prestige of the endangered language; language loyalty; the minority language as a marker of ethnic identity and group membership; etc.

(Adapted and expanded from Campbell and Rehg 2018: 5–6)

Language revitalization

The relationship between language revitalization and language documentation has often been misunderstood. Language revitalization and language documentation are not antagonistic to one another but are interrelated, and revitalization efforts can contribute to language documentation, as obviously language documentation can serve the interests of language revitalization.

Some have thought that language documentation serves only the interests of academics and neglects the language communities who want to revitalize their languages. In reality modern language documentation projects almost never lack a language revitalization component and involvement of the community in decision making. Most scholars involved in language documentation feel a moral commitment to make sure that their language documentation efforts also serve the community whose language is involved, and some granting agencies insist on evidence that this is indeed the case.

Unlike extinct biological species, a dormant language can continue to exist after its last speaker has passed away, but for this, documentation is necessary—an undocumented language that has lost all its speakers is forever irredeemably lost. Not even Hollywood can clone and resurrect a language which has disappeared with no documentation. As has been said various times, if we do not document the languages now while it is still possible, we deserve the contempt of later generations who will have no access to their heritage languages. Without language documentation, what is needed for preparing teaching and learning materials for the language is simply unavailable. Language revival crucially depends on the availability of these materials, the products of language documentation, typically the results of linguistic fieldwork.

Language documentation and language revitalization are often not conducted as independent activities, but are intertwined and mutually supportive. For example, many documentation projects provide training to community members who become part of the documentation team and who at the same time often use their training in service of their communities' language conservation and reclamation efforts. Today, language documentation is very often not just in the hands of a single scholar who is an outsider to the community. Rather, often the documentation is done by teams that have at least some community members as active participants in the documentation and revitalization. In some cases those doing the documentation are themselves linguistically trained members of the community who at the same time are concerned with revitalizing their language. Very often decisions about what is actually documented and how the documentary materials will be used are in the hands of community leaders.

Helping to provide adequate documentation is one of the greatest services linguists and other scholars can render communities whose languages are under threat.

Would fewer languages mean fewer conflicts?

Occasionally some objections to attempting to maintain minority languages are heard, usually in the context of languages in geopolitical conflicts. It is sometimes claimed that if we had fewer languages, we would understand each other better and consequently would live in greater harmony. But this is far from true. That monolingualism does not guarantee nor even foster greater "understanding" is seen throughout history. As David Crystal reminds us, "all of the large monolingual countries of the world have had their civil wars" (2000: 27). It is also shown by the many recent and ongoing armed conflicts among groups speaking the same language—for example, in Colombia, Darfur, Egypt, Iraq, Libya, Northern Ireland, Syria, Thailand, and Yemen[6]—or the horrendous and horrifying 1994 genocide in Rwanda that involved Hutu and Tutsi, both speakers of the same language, Kinyarwanda.

This contrasts with lack of such conflicts in relatively peaceful, officially multilingual Belgium, Belize, Botswana, Canada, Faroe Islands, Finland, Luxembourg, Malta, Netherlands, Paraguay, Singapore, Switzerland, Tanzania, etc. Multilingual and multicultural countries need to recognize that national unity and understanding are not fostered by monolingualism or ethnic cleansing, but that recognition of minority languages' rights can help bring about mutual trust, peace, and ultimately national stability.

We need to expose the erroneous assumption that individuals and countries cannot be both multilingual and successful, and help political leaders and others understand, rather, that there are significant benefits from multilingualism. Several recent research papers report that bilingual children tend to grow up to be more tolerant citizens than monolinguals.[7] In short, there is no evidence that fewer languages might lead to greater harmony and fewer geopolitical conflicts.

Legacies of colonialism

Perhaps vaguely related to this last question involving languages in relation to geopolitical conflicts is another troubling matter. For academics in certain fields and for some Indigenous activists and leaders, there is great concern for "colonialism" and "decolonization." Briefly put, this involves concern for treatment of Indigenous peoples, marginalized ethnic groups, disempowered peoples, and people with no voice in the political affairs that affect them. It includes recommendations for recognizing, empowering, and securing and guaranteeing the rights of these groups. Decolonization is often associated with the following: with ongoing disputes over land rights, ecological extraction and resource exploitation, Indigenous intellectual property rights, and cultural appropriation; with struggles for human, civil, linguistic, and cultural rights; with political position and sovereignty; and with attempts to change how Indigenous and marginalized groups are represented in history, education, and in the view of non-Indigenous people.

Among advocates of decolonization there are some who suspect all non-Indigenous scholars who are engaged in any research involving Indigenous people and their societies, cultures, or languages of being disrespectful and of being perpetrators and perpetuators of evils associated with colonialism. Because of such suspicions, it is important to make clear that today's linguistic fieldwork, language documentation, and language reclamation are just the opposite of those negative things associated with colonialism. Most linguists who do this work share the goals of guaranteeing respect for and the rights of the peoples whose languages are involved, of giving them a voice, particularly in any affairs affecting them or their self-determination, working together with members of these communities to achieve their communities' goals for their languages.

In political and philosophical discussions of identity, some assume and advocate that outside scholars should just get out of the way, with their mentality of the colonizer and the colonized, and instead let those who are marginalized undertake the work themselves.[8] There is another view, perhaps complementary to this one, that scholars privileged with higher education and more extensive resources have an obligation to share knowledge with and to transfer skills to Indigenous communities. In this view we should be available to pitch in to help informed groups as they work towards achieving their own goals for their languages and cultures, and also to help them understand what has worked and not worked in other situations so that they can make informed decisions of their own. It is not the case that outside academics can never get past their colonial baggage sufficiently to be able to practice their craft and deploy their skills in respectful, "decolonizing" ways, with useful, helpful, appropriate results, in collaboration with Indigenous peoples. Just the opposite: we would be remiss if we didn't, in particular given the language endangerment risks faced by so many Indigenous people and their earnest efforts to deal with this problem that is so monumentally important to so many of them.

And what now?

What's to be expected and what's to be done now? What perspective do the some thirty years since Michael Krauss's call to arms for endangered languages in 1991 provide us?[9] When we take stock, there is much to encourage us but at the same time much that is disheartening. We must improve and increase efforts and resources monumentally.

The past thirty years have seen the establishment of funding agencies, both governmental and non-governmental, dedicated to language documentation and work on endangered languages, where before there were none. These agencies have supported documentation of a significant number of languages, though still reaching only a very small portion of the languages that need to be documented. Nevertheless, the amount of funding available is miniscule in comparison to the need. The amount available for even the largest grants for linguistic research projects that involve fieldwork reads like a footnote or afterthought when compared with the award amounts for research grants in physics, chemistry, health sciences, space exploration, super colliders, and so on.

There are now dedicated journals—for example, *Language Documentation and Conservation*. Considerably more grammars, dictionaries, and partial descriptions of endangered and other small languages have been published in recent years than earlier. In spite of many more publications on little-known languages than in earlier times, the languages lacking grammars, dictionaries, or any adequate documentation outnumber by many times over those that do have grammars or dictionaries, or good descriptive materials.

Language documentation work is now generally recognized in linguistics as valid for dissertations. There are also now several international as well as national and local conferences dedicated to endangered languages and language documentation. Several non-profit organizations dedicated to the problem of endangered languages have been established, and there are a number of websites dedicated to fostering endangered languages. A major resource of information is the *Catalogue of Endangered Languages*.[10]

Where before there was very little linguistic archiving and almost no archives with a primary mission of preserving and making accessible materials on the languages of focus in this book, now there are several—for example, AILLA (The Archive of the Indigenous Languages of Latin America, University of Texas at Austin),

DELAMAN (Digital Endangered Languages and Musics Archives Network), ELAR (Endangered Languages Archive, University of London), Kaipuleohone (University of Hawaiʻi at Mānoa), and the Survey of California and Other Indian Languages (University of California, Berkeley).

Unfortunately, the number of linguistics departments offering field methods courses has not increased markedly; however, several departments have expanded course offerings or created tracks for specialized training in language documentation and/or revitalization.[11]

While there have been a number of excellent language-documentation dissertations that have involved substantial fieldwork in the years since 1991, the number is still shockingly small. ProQuest dissertations in linguistics[12] lists 589 dissertations in linguistics from January 1, 2019 to April 6, 2020. Most of these have as their focus second language acquisition, teaching English as a second language, and the English language. Many involve other major languages; for example, a substantial number of them are on Mandarin Chinese and Japanese.

Startlingly, only 3 constitute substantial language-documentation descriptions of one of the thousands of lesser-known languages that need language documentation—that's .5 percent, half of 1 percent! Another 21 concentrate on specific aspects of lesser-known languages often also with theoretical agendas, and 3 are on topics of language endangerment and revitalization generally, not documenting any specific language. Another 15 deal in some way with lesser-known languages but do not involve language documentation. In total, only 44 deal in some way with less well-known minority languages; that's only 7.4 percent of linguistics dissertations in that year and a half that in any way deal with any of the thousands of languages that need language documentation. It is not possible to tell how many of these dissertations rely on any appreciable amount of fieldwork. These numbers can be compared with Paul Newman's (2003) calculation for the years of 1997–2000 where of 1,860 dissertations in linguistics he calculated "5% at most of the Ph.D. dissertations [in linguistics] written during the past four years could be said to represent primary linguistic research involving significant fieldwork" (2003: 5).[13]

The major problems are the urgency—the threat of imminent loss of the severely endangered languages—and not enough trained people for the need, insufficient funding, and inadequate and even wrong-headed policies about language and education.

About funding, obviously circumstances vary widely from case to case, but let's consider costs broadly to get a general though vague idea of the kinds of funding needed to document even the most critically endangered languages. Most larger research grants in linguistics are for a period of three years. Depending on whether the researcher or researchers know something of the language or a related language already and on the amount of time available to dedicate to the project, three years is usually not sufficient time to complete major language documentation, with a grammar, dictionary, and abundant analyzed and processed texts, though it is sufficient time to undertake a significant portion of this.

A typical large research grant for this kind of linguistic research awards around $300,000; that is, $100,000/year. At my university, the indirect costs, overhead charges, are 26 percent if the research is done off campus; that's far less than the indirect costs at most universities, usually negotiated at 40–50 percent, often higher. The indirect costs at 26 percent on such a grant come to $78,000, reducing the $300,000 to only $222,000 that is actually available for research itself.

Typically if leave-time is budgeted for a faculty member to undertake the research, it takes up nearly the entire amount, so for the sake of this exercise in thinking about funding let's assume that much of the work will be carried out by an advanced graduate research assistant, though clearly it would be far better to have a team working on such projects with multiple graduate student researchers, faculty or other professional linguists, and trained members of the language community. At my university a graduate research assistant is awarded on average $22,372 per academic year (i.e. nine months). This is less than graduate assistantships pay at most other universities. That comes to $67,116 for the three-year project. When the graduate research assistant's stipend of $67,116 for the three years is subtracted from the $222,000 that is actually available for the project, $154,884 remains, that is, only $51,628/year. That is often not sufficient to cover the costs of salaries for language consultants, international and local travel, accommodations, recording equipment and supplies, and other expenses. In short, welcome as it is, $300,000 for a three-year project actually turns out to be fairly limited support.

If $300,000 is taken as a rough round figure for documenting a language, to document just the 437 critically endangered languages in the world at that level, $131,100,000 is needed. That might seem like a lot of money, but let's see what it looks like when we put it into perspective.

Like millions of others, I lament and object to many of the things public funds have been spent on and many of the ways these funds have been used and abused, to the squandering of taxpayers' money. I oppose the squandering of opportunities for real solutions and improvements to serious problems affecting society by not deploying at least some of these funds in more useful and productive ways. If we could nudge decisions so that even tiny portions of what seem to many of us as wrong-headed spending so that some otherwise wasteful spending could be deployed instead to support endangered language research, the world would be better off and hardly anyone would notice the money spent for that. In short, political and societal priorities need to change. We need to call for socially more responsible and more effective use of public and other funds. Let's look at some examples.

We can cite the obscene amounts of spending in US election campaigns. For the 2020 US elections candidates spent over $14 billion! On the presidential race, the two main candidates together spent over $6.6 billion (Cillizza 2020; Spring 2020). These amounts are staggeringly obscene and obscenely staggering. With this $6.6 billion we could support the $131,100,000 calculated for grants to document all 437 critically endangered languages more than 50 times over! For the $14 billion spent on campaigns in 2020, we could fund them all 107 times over! Mightn't we respectfully ask for just 1/50 or 1/100 of this mostly wasted money for the most critically endangered languages? Donald Trump's campaign paid $7.9 million just for a recount of votes in Wisconsin, enough to fund 433 graduate research assistants for a year on language documentation projects, essentially one for each of the 437 most critically endangered languages.

With the US military budget for 2020 at $738 billion, our projected $131.1 million for critically endangered languages would come to a miniscule 0.00018 percent of that amount, so small it would not be noticed if that nearly invisible amount were redirected for this purpose. As of 2020, military spending consumed 61 percent of the US federal discretionary budget (Coakley 2020). As Christopher Helman and Hank Tucker (2021) report, "in the 20 years since September 11, 2001, the United States has spent more than $2 trillion on the war in Afghanistan. That's $300 million dollars per day, every day, for two decades. Or $50,000 for each of Afghanistan's 40 million people." The $300 million for just one day would be more than twice the projected $131.1 million needed to address all the world's critically endangered languages! With just over three days of the war cost, all endangered languages of any sort could have been treated.

We could call attention to lost military hardware, downed aircraft in particular. In June of 2019 Iran shot down an American drone that cost about $130 million! **The cost of that one lost drone alone would be sufficient to support documentation for all of the 437 critically endangered languages!** In 2019 US military lost due to crashes, for example:

- a US Marine Corps AH-1Z Viper attack helicopter, $31 million
- a US Air Force F-16, $18.8 million, the cost in 1998
- a US Army Boeing CH-47 Chinook, $38.55 million
- a Sikorsky MH-60 Seahawk, $28.1 million
- a US Air Force E-11A, $50.44–$56 million.

The cost of even the cheapest of these downed aircraft, at $18.8 million, would be sufficient to support language documentation research on 60 languages at the funding level contemplated here.

It is not easy to find clear figures on exactly how much was spent on the construction of Donald Trump's highly unpopular and controversial border wall, though it is beyond doubt several billions. National Public Radio (NPR) estimates $11 billion had gone into its construction by January 2020. Estimates were that it cost $20 million per mile. Usually left unmentioned is the estimated $790 million needed annually for its maintenance (Burnett 2020). The amount for just 1 mile (1.6 kilometers) of wall construction could support grants to document 67 endangered languages; or for the cost of just over 6 miles (10.5 kilometers) of the 1,954 mile (3,145 kilometer) wall, funding could be provided to support documenting all 437 of the critically endangered languages.

In 2018 the average Fortune 500 company CEO was paid $14.5 million per year. College football head coaches in 2019 on average were paid $2.67 million per year; the salary of only one of these coaches would be sufficient to support 45 graduate research assistants each year. In 2019 some 40 university presidents were paid more than $800,000/year, while 17 were paid more than $1 million/year.

Clearly if society reassessed its priorities and its spending regimes, adjusting them to address more urgent needs and to be socially and morally more responsible, it would not be difficult at all to increase support for documentation and revitalization of languages at risk. Oh, please, make it so! For now, we are stuck with the limited funding that is available and with the hope that individuals and organizations will contribute substantially more to the enterprise.

Choosing a language to work on

In the current crisis of language endangerment, many people naturally hope that linguistic scholars will choose to work on an endangered language—the more critically endangered, the greater the urgency for documentation. There are numerous factors that can enter into the choice of which language to work on. For some, the choice involves personal factors such as family, ethnicity, heritage, or a location they identify with. Some choose to continue to work on a language used in a field methods course that they took. For some, the choice reflects their experience or expertise or interest in a particular area or region. Some choose to work on a language that is related to another language they have experience with, since progress can usually be made faster in such a language because of what that language shares with its relatives. For many younger scholars the choice is dictated by perceptions of need. They are attracted to documenting languages that are least well-known and most critically endangered, that is, those most urgently in need of attention. I think almost all of these things have been involved in why I chose to work on some particular languages, all except family or ethnic connection to any particular language.[14]

For those looking for a language urgently in need of language documentation, consulting the *Catalogue of Endangered Languages* is the best resource.[15] It gives information on the status of the endangered languages of the world, with numbers of speakers, their locations, their level of endangerment, and much more.[16]

There are opportunities for and the need for fieldwork on hundreds and even thousands of languages, and that need can feel overwhelming. Rich experiences and rewards lie ahead for those who do this work. It has been my privilege to be part of the effort.

Notes

1. This theme of the Vanishing American Indian has been much written about and hugely castigated, in particular by Indigenous writers. It is often associated with James Fenimore Cooper's romanticization of the "vanishing American Indian" as portrayed in his *The Last of the Mohicans* (1826) and his other books. For example, Renato Rosaldo (1989: 108) laments this romanticization, what he calls imperialist nostalgia, the mourning of the passing of what they themselves (agents of colonialism—officials, constabulary officers, missionaries, etc.) have destroyed. To whatever degree linguistic practices may have been motivated by this sort of nostalgia in the past, it is not appropriate in today's understanding of American Indians and their linguistic interests and needs. They certainly are not vanishing, whether or not the language of any particular group may be endangered. That can be rectified through revitalization efforts.
2. See Campbell (2017b) for more details on this history.
3. Good examples of this sort of work can be found in the papers in Dorian (1989).
4. The relationship between theory and language documentation is treated, for example, by Rice (2018), and Rhodes and Campbell (2018).
5. <http://www.endangeredlanguages.com/>. (Accessed June 28, 2021.)
6. And increasingly in the USA.
7. See, for example, Dewaele and Wei (2013), Singh et al. (2020), and the websites <https://sites.google.com/site/morebenefitsofbilingualism/home/module-1-cultural-awareness-is-well-supported-on-bilingual-people> and <https://www.youtube.com/watch?v=oIKfKnHfnL0> (both accessed July 11, 2021).
8. See, for example, discussion of this in Phipps (2019: 3).
9. In Hale et al. (1992).
10. <http://www.endangeredlanguages.com/>. (Accessed June 28, 2021.)
11. Some graduate programs with coursework and training dedicated particularly to language documentation and revitalization include: Australian National University, SOAS University of London,

University of California Berkeley, University of California Santa Barbara, University of Hawai'i at Mānoa, University of Melbourne, University of Oregon, and University of Texas at Austin.

12. Found at <https://search-proquest-com.eres.library.manoa.hawaii.edu>. (Accessed July 11, 2021.)
13. See Newman (2009) for the number of linguistics departments offering a course in linguistic field methods in 2004.
14. In spite of my Scottish surname, I've never felt any particular allegiance or attraction to Scots Gaelic or Celtic languages. My family, at least the Campbell side of it, came to America in the 1700s, before the American Revolutionary War, and so I've never felt more than the vaguest of connections to Scotland. Rather, growing up in Indian country, I always had a much greater interest in Native Americans and American Indian languages. As for the famous conflicts that in Scotland still bring forth cursing about Campbells there, at the massacre of Glencoe (1692) most of the soldiers were not Campbells and the attack was ordered by the government; and my Campbell forefathers had already left Scotland before the Battle of Culloden in 1746, and in any case, there were Campbells fighting on both sides of that conflict. So, I just laugh at the idea that because of my Campbell surname I should share shame. In any case, shame or those hard feelings against Campbells would scarcely be compelling motivation for me or anyone with my surname to want to work on Gaelic or on Celtic languages. I am, of course, very sympathetic to speakers of those now threatened Celtic languages and supportive of their reclamation efforts.
15. <http://www.endangeredlanguages.com/>. (Accessed June 28, 2021.)
16. Hauk and Heaton (2018) discuss triage, factors that go into decisions about priorities for languages to be documented.

References

Abbi, Anvita. 2001. *A Manual of Linguistic Fieldwork and Structures of Indian Languages*. Munich: LINCOM Europa.

Aragon, Carolina Coelho. 2014. *A Grammar of Akuntsú, a Tupían Language*. PhD dissertation, University of Hawai'i at Mānoa.

Barlow, Russell and Lyle Campbell. 2018. Language classification and cataloguing endangered languages. *Cataloguing Endangered Languages*, ed. by Lyle Campbell and Anna Belew, 23–48. Abingdon and New York: Routledge.

Bechert, Johannes. [1987] 1990. Universalienforschung und Ethnozentrismus. *Proceedings of the 14th International Congress of Linguists (Berlin, 10–14 August 1987)*, ed. by Werner Bahner, Jochen Schildt, and Dieter Vieweger, vol. 3, 2350–2. Berlin: Akademie Verlag.

Bierer, Domnald E., Thomas J. Carlson, and Steven R. King. 1996. Shaman pharmaceuticals: integrating indigenous knowledge, tropical medicinal plants, medicine, modern science, and reciprocity into a novel drug discovery approach. Retreat Ayahuasca. <http://www.retreatayahuasca.com/Ethnobotanique/feature11.html>. (Accessed June 28, 2021.)

Bloomfield, Leonard. 1917. *Tagalog Texts with Grammatical Analysis*.

(University of Illinois Studies in Language and Literature, 3 vols.). Urbana: University of Illinois.

Bloomfield, Leonard. 1933. *Language*. New York: Holt, Rinehart and Winston.

Boas, Franz. 1917. El dialecto mexicano de Pochutla, Oaxaca. *International Journal of American Linguistics* 1: 9–44.

Bouquiaux, Luc and Jacqueline M. C. Thomas. 1992. *Studying and Describing Unwritten Languages*. Dallas: Summer Institute of Linguistics. [Originally published in French.]

Bowern, Claire. 2008. *Linguistic Fieldwork: A Practical Guide*. (1st edition.) Basingstoke: Palgrave Macmillan.

Bowern, Claire. 2015. *Linguistic Fieldwork: A Practical Guide*. (2nd edition.) New York: Springer.

Brinton, Daniel G. 1885. *The Annals of the Cakchiquels*. Philadelphia: Library of Aboriginal American Literature.

Burling, Robins. 1984. *Learning a Field Language*. Ann Arbor: University of Michigan Press. (Reprint: 2000. *Learning a Field Language*. Prospect Heights, IL: Waveland Press.)

Burnett, John. 2020. $11 billion and counting: Trump's border wall would be the world's most costly. *NPR*, January 19. <https://www.npr.org/2020/01/19/797319968/-11-billion-and-counting-trumps-border-wall-would-be-the-world-s-most-costly>. (Accessed June 28, 2021.)

Campbell, Lyle. 1973. On glottalic consonants. *International Journal of American Linguistics* 39: 44–6.

Campbell, Lyle. 1977. *Quichean Linguistic Prehistory*. (University of California Publications in Linguistics, 81.) Berkeley: University of California Press.

Campbell, Lyle. 1978. Quichean linguistics and philology. *World Anthropology: Approaches to Language, Anthropological Issues*, ed. by William McCormack and Stephen Wurm, 223–33. The Hague: Mouton.

Campbell, Lyle. 1985. *The Pipil Language of El Salvador*. Berlin: Mouton de Gruyter.

Campbell, Lyle. 1987. Tzeltal dialects: new and old. *Anthropological Linguistics* 29: 549–70.

Campbell, Lyle. 1988. *The Linguistics of Southeast Chiapas.* (Papers of the New World Archaeological Foundation, 51.) Provo, UT: New World Archaeological Foundation, Brigham Young University.

Campbell, Lyle. 1990. Philological studies and Mayan languages. *Historical Linguistics and Philology*, ed. by Jacek Fisiak, 87–105. Berlin: Mouton de Gruyter.

Campbell, Lyle. 2014. How to "fake" a language. *Estudios de Lingüística Chibcha* 33: 63–74.

Campbell, Lyle. 2017a. Language contact and language documentation: whence and whither? *Proceedings of SALSA 25, Texas Linguistics Form 60*, ed. by Hannah Foster, Michael Everdell, Katie Bradford, Lorena Orjuela, Frances Cooley, Hammal Al Bulushi, and Ambrocio Gutierrez Lorenzo. <http://salsa.ling.utexas.edu/proceedings/2017/Campbell.pdf>. (Accessed June 28, 2021).

Campbell, Lyle. 2017b. The history of linguistics: approaches to linguistics. *Handbook of Linguistics* (2nd edition), ed. by Mark Aronoff and Janie Rees-Miller, 97–118. Oxford: Wiley-Blackwell.

Campbell, Lyle. 2018. How many language families are there in the world? *Studia Diachronica et Philologica in Honorem Joakin Gorrotxategi: Vasconica et Aquitanica* (Diachronic and Philological Studies in Honor of Joaquín Gorrochategi: Basque and Acquitanian). Special issue of *ASJU [Anuario del Seminario de Filología Vasca "Julio de Urquijo"* (Yearbook of the "Julio de Urquijo" Seminar of Basque Philology)] 52: 133–52. Gasteiz: Universidad del País Vasco.

Campbell, Lyle. 2020. *Historical Linguistics: An Introduction.* (4th edition.) Edinburgh: Edinburgh University Press.

Campbell, Lyle and Anna Belew (eds.). 2018. *Cataloguing the World's Endangered Languages.* London: Routledge

Campbell, Lyle, Luis Díaz, and Fernando Ángel. 2020. *Nivaclé Grammar.* Salt Lake City: University of Utah Press.

Campbell, Lyle and Brant Gardner. 1988. Coxoh. *The Linguistics of Southeast Chiapas*, by Lyle Campbell, 315–38. (Papers of the New World Archaeological Foundation, 51.) Provo, UT: New World Archaeological Foundation, Brigham Young University.

Campbell, Lyle and Verónica Grondona. 2010. Who speaks what to whom?: Multilingualism and language choice in Misión La Paz—a unique case. *Language in Society* 39: 1–30.

Campbell, Lyle and Martha Muntzel. 1989. The structural consequences of language death. *Investigating Obsolescence: Studies in Language Death*, ed. by Nancy Dorian, 181–96. Cambridge: Cambridge University Press.

Campbell, Lyle and Kenneth L. Rehg. 2018. Introduction. *The Oxford Handbook of Endangered Languages*, ed. by Kenneth L. Rehg and Lyle Campbell, 1–18. Oxford: Oxford University Press.

Centers for Disease Control and Prevention. 2019. Tick removal. Centers for Disease Control and Prevention, September 6. <https://www.cdc.gov/ticks/removing_a_tick.html>. (Accessed June 28, 2021.)

Centers for Disease Control and Prevention and Gary W. Brunette. 2020. *CDC Yellow Book 2020: Health Information for International Travel*. Oxford: Oxford University Press.

Chelliah, Shobhana T. and Willem J. de Reuse. 2010. *Handbook of Descriptive Linguistic Fieldwork*. Dordrecht, Heidelberg, London, New York: Springer.

Chomsky, Noam. 1957. *Syntactic Structures*. The Hague: Mouton.

Chomsky, Noam. 1964. *Current Issues in Linguistic Theory*. The Hague: Mouton.

Cillizza, Chris. 2020. The absolutely stunning price tag of the 2020 election. *CNN*, October 29. <https://www.cnn.com/2020/10/29/politics/2020-election-cost-money-trump-biden/index.html>. (Accessed June 28, 2021.)

CliffsNotes. n.d. Why should literature be studied? *CliffsNotes*. <https://www.cliffsnotes.com/cliffsnotes/subjects/literature/why-should-literature-be-studied>. (Accessed June 28, 2021.)

Coakley, Carol. 2020. The Pentagon's immoral budget. *Milford Daily News*, March 14. <https://www.milforddailynews.com/opinion/20200314/column-pentagons-immoral-budget>. (Accessed June 28, 2021.)

Cox, Paul Alan. 1993. Saving the ethnopharmacological heritage of Samoa. *Journal of Ethnopharmacology* 38: 181–8.

Cox, Paul Alan. 2001. Will tribal knowledge survive the millennium? *Science* 287.5450: 44–5.

Cox, Paul Alan and Michael J. Balick. 1994. The ethnobotanical approach to drug discovery. *Scientific American* 270.6: 82–7.

Crowley, Terry. 2007. *Field Linguistics: A Beginner's Guide.* Oxford: Oxford University Press.

Crystal, David. 2000. *Language Death.* Cambridge: Cambridge University Press.

Derbyshire, Desmond C. 1977. Word order universals and the existence of OVS languages. *Linguistic Inquiry* 8: 590–99.

Darnell, Regna and Judith T. Irvine. 1997. *Edward Sapir 1884–1939: A Biographical Memoir.* Washington, DC: National Academies Press. <http://www.nasonline.org/publications/biographical-memoirs/memoir-pdfs/sapir-edward.pdf>. (Accessed June 28, 2021.)

Davis, Jenny L. 2019. *Talking Indian: Identity and Language Revitalization in the Chickasaw Renaissance.* Tucson: University of Arizona Press.

Dewaele, Jean-Marc and Li Wei. 2013. Is multilingualism linked to a higher tolerance of ambiguity? *Bilingualism: Language and Cognition* 16.1: 231–40.

Dixon, R. M. W. 1983. *Searching for Aboriginal Languages: Memoirs of a Field Worker.* Brisbane: University of Queensland Press.

Dixon, R. M. W. 2007. Field linguistics: a minor manual. *Sprachtypologie und Universalienforschung/Language Typology and Universals* (STUF) 60.1: 12–31. <http://www.romanistik.uni-freiburg.de/pusch/Download/korpuslinguistik_2010/Dixon_2007.pdf>. (Accessed July 11, 2021.)

Dixon, R. M. W. 2011. *I Am a Linguist.* Leiden: Brill.

Dorian, Nancy (ed.). 1989. *Investigating Obsolescence: Studies in Language Death.* Cambridge: Cambridge University Press.

Felger, Richard and Mary Beck Moser. 1973. Eelgrass (*Zostera marina L.*) in the Gulf of California. *Science* 181.4097: 355–6.

Fisher, Danielle. n.d. How to become an Army linguist. *HowStuffWorks.* <https://science.howstuffworks.com/military/army-careers/how-to-become-army-linguist.htm>. (Accessed June 28, 2021.)

Fishman, Joshua A. 1990. What is reversing language shift (RLS) and how can it succeed? *Journal of Multilingual & Multicultural Development* 11: 5–36.

Fishman, Joshua A. 1991. *Reversing Language Shift: Theoretical and Empirical Foundations of Assistance to Threatened Languages*. Clevedon: Multilingual Matters.

Galla, Kaleimamaoowahinekapu and Alanaise Goodwill. 2018. Talking story with vital voices: making knowledge with indigenous language. *Journal of Indigenous Wellbeing* 2: 67–75.

Gippert, Jost, Nikolaus Himmelmann, and Ulrike Mosel (eds.). 2006. *Essentials of Language Documentation*. Berlin: Mouton de Gruyter.

Greenberg, Joseph H. 1970. Some generalizations concerning glottalic consonants, especially implosives. *International Journal of American Linguistics* 36: 123–45.

Greenberg, Joseph H. 1978. Introduction. *Universals of Human Language*, ed. by Joseph H. Greenberg, Charles A. Ferguson, and Edith A. Moravcsik, vol. 2, 1–6. Palo Alto, CA: Stanford University Press.

Grenoble, Lenore A. and N. Louanna Furbee (eds.). 2010. *Language Documentation*. Amsterdam: Benjamins.

Gutiérrez, Analía. 2015. *Segmental and Prosodic Complexity in Nivaĉle: Laryngeals, Laterals, and Metathesis*. PhD dissertation, University of British Columbia.

Hale, Kenneth, Colette Craig, Nora England, Laverne Jeanne, Michael Krauss, Lucille Watahomigie, and Akira Yamamoto. 1992. Endangered Languages. *Language* 68: 1–42.

Hauk, Bryn and Raina Heaton. 2018. Triage: setting priorities for endangered language research. *Cataloguing the World's Endangered Languages*, ed. by Lyle Campbell and Anna Belew, 259–304. London: Routledge.

Healey, Alan (ed.). 1975. *Language Learner's Field Guide*. Ukarumpa, EHD, Papua New Guinea: SIL.

Healy, Jack. 2021. Tribal elders are dying from the pandemic, causing cultural crisis for American Indians. *New York Times*, January 12.

Helman, Christopher, and Hank Tucker. 2021. The War in Afghanistan Cost America $300 Million per Day for 20 Years, with Big Bills Yet to Come. *Forbes* Aug 16. <https://www.forbes.com/sites/hanktucker/2021/08/16/the-war-in-afghanistan-cost-america-300-million-per-day-for-20-years-with-big-bills-yet-to-come/?sh=30c1d5c37f8d>. (Accessed Aug 24, 2021.)

Himmelmann, Nikolaus. 1998. Documentary and descriptive linguistics. *Linguistics* 36: 161–95.

Himmelmann, Nikolaus. 2006. Language documentation: what is it and what is it good for? *Essentials of Language Documentation*, ed. by Jost Gippert, Nikolaus P. Himmelmann, and Ulrike Mosel, 1–30. Berlin: Mouton de Gruyter.

Himmelmann, Nikolaus. 2012. Linguistic data types and the interface between language documentation and description. *Language Documentation & Conservation* 6: 187–207. <https://scholarspace.manoa.hawaii.edu/handle/10125/4503>. (Accessed June 28, 2021.)

Holloway, Charles. 1993, *The Death of a Dialect: Brule Spanish in Ascension Parish, Louisiana*. PhD dissertation, Louisiana State University. <https://digitalcommons.lsu.edu/gradschool_disstheses/5514>. (Accessed June 28, 2021.)

Kipp, Darrell. 2008. Encouragement, guidance, and lessons learned: 21 years in the trenches of Indigenous language revitalization. Address at the 15th Stabilizing Indigenous Languages Symposium, 2008, Northern Arizona University. <https://jan.ucc.nau.edu/~jar/ILR/ILR-1.pdf>. (Accessed June 28, 2021.)

Ladefoged, Peter and Ian Maddieson. 1996. *The Sounds of the World's Languages*. Cambridge: Blackwell.

Lange, Katie. 2018. 64 weeks to fluency: how military linguists learn their craft. US Dept. of Defense, April 27. <https://www.defense.gov/Explore/Inside-DOD/Blog/Article/2061759/64-weeks-to-fluency-how-military-linguists-learn-their-craft/>. (Accessed June 28, 2021.)

Macaulay, Monica. 2005. Training linguistics students for the realities of fieldwork. *Anthropological Linguistics* 46: 184–209.

McCoy, Terrence and Heloísa Traiano. 2020. "There are no words": as coronavirus kills Indigenous elders, endangered languages face extinction. *Washington Post*, October 5. <https://www.washingtonpost.com/world/the_americas/coronavirus-brazil-indigenous-endangered-language/2020/10/06/59fa1aa8-f42b-11ea-999c-67ff7bf6a9d2_story.html>. (Accessed July 6, 2021.)

Mac Kenzie, Josefina López. 2020. La CIDH impone a Argentina garantizar tierra, agua potable y alimentos a comunidades indígenas. *El País*, April 7. <https://elpais.com/sociedad/2020-04-07/la-cidh-impone-a-argentina-garantizar-tierra-agua-potable-y-alimentos-a-comunidades-indigenas.html>. (Accessed June 28, 2021.)

Maddieson, Ian. 1984. *Patterns of Sounds*. Cambridge: Cambridge University Press.

Maddieson, Ian. 2013. Lateral consonants. *The World Atlas of Language Structures Online*, ed. by Matthew S. Dryer and Martin Haspelmath. Leipzig: Max Planck Institute for Evolutionary Anthropology. <http://wals.info/chapter/8>. (Accessed June 28, 2021.)

Maddieson, Ian and Karen Emmorey. 1984. Is there a valid distinction between voiceless lateral approximants and fricatives? *Journal of Phonetics* 41: 181–90.

Meakins, Felicity, Jennifer Green, and Myfany Turpin. 2018. *Understanding Linguistic Fieldwork*. Abingdon and New York: Routledge.

Meek, Barbra. 2012. *We Are Our Language: An Ethnography of Language Revitalization in a Northern Athabaskan Community*. Tucson: University of Arizona Press.

Newman, Paul. 2003. The endangered languages issue as a hopeless cause. *Language Death and Language Maintenance: Theoretical, Practical and Descriptive Approaches*, ed. by Mark Janse and Sijmen Tol, 1–13. Amsterdam: John Benjamins.

Newman, Paul. 2009. Fieldwork and field methods in linguistics. *Language Documentation and Conservation* 3: 113–25.

Newman, Paul and Martha Ratliff (eds.). 2001. *Linguistic Fieldwork*. Cambridge: Cambridge University Press.

O'Grady, William. 2018. The linguistics of language revitalization: problems of acquisition and attrition. *The Oxford Handbook of Endangered Languages*, ed. by Kenneth L. Rehg and Lyle Campbell, 490–509. Oxford: Oxford University Press.

Palosaari, Naomi and Lyle Campbell. 2011. Structural aspects of language endangerment. *The Cambridge Handbook of Endangered Languages*, ed. by Peter K. Austin and Julia Sallabank, 100–19. Cambridge: Cambridge University Press.

Payne, Thomas. 1997. *Describing Morphosyntax: A Guide for Field Linguists*. Cambridge: Cambridge University Press.

Pfeiffer, Anita and Wayne Holm. 1994. Laanaa Nisin: Diné education in the year 2004. *Journal of Navajo Education* 11: 35–43.

Phipps, Alison. 2019. *Decolonising Multilingualism: Struggles to Decreate*. Bristol: Multilingual Matters.

Reality Check Team. 2021. Afghanistan war: what has the conflict cost the US? *BBC News*, April 15. <https://www.bbc.com/news/world-47391821>. (Accessed June 28, 2021.)

Rehg, Kenneth L. 2007. The language documentation and conservation initiative at the University of Hawaiʻi at Mānoa. *Language Documentation and Conservation*, Special Publication No. 1, *Documenting and Revitalizing Austronesian Languages*, edited by D. Victoria Rau and Margaret Florey, 13–24. <http://hdl.handle.net/10125/1350>. (Accessed June 28, 2021.)

Rehg, Kenneth L. and Lyle Campbell (eds.). 2018. *The Oxford Handbook of Endangered Languages*. Oxford: Oxford University Press.

Rhodes, Richard A. and Lyle Campbell. 2018. The goals of language documentation. *The Oxford Handbook of Endangered Languages*, ed. by Kenneth L. Rehg and Lyle Campbell, 107–22. Oxford: Oxford University Press.

Rice, Keren. 2006. Ethical issues in linguistic fieldwork: an overview. *Journal of Academic Ethics* 4: 123–55.

Rice, Keren. 2018. Documentation, linguistic typology, and formal grammar. *The Oxford Handbook of Endangered Languages*, ed. by Kenneth L. Rehg and Lyle Campbell, 123–46. Oxford: Oxford University Press.

Rice, Keren and Nicholas Thieberger. 2018. Tools and technology for language documentation and revitalization. *The Oxford Handbook of Endangered Languages*, ed. by Kenneth L. Rehg and Lyle Campbell, 225–70. Oxford: Oxford University Press.

Robins, Robert H. and Eugenius M. Uhlenbeck (eds.). 1991. *Endangered Languages*. Oxford: Berg.

Rogers, Chris. 2018. Xinkan vowel harmony revisited. *Anthropological Linguistics* 60: 320–45.

Rosaldo, Renato. 1989. Imperialist nostalgia. *Representations* 26: 107–22.
Sakel, Jeanette and Daniel L. Everett. 2012. *Linguistic Fieldwork: A Student Guide*. Cambridge: Cambridge University Press.
Samarin, William, J. 1967. *Field Linguistics: A Guide to Linguistic Field Work*. New York: Holt, Rinehart and Winston.
Sapir, Edward. 1930. Southern Paiute, a Shoshonean language. *Proceedings of the American Academy of Arts and Sciences* 65.1: 1–296.
Sapir, Edward. 1933. Language. *Encyclopaedia of the Social Sciences*, vol. 9, 155–69. New York: Macmillan.
Singh, Leher, Paul C. Quinn, Miao Qian, and Kang Lee. 2020. Bilingualism is associated with less racial bias in preschool children. *Developmental Psychology* 56.5: 888–96.
Spring, Marianna. 2020. US election 2020: how to spot disinformation. [Video.] *BBC News*, October 14. <https://www.bbc.com/news/av/world-us-canada-54518196>. (Accessed June 28, 2021.)
Stearns, Peter. n.d. Why study history? American Historical Association. <https://www.historians.org/teaching-and-learning/why-study-history>. (Accessed June 28, 2021.)
Thieberger, Nicholas (ed.). 2012. *The Oxford Handbook of Linguistic Fieldwork*. Oxford: Oxford University Press.
Treuer, Anton. 2020. *The Language Warrior's Manifesto: How to Keep Our Languages Alive No Matter the Odds*. St. Paul: Minnesota Historical Society Press.
US Dept. of Defense. 2018. Military linguists: rapid training track with no experience required. US Dept. of Defense, October 3. <https://www.defense.gov/Explore/Features/story/Article/1650937/military-linguists-rapid-training-track-with-no-experience-required/>. (Accessed June 28, 2021.)
Vaux, Bert and Justin Cooper. 1999. *Introduction to Linguistic Field Methods*. Munich: Lincom Europa.
Vaux, Bert, Justin Cooper, and Emily Tucker. 2007. *Linguistic Field Methods*. Eugene, OR: Wipf and Stock.
Warner, David. 2015. *Where There Is No Doctor*. Berkeley: Hesperian Foundation. <https://hesperian.org/books-and-resources/> (Accessed June 28, 2021.)

Watahomigie, Lucille. 1998. *The Native Language Is a Gift: A Haualapai Language Autobiography*. Berlin: Walter de Gruyter.

Wolff, John U. 1987. Bloomfield as an Austronesianist. *Leonard Bloomfield: Essays on His Life and Work*, ed. by Robert A. Hall, Jr., 173–8. Philadelphia: John Benjamins.

World Health Organization. 2021. Chagas disease (also known as American trypanosomiasis). World Health Organization, April 1. <https://www.who.int/news-room/fact-sheets/detail/chagas-disease-(american-trypanosomiasis)>. (Accessed June 28, 2021.)

World Population Review. 2021. Murder rate by country 2021. World Population Review. <https://worldpopulationreview.com/countries/murder-rate-by-country>. (Accessed June 28, 2021.)

Zepeda, Ofelia. 1990. American Indian language policy. *Perspectives on Official English: The Campaign for English as the Official Language of the USA*, ed. by Karen L. Adams and Daniel T. Brink, 247–56. Berlin: De Gruyter Mouton.

Subject index

Acompañamiento Social de la Iglesia Anglicana en el Norte Argentino *see* ASOCIANA
Aeromexico, 197
Afghanistan, 257
Africa, 20, 134, 175
Agua Azul, Chiapas, Mexico, 132
aguardiente, 36
AILLA (Archive of the Indigenous Languages of Latin America), 253
alcohol, 122, 155, 158–9
Alka-Seltzer, 169
alligator *see* caiman
Alonso, don Alonso, 32–3
Alta Verapaz, 145, 199, 206
Altín, don Altín, 63, 67, 72, 95–7, 126, 208
American Indian, American Indian languages, 3, 244, 246, 236, 260n, 261n
American Revolutionary War, 261n
amoebas, amoebic dysentery, 119–20, 166–8
Ampú, Josefa, 112, 130

anaconda, 126
Andes, 28, 29, 156
Ángel, Fernando, don Fernando, 129, 131–2
Ángeles Verdes (Green Angels), 187
Anglican, 123, 125, 150–1
Anselmo, don Anselmo, 79–80
anteater, 207–8
anthrax, 177
anthropology, anthropologist, anthropological, 2, 3, 44, 75, 77, 87, 91, 186, 202, 216, 236
antibiotics, 172, 230
Antigua, Guatemala, 41, 42, 80, 146, 152, 154
ants, 66, 152, 165
Apolo, 27–30
approximant, 43
Aquespala, 46
Arab countries, 218
Aragon, Carolina, 112–13, 115n
Arana Osorio, Carlos, 152
archaeology, archaeologist, archaeological, 87, 186

Archive of the Indigenous Languages of Latin America *see* AILLA
archive, archiving, 21, 22, 23, 54, 115, 219, 234n
Argentina, Argentinian, 10, 18, 37, 42, 50, 63, 67, 69, 71, 72, 76, 94, 95, 96, 97, 98, 99, 104, 112, 123, 124, 125, 126, 127–32, 134, 139–41, 143, 144, 150–2, 155, 156–7, 163, 166, 173, 176, 189, 190–1, 204, 207–8, 211–12, 220, 223, 224, 228, 228
armadillo, 27
Arte de la Lengua Vulgar Mexicana de Guatemala qual se habla en Escuintla y otros Pueblos deste Reyno, 55, 73n
Ascension Parish, 100
Asencio, 132, 163n
ASOCIANA (Acompañamiento Social de la Iglesia Anglicana en el Norte Argentino), 151
attitudes, 247–8
auxiliary (shaman's), 131
Aztec two-step, 172

backpack, 133, 137, 160, 225
bathing, 204, 205–7, 230
bats, 138, 142–4
batteries, 89, 188, 194, 213, 227, 234
Baygon, 119, 232
Beatriz, 86
Bechert, Johannes, 240
bee, bees, 62–4, 70
behaviorist psychology, 238
Belgium, 79, 199, 250
Belisario Domínguez, 148
Belize, 186, 250
Bible, 10, 95, 150, 151–2, 170
bicycle, 66
bilabial, 95
binoculars, 160, 213
biologists, 12, 42

birds, 138–42
bloodletting, 66–7
Bloomfield, Leonard, 52, 238
blowgun, 65
Boas, Franz, 55, 236–9, 241
boat, 180, 196, 213
books, 55, 98, 126, 167, 170, 213, 225, 231, 234, 260n
boot, boots, 122, 123, 180, 229
border crossing, 148, 172, 202–3
border wall, 258
Botswana, 250
bottlegourd, 61–2
botulism, 171
Bowern, Claire, 25n, 37, 115n
Brasseur de Bourbourg, Abbé Charles-Étienne, 55
BRAT diet, 172
Brazil, 17, 111, 112, 121, 203
bribe, 188–9, 198, 202
bridge, 184–5, 190, 204
bring 'em back alive, 1, 81
Brinton, Daniel G., 55, 73n
brujo, 31–2, 78, 131; *see also* witch
brush, 207
bubonic plague, plague, 28, 120, 301
Buck, Frank, 81
buckets, 203–4, 232, 232
Buenos Aires, 189, 223
Burkina Faso, 175
bus, buses, 80, 81, 118, 145, 158, 159, 160, 162, 180–2, 200
bush plane, 27–31, 180

caiman, 96, 165
California, 183, 254
camera, 137, 213, 225, 227, 160
Campbells, 261n
Canada, 20, 250
Canary Islander, Canary Islands, 100, 115n
canoe, 180, 195, 213

SUBJECT INDEX | 275

car, 180, 182–9, 200
Caribbean, 61
Carlisle Indian Industrial School, 8, 93
Carmen Xan (Carmen Xhan), 44
Casa de Cultura (cultural center), 147
cat scratch disease, cat scratch fever, 120, 136
Catalogue of Endangered Languages, 11, 24n, 245, 253, 259
Catholic, Roman Catholic, 78, 79, 216
cats, 78, 133, 136
causes of language endangerment, 245–8
cayuco see dugout canoe
CDC *see* Centers for Disease Control and Prevention
Centers for Disease Control and Prevention (CDC), 122, 173, 178
Central America, 55, 78, 84, 104, 105, 107, 118, 134, 143, 148, 158, 167, 180–1, 182–3, 188, 192, 202, 203
ceramics, 87
cetaceans, 12
Chaco, Gran Chaco, 123, 124, 126, 127, 128, 134, 139, 152, 211, 219–23, 228, 233
Chaco language documentation project, 76, 98, 189
Chaculá, 45
Chagas disease, 124–5
Chiapas, Mexico, 30, 45, 73n, 87, 88, 105, 108, 132, 136, 145, 148, 182, 183, 192–3, 198, 216, 218
chicha, 62–3, 70–1, 74n
chickens, 30, 138
Chicomuselo, 183, 192, 194
chief, 98, 151, 218
Chilanga, 57, 59
children and fieldwork, 176–7
China, 203
Chinautla, 145
Chomsky, Noam, 238–9, 244

Christmas, 146, 197
Christopher Columbus, 61
cigarettes, cigarettes, 158, 218
Cipriano, don Cipriano, 32, 34
civil rights, 251
civil war, 147, 150, 250
clay balls, clay slingshot balls, 139–40
climate, 210–11, 213, 214, 223, 226, 229, 246
clipboard, 228, 234
Coapa, 46
Cobán, 145, 146, 199, 200, 206
Coca-Cola, 5, 157, 168–9, 172, 195
coca, 155, 156–8, 163n
Code of the West, 4, 23n, 192
cognition, 9, 17, 18, 37, 43, 240
Colombia, 250
colonialism, 251, 260n
Columbus, Christopher *see* Christopher Columbus
comandancia (military headquarters), 30, 149
comandante (military commander), 29–30
Comapa, 108
comb, 207–8, 233
Comitán, 46
communism, 149
compensation, 102–5, 222
competence, 106, 110, 238, 247
computer, 83, 211–13, 227; *see also* laptop
Coneta, 46
conservation, language conservation, 19, 76, 249
consultant, 20, 21, 23, 31–2, 34, 38, 75, 77–8, 80–3, 85–6, 89, 91–3, 95, 99, 101–8, 110–15
consultant compulsions, 105
contact language, 52, 110–13, 225
contact-induced language change, 10
contraband, 29, 145

converge, converging, convergence, 52
Cooper, James Fenimore, 260n
coral snake, 127–8, 130
corpus, 241–2
Corpus Christi, Texas, 187
COVID-19, 246–7
Cox, Paul Alan, 16
Crystal, David, 250
Cuisnahuat, 62, 85
Culloden (Battle of), 261n
cultural appropriation, 251
culture, cultures, 2, 9, 10, 14, 16, 21, 36, 55, 59, 98, 101, 134, 143, 177, 182, 214–15, 218, 219, 225, 236, 247, 248, 251, 252
culture shock, 214–15
curandero, 35

dampness, 213
Darfur, 250
dark glasses, 225, 234
Das grammatische Raritätenkabinett, 69
DDT, 28, 118–19
decolonization, 251
definition of fieldwork, 7–8
dehydration, 169, 172
DELAMAN (Digital Endangered Languages and Musics Archives Network), 254
Delhi belly, 172
Demetrio, don Demetrio, 44–5
demonstrative, 49–50
dengue, 120–1
dialect, dialects, 28–30, 44, 46, 50, 73n, 76, 87, 89, 90, 100, 152, 180, 196, 201, 223, 234
dialectology, 44, 76
diarrhea, 68, 168–9, 171–2, 230
Díaz, Luis, don Luis, 71, 93–5
Dick Nixons Band, 101
dictionary, 21, 75, 225, 241–2, 255
diesel, 190

discovery procedures, 238
diverge, diverging, divergence, divergent, 46, 52, 55
document, colonial document, 7, 46, 53–6
document, official document, 28–30, 189, 223–4
documentary linguistics, 241, 244
documentation, documenting, 1, 6, 7, 9, 10–15, 17–22, 31, 40, 41, 43, 51, 57, 59, 76–7, 89, 98, 100–1, 103, 106, 113, 114, 126, 131, 145, 148, 165, 173, 175, 203, 217–18, 222, 223, 235, 239–44, 248–51, 253–9, 260n, 261n
dog, dogs, 78, 118, 122, 133–6, 138, 139, 143–4, 200–1
Donaldsonville, Louisiana, 101
donkey, 64, 139, 165
dormant, 6–7, 11, 13, 15, 18, 24n, 46, 55, 57, 192, 239, 245, 249
drone, 257
drug, drugs, 16, 155–6, 158, 159, 172, 174
drunk, drunkenness, 29, 85, 158–9, 202
dry bags, 213
dual-lingualism, 50–1
duct tape, 186, 188, 204, 224
dugout canoe (*cayuco*), 180, 195
dust, 60, 119, 128, 185, 210, 211–12

earplugs, 200, 226
ecological extraction, 251
ecology, 16, 58
eelgrass, 15
Egypt, 250
ejectives, 37n
El Gran Rey Catarral del Mar (The Great Catarrhal King of the Sea), 34

El Salvador, 54, 57, 79–80, 84–7, 101, 107, 108, 118, 139, 147, 149–50, 176–7, 186, 199, 200, 234
ELAR (Endangered Languages Archive), 234n, 254
election, 149–50, 152, 256
electric currency converter, 228
elicitation, elicit, 21–2, 87, 101, 105, 106, 109, 111–12, 115
Emmorey, Karen, 43
endangered language, endangered languages, 1, 2, 6, 9, 10, 11–12, 14, 18, 19, 23n, 24n, 27, 31, 44, 58–9, 77, 113, 115n, 148, 165, 196, 234n, 235–6, 239, 240, 242, 244, 245–8, 252–9, 260n
Entamoeba histolytica see amoebic dysentery
environment, 7, 16, 58, 110, 118, 126, 152, 214
Escuintenango, 46
Escuintla, 55
ethics, ethical, 7–8, 16, 20, 117, 173
ethnobotany, ethnobotanical, 10, 16, 77
ethnogeography, 77
Ethnologue, 11, 24, 24n
ethnomusicology, 97
ethnozoology, 10
Europe, European, 20, 35, 65, 79, 85, 97, 134, 154, 159, 200, 215, 237
extinct, extinction, 6–7, 239, 245, 246, 249

fake, faker, 107–10, 115n
Falklands War, 150
Faroe Islands, 250
felids, 12
Felipa, 86
ferry, 199
field methods, field methods course, 21–3, 37, 82, 223, 254, 259, 261n
Finland, 199, 250
first peoples, first nations, 3
fish, fishing, 16, 19, 49, 68, 94, 220
Fishman, Joshua, 240
flashlight, 133, 134–5, 188, 213, 227
flavanone, 16
fleas, 28, 41, 118–20, 134, 136, 180, 192, 194
Flores, Petén, Guatemala, 123, 196
Floresta, 34
food, 15, 26, 103, 117, 137, 152, 164, 170, 171, 194, 203, 210, 211, 213, 220–1, 231
food poisoning, 168, 171
Franciscans, 79
Francisco Calvo Pérez, don Francisco, 34–6
Franco, 126, 132, 141
fricative, 43, 95
FUNAI, 113
Fundação Nacional do Índio (National Indian Foundation) *see* FUNAI
funding, funds, 102–4, 148, 165, 182, 223–4, 233, 247, 253, 255–9
funeral, 85, 219

gangs, 148
García, Nancy, 18, 100
gasoline filter, fuel filter, 185–6
gasoline, gas, 161, 182, 185–7, 190
gay relationships, 217
conflict, conflicts, 45, 117, 148, 149, 151, 162, 246, 250–1, 261n
Ghana, 138, 175
giardia (giardiasis), 136, 169
Glencoe, 261n
glottalic, 47–8
glottalized consonant, glottalization, 32, 37n, 38, 106–7
Gonzáles, Hugo, 98–100

Gracias a Dios, 44–5
grammar, 6, 21, 28, 49, 52, 54–5, 75, 106, 112, 115n, 148, 237, 238, 241–2, 253, 255
Grammatical Rarities Cabinet, 74n
Gran Chaco *see* Chaco
grasshoppers, 165
Great Britain, 150; *see also* UK
Greenberg, Joseph, 17, 47
gringo, 29, 32–3, 34, 77–8, 108, 119, 140, 150, 181
grubs, 165
Guajiquiro, 89, 194–5, 201
guaro, 159
Guatemala, Guatemalan, 31, 32, 33, 40, 41, 44–5, 47, 48, 54–5, 73n, 77–81, 89–91, 97, 101, 107, 108, 110, 119, 123, 142, 145–8, 152, 154, 159, 166, 168, 180, 181–2, 186, 192, 193, 195, 199–200, 202, 206, 215, 216, 218, 234
Guatemala City, 54, 97, 145, 167, 199, 234
Guazacapán, 31–3, 34, 40, 54, 57, 78, 106, 107, 142
guerrilla, 28, 30, 146, 153, 154, 159
gun, shotgun, 65, 69, 149–50, 152, 159

hair, 61, 78–9, 120, 137, 153, 176–7, 204, 207–8
health, 23, 84, 117, 121–2, 154, 164–5, 168, 169–70, 173, 176–8, 210, 247, 253
helicopters, 152–3
Helman, Christopher, 257–8
Helsinki, 199
heritage language, 6, 7, 81, 87, 179, 249
hero, 60, 163n
hiking, 200–1
Himmelmann, Nikolaus, 240–2
historical linguistics, 76

history, 6, 13, 14, 54, 55–6, 60, 76–7, 214, 235, 250, 251
HIV, HIV/AIDS, 16, 174–6
Holloway, Charles ("Chip"), 101
homeland, 14
honey, 62–4, 70, 74n
horse, 65, 165, 171, 180, 192, 195
hot chocolate, 170, 207, 232
hot water wand *see* immersion heater
human rights, 13, 152, 246, 247
Humboldt, Wilhelm von, 238
Hunahpu, 60
hunt, hunting, 16, 58, 66, 81, 134
hunters and gatherers, hunting and gathering, 58, 64, 221
hygiene, 203–4, 207

ice, 170
identity, 1, 13, 152, 216, 246, 248, 252
ignorance, 89–91
iguana, 134, 165
immersion heater, 206
imploded, 47
Indian, 3, 79, 154, 261n; *see also* American Indian
Indiana Jones, 37
Indigenous, Indigenous people, 2, 3–4, 13, 14, 15–16, 24n, 33, 60, 78, 79–80, 82, 83, 84, 86, 89–90, 95, 97, 103, 108, 127, 146, 151–2, 154, 155–8, 176, 182, 201, 203, 209, 216, 218, 246, 251–2, 260n
Indigenous language, 20, 27, 44, 51–2, 54, 77, 79–80, 87, 98, 99, 107, 192, 253
Indonesia, 111, 137
informant, 75, 93, 115n
insect repellent, insecticide, 118–19, 121, 230, 232
institutional review board (IRB), 20, 117, 148

institutional support, 247
intellectual property rights, 15–16, 251
Inter-American Court of Human Rights (Corte Interamericana de Derechos Humanos), 152
International Phonetic Alphabet *see* IPA
IPA (International Phonetic Alphabet), 47, 94–5
Iraq, 250
IRB *see* institutional review board
Irish, 79, 150
Italy, 79

jacket, 228
jail, 45, 85, 194
Jesuits, 79
journalists, 39
jugs, 203
Jumaytepeque, 40–1, 57, 107

Kab'raqan (Cabrakan), 60
Kaipuleohone (archive), 254
Kaufman, Terrence (Terry), 41, 80, 152
Ken Hale Prize, 98
knife, 69, 226, 230
knowledge system, endangered knowledge system, 10, 37, 58–9, 60, 77
Krauss, Michael, 239–40, 252

La Calavera see tsuntekumat
La Paz (Bolivia), 28–9
labiodental, 95
Lake Atitlán, 196
Lake Petén, 196
Lalo, don Lalo, 149
land rights, 251
landslides, 190
Language (journal), 240
language acquisition, 6, 76, 254

language attrition, 178n
language contact, 10, 51–2, 64, 247
language death, 239–40
Language Documentation and Conservation, 253
language ecology, 10
language endangerment *see* endangered language
language family, language families, 12, 31
language rights, linguistic rights, 250, 251
Lanquín, 152–3
Lanquín Cave, 153
laptop, 83, 160, 108, 224, 225–6, 231; *see also* computer
Las Cumbres, Chiapas, 108
Las Pacayas, 90
lateral, laterals, 42–3
Latin America, 20, 27, 74n, 81, 82, 110, 124, 146, 167, 169, 174, 176, 188, 197, 218, 253
lexical suffix, 58, 68–73
lexicon, 242
liberation theology, 146
Libya, 250
lice, 208, 229, 233
linguistic anthropology, 77
linguistic diversity, 9, 11, 12, 14, 16, 17, 245
linguistic exogamy, 50–1
linguistic rights *see* language rights
Linguistic Society of America, 239
linguistic theory, 18, 242–4
liquids, 42
literature, 13–14, 60, 114, 149
Lucio, don Lucio, 31–2
Luxembourg, 250

macho bus drivers, 181
Maddieson, Ian, 42–3
malaria, 120–1, 174–5

Mali, 175
Malta, 250
mamala plant, 16
marriage, 50, 217, 246
Maryknoll (Maryknoll Fathers and Brothers, Catholic Foreign Mission Society of America, 79
matanza, 79–80
Mauigoa, Epenesa, 16
Maxwell, Judith, 106–7
Maya calendar, 91
Mayanist, 56, 106, 193
measles, 77–8, 154–5
medical kit, 173, 231
medicine, medicinal plants, 10, 15–16, 34, 58, 67–8, 119–20, 124, 167–8, 172–5, 178, 230, 233
mefloquine, 175
memory sticks, memory cards, 225, 227
mentalism, 238–9
Mesoamerica, 31, 40
Mexico City, 189, 197, 199
military linguist, 5
Millen, Jack, 101
Misión La Paz, MLP, 10, 18, 19, 27, 50–3, 62, 63, 67, 69, 71, 72, 76, 94, 96, 97, 98–9, 100, 112, 123, 125, 126, 127, 128–30, 131, 132, 134–5, 140, 141, 143, 144, 156, 157, 166, 173, 189, 208, 211, 220
missionary, missionaries, 10, 44, 84, 123, 125, 150, 167, 184, 260n
Missouri, 183
mites (scabies), 136
MLP *see* Misión La Paz
money, 80–1, 84, 103, 108, 143, 148, 159, 160, 165, 182, 187, 188, 198, 200, 220, 224, 234, 256–257
monkey, monkeys, 106, 136–8, 165–6, 216
monolingual, monolingualism, 250–1

monolingual elicitation, 111–13
monolingual fieldwork, 112
Montaña de la Flor, 184
Monte Bello (lakes of), 44
Montezuma's revenge, 172
mordida see bribe
morphology, 22
morral, 89–90, 234
Moscow, 97
mosquito net, 226
mosquitos, 119, 121, 123, 127, 226, 228
motorcycle, motorbike, 66, 98, 155–6, 182
MTV, 101
mule, 40, 89, 96, 180, 192, 194–5
multilingual, multilingualism, 5, 51–3, 64, 247, 250–1
Museum Library of the University of Pennsylvania, 54–5
music, musician, 81, 97–101, 231, 247, 254
mystery language, 108

nahual, nagual, 31
nailon, 90
National Public Radio (NPR), 258
nebulizer, 173, 233
Netherlands, 250
New Orleans, 115n
New York, 183, 188
New York Times, 246
Newman, Paul, 254, 261n
Nicaragua, 57, 196
Northern Ireland, 250
Nueva Santa Rosa, 41

Oaxaca, Mexico, 55
obscene, obscenity, 64–5, 105–7
obscenity avoidance, 64
O'Grady, William, 178n

SUBJECT INDEX | 281

Opatoro, 194
Oregon, 1
owl, 109, 141–2

Panchimalco, 108
Papua New Guinea, 81, 216
Paraguay, 42, 125, 130, 156, 204, 207, 250
Paris, 97
parrot, parrots, 139, 144–5
Paso Hondo, Chiapas, 105, 193
passport, 161, 202, 223
Peace Corps, 28, 78, 168, 169
peccary, 165
pensión, 123–4, 160, 168, 200, 210, 234
people-eater, 31–4, 78
pharmaceuticals, 15–16
pharmacists, 174
Philippine, 146
philology, philological, 55–6
phonetics, phonetic, 48, 73n, 76, 94, 109
phonology, phonological, 22, 49, 52, 72, 73n, 76, 106
Pilcomayo, 19, 98, 128, 139, 156, 211, 223
pilgrimages, 34
Pinart, Alphonse L., 55
pipián sauce, 165
piqueteros ("picketers"), 190–1
piranha, 69
plague, 28, 120; *see also* bubonic plague
plane, planes, airplane, 28–31, 34, 180, 197–200, 223, 226, 228; *see also* bush plane
plastic bags, 183, 206, 212, 213, 228
Pleiades, 59–60
PLFM *see* Proyecto Lingüístico Francisco Marroquín
police, 75, 82, 84, 145, 147, 156, 159, 173, 188, 191

politicians, 152–3, 198
politics, 117, 149–54
polyglot, 5
Polynesia, 218
Poor Clares, 79
Popol Vuh, 60
poverty, 104, 146, 157, 158, 215, 237, 248
primitive, 236–7
private ownership, private property, 219, 221–2
prostratin, 16
Proyecto Lingüístico Francisco Marroquín (PLFM), 41, 80–1, 146
pulse (*pulsar*), 35–6
purple burps, 169

questionnaire, 89, 101–2, 106, 110, 225, 234

Rafael Hernández, don Rafael, 87–8
Raid, 119, 232
rainy season, 41, 84–5, 211, 213
Ramos, Teresa, doña Teresa, 112
rattlesnake, 131
REC *see* research ethics committee
reclamation, language reclamation, 9, 76, 103, 240, 247, 249, 251, 261n
recorder, recording equipment, 21, 22, 83, 89, 99, 103, 205, 211–13, 225, 227, 234, 256
recording, recordings, 91, 95, 98, 114, 115, 131, 136, 139–40, 219, 235, 241–2
Rehg, Kenneth, 23n, 116n, 242–4, 248
religion, 2, 151, 215–17, 246
rememberer, 57, 80
research ethics committee (REC), 117
restroom, 200, 209

revitalization, revitalize, 6, 7, 9, 11, 13, 19, 21, 76, 103, 114, 147, 149, 163n, 175, 235, 240, 241, 245, 246–7, 248–9, 254, 258, 260n
right whale, 12
ritual drinking, 218
robberies, robbed, robbing, 160, 162, 181, 215, 246; *see also* theft
Robins, Robert, 240
rockslides, 190
Rogers, Chris, 73n
Rolling Skull *see tsuntekumat*
Rosaldo, Renato, 260n
runs, 172
Rwanda, 250

Sabina airline, 199
salad, 171
salami, 165, 233
salmonella, 136, 169, 171
Salta, 50, 152, 156
salvoconducto, 28–30
San José Petén, 196
San Luis Potosí, 193
San Salvador, 147
Santa María Ixhuatán, 54
Santa Rosa, 40
Santo Domingo de Guzmán, 62, 86–7, 139, 149
Sapir, Edward, 8, 93, 237
sarsaparilla, 185
scam, scams, 89, 160–2
scented, 120
school, 5, 18, 24n, 95, 98, 99, 104, 110, 146, 192, 233
scorpion, 122–4, 133
Segovia, Laureano, Don Laureano, 98–9
semispeaker, 38, 58, 80, 106
shaman *see* witch
shampoo, 120, 204, 229
sharing, 221–2

shoes, 122, 195, 201, 213, 218, 229, 234
Siberian tiger, 12
sibilant, 93
SIL *see* Summer Institute of Linguistics
síndico (town treasurer and secretary), 54
Singapore, 250
skletsex (*Jacaratia hassleriana*), 58–9
slingshot, 139–40
snake, 126–33
soap, 120, 122, 170, 204, 209, 229, 231, 233
social justice, 10, 13
Society for the Study of the Indigenous Languages of the Americas (SSILA), 98
sociolinguistic, sociolinguistics, 53, 76, 240
soldier, 45, 66, 79, 130, 146, 149, 150, 152–3, 159, 216, 261n
Sololá, 168
Solomon Islands, 202
songs, 219
South America, 77, 134, 143, 158, 219, 236
soul, souls, 131, 136; *see also* spirit
sovereignty, 251
Spaniards, 61, 216
Spanish tummy, 172
species, 12, 17, 42, 62, 66, 122, 126, 130, 139, 143, 249
spirit, spirits, 31, 32, 36, 136, 142, 192; *see also* soul
SSILA *see* Society for the Study of the Indigenous Languages of the Americas
stab ritually *see* bloodletting
street food, 171
Summer Institute of Linguistics (SIL), 184
Survey of California and Other Indian

Languages, 254
survival, human survival, 15, 17, 59, 221
swashbuckler, swashbuckling, 1, 26, 34, 37
Switzerland, 250
Syria, 250
syringes, 172–3, 233

taboo, 64–5
TACA, 199–200
Tacuba, 200–1
Tanzania, 250
tapeworm, 120, 134
tapir, 165–6
Tartagal, 156–7, 191, 256
tea, 170, 172, 207, 232
TEK (traditional ecological knowledge, 77
temperature, 170, 212, 226
TESL (teaching English as a second language), 254
Texas, 182, 187, 197
Thailand, 250
The Annals of the Cakchiquels, 8n
The Hitchhiker's Guide to the Galaxy, 205
The Last of the Mohicans, 260n
The Oxford Handbook of Endangered Languages, 242
The Skull *see tsuntekumat*
theft, 15, 26, 160–2, 180; *see also* robberies, robbed, robbing
Tibet, 21, 203
tick key, 121
tick, ticks, 119, 121–2
Tillohash, Tony, 8, 93
tinderhorn, 72
título único, 151–2
toad, 133
tobacco, 158, 218
toilet, 122, 168, 172, 209–10

toilet paper, 209–10
toothbrush, 207–9, 213
torch *see* flashlight
tortillas, 172
towel, 170, 205–6, 212, 229
traditional ecological knowledge *see* TEK
transcription, transcribing, transcribe, 22, 92–5, 212, 216
traveler's diarrhea *see turista*
tribal council, 82
Trinitaria, 34–5, 44, 46, 108
trots, 172
Trump, Donald, 257, 258
tsuntekumat, 61–2
Tucker, Hank, 257
turista (traveler's diarrhea), 171–2
turtle, 165
Tuxtla Gutiérrez, 198
Tuzantán, 148
tweezers, 121–2, 230
typhoid, 169
typhus, 120
typology, typological, 50, 68, 235

UCLA, 244
Uhlenbeck, Eugenius, 240
UK, 150
universal, universals, 17, 47–8, 53
universal grammar, 238, 244
University of Washington, 22
unscented, 120
US State Department, 162

vaccination, 77–8, 154, 169
vampire bats, 142–4
Vanuatu, 81
Venezuela, 202
Venus, 60
Veracruz, 92, 193
vinchuca, 124–5
violence, 13, 117, 145–9, 162

visa, 45, 202–3
vitamin B, 119
voiceless "l", 42–3, 52, 150–1
Volkswagen van, 147, 182, 188
vowel harmony, 48–9
Vucub Caquix, 60

war, 147, 150, 250, 246, 261n
Washington Post, 246
water tower, 204
weather, 198, 210, 212
Where There Is No Doctor, 167, 178
Wikipedia, 157
wind, 60, 61, 195–6, 212, 229

witch, 1, 31–2, 34, 131, 141–2; *see also* brujo
witchcraft, 42, 78, 105
word order, basic word order, 17–18
World Health Organization, 163n, 173
worms, 68, 78, 136, 154

Xbalanque, 60
Xuraqan (Hurakan), 60–1

yarará, 130, 132
Yemen, 250

Zapaluta *see* Trinitaria

Languages, language families, and ethnic groups index

African languages, 244
Akuntsú, 112–13
Amazonian, 17

Bimanese, 111
Brulé Spanish, 100–1

Cacaopera, 57, 80
Cariban, Cariban language, 17
Cathlamet, 236
Celtic languages, 261n
Chemakum, 236
Chiapanec, 57
Chicomuceltec, 57, 87, 183, 192–3
Chicomuselo, 183, 192, 194
Chilanga, 57, 59
Chiquimulilla Xinka, 57
Chorote, 19, 50, 52–3, 66, 76, 95, 99–100, 112, 139, 144
Chuj, 87
Coxoh, 45–6
Cuzco Quechua, 28

English, 31, 32–3, 37n, 53, 61, 64, 65, 69, 81, 82, 90, 106, 110, 124, 150, 254

Finnish, 23n
French, 61, 100, 110, 176

Guazacapán, Guazacapán Xinka, 31–3, 34, 40, 54, 57, 78, 106, 107, 142

Hixkaryana, 17
Huastec, 92, 193
Hutu, 250

Indonesian, 111
Irish, 79, 150
Isleño, 115n
Itza', 196

Jakaltek, 105–6
Japanese, 254
Jicaque *see* Tol
Jumaytepeque, Jumaytepeque Xinka, 40–1, 57, 107

285

Kakchikel, 56, 89, 119, 168, 196
K'iche', 23n, 60–1, 65, 89
Kinyarwanda, 250

Lenca, 5, 7, 79, 80, 89, 194

Mam, 193
Mandarin, 254
Matacoan, 42, 50, 66
Maya, 45, 60, 61
Mayan language, Mayan languages, 2, 34, 45–6, 47, 56, 75, 77, 89, 90, 91, 92, 101–2, 146, 148, 168, 183, 193, 196
Misumalpan, 57, 196
Mocho', 87

Nahua, 55
Nahuatl, 23n, 54–5, 141
Nawat *see* Pipil
Nivaclé, 19, 42–3, 49–50, 52, 58, 59, 62, 64, 66–70, 76, 93, 95, 112, 131, 132, 139, 145, 221–2
Nootka *see* Nuu-chah-nulth
Nuu-chah-nulth, 4, 21, 66

Otomanguean, 57

Papago *see* Tohono O'odham
Pentlach, 236
Pipil (Nawat), 54–5, 61–2, 80, 85, 86, 101–2, 108–9, 139, 147, 149, 200
Pochuteco, 55, 236
Poqomam, 56, 89, 145, 166
Poqomchi', 56, 89
Portuguese, 29, 110, 111
Puris, 236

Q'eqchi', 56, 89, 145, 146, 152, 154, 206
Quechua, 23n, 27–30

Salvadoran Lenca *see* Chilanga
Scots Gaelic, 261n
Seri, 15
Southeastern Tzeltal, 34, 44–6
Southern Paiute, 8, 93
Spanish, 23n, 29, 31, 32, 36, 38, 46, 50–1, 56, 60, 61, 62, 64–5, 70, 81, 82, 93–4, 5, 97, 99, 100–1, 105–7, 109, 110–12, 115n, 123, 139, 159, 163n, 177, 188
Subtiaba, 57

Taensa, 115n
Taino, 61
Tetum, 111
Tibetan, 21
Tohono O'odham, 3, 22
Tojolabal, 34, 35, 87
Tol (Jicaque), 184–5
Tsetsaut, 236
Tupían, 112, 115n
Tutsi, 250
Tuzanteco, 148
Tzeltal, 34, 35, 44–6, 87; *see also* Southeastern Tzeltal
Tzotzil, 34
Tz'utujil, 89

Uspantek, 89–90
Uto-Aztecan, 22, 54–5

Wichí, 19, 50, 52, 76, 98, 99, 150–2, 176, 190–1

Xinka, Xinkan, 31–2, 34, 38, 40–1, 48, 54, 57, 78, 106–7, 142

Yupiltepeque, 31

Zoque, 145